Crypto Crises

Crypto Crises

Lessons From the Booms and Busts

Tarek Omraneh

Mindful Pages

Published in 2026

ISBN: 9789374592939 (PB)
ISBN: 9789374590959 (eBook)

Published by

Mindful Pages
Imprint of Alpha Editions LLC
312 W. 2nd St #1834
Casper, WY 82601, USA

This book was developed using advanced writing tools to support the drafting and ideation process. All content has been thoughtfully curated, refined, and reviewed to ensure quality and relevance.

Content

Introduction

The first thing people notice in a crypto bull market is the noise. Screens glow green, timelines churn with declarations of a new era, and ordinary individuals feel a once-in-a-lifetime opportunity—perhaps the only one they will ever see—unfolding before their eyes. Stories arrive faster than anyone can examine them: banking without banks, internet money for a borderless world, immutable property rights for the many rather than the few. Fear of being too late collides with fear of being left behind. Fortunes multiply in the time it takes to refresh an app. Every conversation is charged with the question, whispered or shouted: what if this is the moment everything changes?

Then, in what feels like an instant, that same world is declared irrational, dangerous, or doomed. Screens turn red. The once-celebrated projects become cautionary tales. Politicians call for protection, critics call for restraint, and those who believed hardest sit with the haunting thought that they should have known better. Once more, technology promised transformation; once more, human behaviour delivered chaos. It is tempting to view these cycles as proof that crypto is a bubble or a scam, an empty carnival built on speculation rather than substance. Yet this conclusion misses the deeper truth. We are witnessing something far more complex and far more revealing.

Crypto markets expose what we want from money: sovereignty or safety, fairness or familiarity, a system that treats us equally or a system that guarantees us comfort. They reveal our instincts under pressure—our willingness to trust strangers, to believe in a story, to imagine a future different from the present. They turn the abstractions of economics into the lived drama of hope and fear. To study crypto cycles is to study ourselves.

The paradox at the heart of this new financial frontier is deceptively simple. Code is supposed to reduce the need for trust. If rules are publicly verifiable—if no middleman can change the numbers—then fraud and favouritism should fade. Yet markets are not mathematics; they are human arenas. The prices we watch so obsessively are built on confidence, liquidity, and narrative—things that do not live on a blockchain. Even the most elegant protocol becomes volatile when emotions take control of capital. Crypto promises rational money. The crowd delivers raw psychology.

This tension—between what computers guarantee and what humans believe—defines every crypto boom and every crypto crash. Understanding that tension is the first step toward navigating this space with clarity rather than confusion. It means recognising that technology can improve systems but cannot eliminate the passions that animate them. It means seeing that progress is not a straight line and that the lessons of the past are not erased simply because the code base has been rewritten.

The stories that drive digital assets do not emerge randomly. They follow patterns as old as markets themselves. At the start of a cycle, enthusiasts speak quietly among themselves. Funding is scarce, hope is fragile. Then an innovation—sometimes major, sometimes cosmetic—catches fire. A new narrative takes hold: digital gold, decentralised finance, the metaverse, tokenised everything. Capital flows in. Liquidity makes prices rise; rising prices draw attention; attention creates more capital. A feedback loop forms, and a movement that once looked speculative now looks inevitable.

Inevitability is always expensive.

Eventually, reality intrudes. Scarcity becomes congestion. Promised yields reveal leverage rather than productivity. A platform's security assumptions are tested and found wanting. An exchange that seemed impregnable is exposed as a brittle pile of incentives and shortcuts. Overnight, trust, once abundant, becomes a rare commodity. Liquidity evaporates. The same mechanisms that fuelled the ascent now accelerate the fall. The cycle turns.

We convince ourselves each time that this cycle is unique; that this narrative is stronger, that this technology is sounder, that this time will finally prove the sceptics wrong. And to be fair, sometimes we are right. Each major downturn has left behind survivors whose ideas were vindicated over time. Bitcoin has weathered countless obituaries. Ethereum has matured through crises that would have ended weaker systems. Yet, surrounding the enduring innovations, there are always the same wreckages: over-leveraged dreams, reckless shortcuts, and a marketplace dazzled by the speed of change rather than the substance of it.

The aim of this book is not to cheerlead for the future or chastise the past. It is to offer a practical, historically-literate, behaviourally-aware way of seeing crypto markets as they are. You will not find predictions of prices here. What you will find are the recurring indicators—narrative, liquidity, reflexivity—that influence the turning points far more than logic does. You will learn why some flaws are structural rather than accidental; why the incentives built into exchanges, miners, validators, and protocols shape outcomes more than whitepapers do; why stablecoins can appear as calm as a lake yet hide the threat of undertow.

Most importantly, you will be invited to develop your own rules—rules that keep you steady when the collective pulse quickens. In crypto, indecision is a decision, and not having a plan is a plan to be ruled by others' emotions. There is no shame in caution, and no glory in reckless conviction. To survive and learn from these markets is to respect both the promise of the technology and the inevitability of human error.

Crypto is often framed as a rebellion against traditional finance, yet in many ways it recapitulates its hard-won lessons. Bank runs predate blockchains. Leverage has toppled powerful institutions long before stablecoins existed. Media-driven manias have been a feature of markets since the first exchange floors. What is novel is not the behaviour but the speed and transparency with which we now watch it unfold. A rumour can trigger billions in liquidations before regulators finish their morning coffee. A meme can move more capital in an hour than a central bank can deploy in a week. The timeline, quite literally, is on fire.

This velocity changes the stakes. A misjudged click, a misleading headline, a bug overlooked by auditors can set off cascades that drag down entire networks. The distance between curiosity and catastrophe has never been shorter. That is why this field demands discipline, not dogma; patient observation, not perpetual panic. Crypto rewards those who can distinguish between temporary noise and structural change.

Across these chapters, we will map the anatomy of crypto cycles—where they echo history, where they deviate, and where they surprise even the most seasoned observers. Bitcoin will serve as our teacher in durability and distrust; exchanges will reveal the fragility of centralisation in a decentralised world; stablecoins will show how still water can be an illusion maintained only by relentless activity below the surface. In decentralised finance, we will confront the double-edged sword of composability—a system that can build marvels but also unleash chain reactions when one component slips. And throughout, we will anchor our understanding in behavioural finance: the simple truth that the greatest vulnerabilities in this market exist not in codebases but in the hearts and minds of participants.

You may approach these ideas as a curious newcomer or as a veteran who has already lived through booms and heartbreaks. Either way, the goal is the same: to replace the roller-coaster of euphoria and despair with a more durable state of informed calm. To become someone who can witness frenzy without joining it, who can see opportunity without abandoning caution, who can participate with eyes open.

There is a future for this technology—one that extends far beyond speculative assets and trading screens. It lies in systems that are open, auditable, and harder to corrupt than what came before. It lies in financial tools that grant agency without requiring permission. It lies in communities that form not around a promise of riches but around a commitment to shared infrastructure. But futures are fragile things. They depend on our ability to learn, both individually and collectively.

So, the questions before us are both practical and philosophical. How do we build and adopt technologies that make society more resilient rather than more reckless? How do we allocate capital in ways that foster innovation without fuelling collapse? How do we design incentives that reward stewardship rather than exploitation? How do we protect ourselves from the wolves without losing the curiosity that leads us into the forest?

These are not questions that markets answer for us. They are questions that demand judgement.

This book will not promise safety. It will not promise wealth. It will not pretend that risk can be engineered away or that technological progress makes us immune to ancient temptations. What it offers is perspective: the ability to recognise where the ground is firm, where it is slippery, and where it is simply too early to tell. Perspective is not protection, but it is the beginning of wisdom.

Crypto cycles will continue. There will be more euphoria, more despair, more arguments about whether change is real or illusion. But there will also be learning. We will get better at recognising the difference between substance and spectacle. We will cultivate habits that help us navigate both the excitement of invention and the discomfort of uncertainty. We will develop a language for discussing risk without shame and for embracing innovation without naïvety.

If history teaches one thing, it is that every financial revolution is born doubted, grows disorderly, and matures painfully. Crypto will be no exception. Yet those who engage with it thoughtfully can avoid becoming collateral in the battles between zealotry and cynicism. They can harness its creativity while sidestepping its traps. They can insist that technology serve human flourishing rather than consuming it.

As you turn the page, hold on to this simple idea: markets may repeat themselves, but you do not have to repeat your mistakes. You can read the signals others overlook. You can help build the structures that survive. And you can keep your head clear when the crowd loses theirs.

In every bull run, a new story will try to convince you that money has finally been reinvented. In every crash, you will discover how familiar the chaos truly is. This book exists for the space between those extremes—the space where rational hope lives. Let us step into that space together, prepared not merely to witness the next boom and bust, but to understand it.

Chapter 1
The Pattern Behind the Hype

At the height of a crypto bull market, rationality takes on a peculiar form. A whitepaper sketched in broad strokes becomes a prophecy. A token with no functioning product trades at valuations that would make seasoned financiers blush. People speak in absolutes: *this is the future of finance, this is the new internet, this is the end of the old system*. If you question the fever, you are simply not "getting it". The charts are pointing up. Influential figures are convinced. Liquidity is flowing. What else matters?

Yet when the tide turns, certainty crumbles just as quickly. Where once there was conviction, there is now bewilderment: how could so many supposedly rational participants get swept into such unsustainable narratives? How did we confuse speculation with inevitability? How can the same token that once represented transformation now be dismissed as worthless?

Crypto's most dramatic cycles are not accidents. They are the predictable consequence of a market built on three interlocking forces: *narratives,* which explain the world; *liquidity,* which animates belief; and *reflexivity,* which binds the two into a feedback loop strong enough to reshape reality, at least temporarily. When these elements align, prices detach from fundamentals—not because participants are foolish, but because markets are social organisms that reward collective enthusiasm. And when the alignment breaks, rationality returns with a vengeance.

Consider the retail investor who enters the market during a period of intense excitement. Perhaps they see a friend post a screenshot of life-changing gains. Perhaps they read that pension funds are investing in the same assets. Perhaps they simply notice that every headline carries the scent of the inevitable. New on-ramps—easy-to-use apps, frictionless exchanges, copy-trading platforms—open their gates. Capital flows in faster than new supply can adjust. The price rises because demand rises, and demand rises because the price rises. The loop tightens. The charts become a story, and the story becomes a justification for the charts.

This is not stupidity; it is pattern recognition misapplied to a rapidly changing environment. Human beings are exquisitely tuned to momentum. We chase what others are chasing, because in evolutionary terms, that strategy often kept us alive. In markets, however, the same instinct can drive us towards cliffs as well as fields of abundance.

Media accelerates this dynamic. What once required months of speculation now unfolds in days. A single viral thread can ignite a movement, sending millions to search for a token they had never heard of an hour earlier. Due diligence—slow, sceptical, essential—gets compressed into a few glances at charts or the credentials of an influencer. Memes become models. Attention becomes validation. The speed at which sentiment shifts leaves little room for caution.

And yet it would be a mistake to dismiss the cultural power of these narratives. Memes are not merely jokes; they are social signals. They communicate belonging, direction, and possibility. A project that captures the cultural imagination is already halfway to attracting the liquidity it needs. In crypto, people invest not only in technology but in community. And communities, when they scale rapidly, behave like crowds: energised, optimistic, prone to groupthink.

Even when the underlying technology is robust, incentives can corrode outcomes. Miners and validators who secure networks are rational economic actors; when rewards fall, loyalty falters. Exchanges that serve as the central marketplaces for crypto trading often rely on revenue models that prioritise volume over prudence. During periods of stress, fees spike, withdrawals slow, and users discover the uncomfortable truth that efficiency in calm times does not guarantee resilience in crisis. Elegant protocols buckle not because the code is flawed, but because participants respond to incentives that the designers failed to anticipate—or simply ignored.

Cycles expose these incentive misalignments with brutal clarity. In the heat of a bull market, the assumption that "technology will fix it" allows unresolved risks to accumulate. Hacks are dismissed as growing pains. Centralised control structures are tolerated in the name of convenience. Token economics that reward speculation over usage are seen as clever mechanisms rather than traps. Optimism smooths over contradiction. Until it does not.

Yet beneath the frenzy, there are reliable signals—markers that reveal when hype is overtaking reality. When funding rates soar, leveraged traders are crowding into the same direction. When exchange reserves fall sharply, someone is preparing for trouble or for triumph, and the distinction matters. When new account registrations surge, particularly among first-time traders, the market's immune system weakens: inexperienced capital is always the most excitable capital. When governance forums fall silent, apathy is whispering a warning: the community may be checking out before the price does.

These signs do not tell us exactly when the music will stop. But they remind us that markets do not defy gravity forever. Crypto does not operate outside the laws of financial physics. It only expresses them in a more distilled form.

This chapter is not about predicting crashes or calling tops. It is about recognising the machinery behind momentum. It is about understanding why good technology can become bad investment at the wrong moment. It is about seeing that markets create their own weather, and that storms form long before the first raindrop falls.

We will explore how narratives emerge and mutate, why liquidity acts as both oxygen and accelerant, and how reflexivity turns belief into price and price into stronger belief. We will examine how memes can perform the cultural work that whitepapers cannot, amplifying a project's reach faster than any marketing department ever could. We will look closely at incentives—not the ones stated proudly on websites, but the ones embedded in the structures that participants actually respond to under pressure.

Above all, this chapter will help you build a mental model: one capable of distinguishing between signals of sustainable adoption and symptoms of speculative swelling; one that allows you to move through cycles with a steadier hand and a clearer mind.

Markets may appear chaotic, but they are not entirely unpredictable. They follow rhythms shaped by human psychology, institutional design, and the availability of capital. The hype cycles that define crypto are not aberrations—they are features of a system where belief and value intertwine more tightly than ever before.

Understanding these patterns is the first step in transforming how you engage with this market. Instead of being pushed and pulled by waves of enthusiasm, you can learn to see the tide. Instead of reacting to excitement, you can analyse its source. Instead of being surprised when volatility returns, you can anticipate it.

The stories that define each cycle will change. The mechanics will not. And once you start to recognise how narratives, liquidity, and incentives interact, you will find that the turbulence becomes less bewildering. You will be able to appreciate both the creativity and the folly of the crowd—without being swallowed by either.

As we move deeper into the chapter, we will dissect each of these forces in detail. We will uncover how hype is constructed, how it becomes self-reinforcing, and how it inevitably outgrows the fundamentals that first justified it. Along the way, we will connect these insights to behavioural patterns as old as trade itself. Because while the tools of finance may evolve, the instincts of the trader rarely do.

The point is not to stand above the crowd, cynical and aloof. Nor is it to join the crowd blindly. It is to observe the crowd with clear eyes. To know that hype has a pattern—and that once you see the pattern, you cannot unsee it.

Turn the page, and we will begin tracing those patterns—not to spoil the excitement of the market's rises and falls, but to understand them. Because understanding, in a space where certainty is always in short supply, might just be the most valuable asset you can hold.

Narratives, Liquidity, and Reflexivity

On 12 May 2021, in Austin, Texas, Coinbase reported that its mobile app had climbed to the number one spot on the Apple App Store in the United States. The previous time a crypto exchange topped that chart was December 2017, just days before Bitcoin reached its then-all-time-high. The surge in downloads was not simply a reflection of technological progress or broader awareness. It showed a far older force at work: the crowd discovering a door to fast money. New capital was arriving faster than supply could adjust. Price did not merely reflect belief; it manufactured it.

Liquidity is not a neutral ingredient in markets. It shapes behaviour, accelerates hope, and compresses time. When fresh capital pushes against a finite asset pool, price leaps ahead of fundamentals. The narrative—that crypto was unavoidable, that digital assets were a ticket to the future—began to feel confirmed by the charts. The rise itself became the reason to believe. We see the loop form: story fuels capital, capital fuels price, price strengthens story. Then the cycle repeats with greater force.

This is reflexivity in motion: perception altering reality. It is not unique to crypto, yet crypto puts the loop under a microscope. Participants can watch in real time as social sentiment converts into deep liquidity, and as deep liquidity hardens into a still more persuasive narrative.

The seed of every speculative rush is a story that solves a desire. Bitcoin answered distrust in institutions after the 2008 financial crisis. Ethereum promised programmable finance. NFTs promised ownership of digital culture. Each narrative gives the market a reason to buy before knowing what comes next. The logic often follows later. Hope moves first.

The philosopher George Soros, who coined the term *reflexivity,* argued that markets do not passively track reality; they generate new realities (Soros, *The Alchemy of Finance*, 1987). In crypto, this alchemy is more visible because fundamentals are, in many cases, still emerging. A network's value depends on adoption that has not happened yet. A token's worth reflects potential utility rather than present cashflows. When a future-focused market meets a liquidity tidal wave, prices are no longer anchored by present function. They float on belief.

Consider the arrival of retail on-ramps. Before mid-2019, acquiring crypto typically required navigating clunky exchanges or slow bank transfers. But as PayPal expanded crypto buying access in October 2020, and as platforms like Robinhood and Revolut simplified onboarding, millions encountered digital assets via familiar interfaces. The demand curve bulged. Bitcoin's supply schedule remained stubbornly fixed. The inevitable outcome was a rapid rise in price, and that rise fed a louder claim: *this revolution is unstoppable*. The technology did not change overnight. Access did. Access is liquidity.

Liquidity is also emotional. When markets are thin, uncertainty feels expensive. When markets are deep, boldness feels safe. A crowded route in makes the exit seem secure—until everyone heads for the door at once.

The media intensifies this movement. A tweet from Elon Musk in February 2021 declaring "Bitcoin is a good thing" preceded Tesla's $1.5 billion purchase reported that month. The market responded within minutes. A thread on a popular forum can pivot sentiment within 48 hours. The attention economy rewards speed over scrutiny. Headlines narrate rises as inevitabilities, falls as failures. The crowd scours stories for cues about how others will behave.

It is tempting to dismiss memes and viral sentiments as fluff. But they are signals of coordination. A meme compresses a complex worldview into a recognisable icon—Dogecoin as the cheerful protest against financial elitism; "HODL" as a manifesto of persistence; "WAGMI" assuring believers that their collective future is bright. Memes express not only belief but belonging. And belonging is a powerful allocative force.

Still, a counterpoint: markets can move in the absence of narrative, driven instead by macro liquidity shifts. When central banks expanded balance sheets aggressively during the pandemic (Bank of England data for March–December 2020), risk assets of all sorts rallied—equities, technology stocks, and cryptocurrencies alike. The story followed the movement, not the other way round. Liquidity acted as the unseen hand. The reconciliation is simple: narratives and liquidity are not alternatives. They are co-pilots. Narrative answers the question *why now?* Liquidity answers the question *how far?*

The motif of the tide returns here. When liquidity pours in, distinctions blur: sound projects and fragile ones float together. Even genuinely transformative networks become overpriced in this environment. Not because their technologies are flawed, but because markets are paying for the future too quickly. Prices overshoot adoption. The risk is not that the idea is wrong, but that its timeline cannot catch up with its valuation.

Ethereum in early 2021 demonstrated this tension. Decentralised finance and NFTs were expanding rapidly, and transaction volumes surpassed $1 billion a day on multiple occasions (data: Dune Analytics, March 2021). Fees soared during periods of congestion; the very success of network usage created user pain. The core tech had proven valuable. Yet valuations assumed that these strained pipes could carry limitless growth without friction. When the tide receded, it revealed unaddressed scalability bottlenecks—and showed that not every price reflects durable reality.

Reflexivity also reveals itself in incentives at the edges of systems. Miners during high-fee periods have a rational incentive to prioritise profitable transactions, which can distort fairness. Validators in proof-of-stake systems may focus on yield opportunities that introduce new risks. Centralised exchanges, rewarded for volume, may list dubious projects that attract desperate crowds. Each actor behaves sensibly for themselves; collectively, they can push markets into precarious territory.

The temptation is to attribute these distortions to malice or incompetence. But the truth is more structural: incentives drive outcomes even when intentions are noble. A protocol designed to decentralise finance can, under pressure, encourage concentration of power in the hands of those who control liquidity. The paradox: the stronger the narrative of liberation, the more entrenched new gatekeepers can become if liquidity pools around them.

Reflexive loops do not only inflate bubbles; they can accelerate collapse. As soon as confidence wavers, price falls become proof of failure. The same mechanisms that fuelled ascent now hasten decline. The narrative inverts: from "too big to fail" to "obviously doomed". Traders reduce risk by selling; their exit worsens the fall. Long-term believers grow quieter, drowned out by panic. The loop continues in reverse.

The 2022 unwinding of TerraUSD and Luna offers a harsh example. In Seoul, South Korea, Terraform Labs promoted an algorithmic stablecoin whose peg relied on reflexive confidence. As long as traders believed in the mechanism, it worked. When belief cracked in May 2022, billions evaporated within days. The collapse revealed how the same forces that elevate innovation can, when misaligned, turn stability into illusion.

Reflexivity's danger lies in its persuasive speed. It turns predictions into prices so quickly that distinguishing signal from noise becomes a challenge. The crowd can be right for the wrong reasons and wrong for the right ones. Efficiency does not guarantee truth. It guarantees consequence.

Yet there is a constructive view. Reflexivity enables radical experiments. It gives new entrants access to capital before they have proven anything. It rewards boldness and creativity. The risk is that experimentation becomes a substitute for execution. But the reward is that breakthroughs arrive faster than established systems would permit. Without narrative and cheap capital, Ethereum might have remained an obscure research project. Without waves of speculative interest, DeFi would not have reached maturity. Liquidity funds learning.

The challenge is not to extinguish hype but to recognise its mechanics. Intelligence lies in identifying when a story has escaped its fundamentals. If the price is rising while active users stagnate, the tide is doing the lifting. If token supply is expanding while narrative becomes louder, enthusiasm may be masking dilution. Metrics tether us to the seabed beneath the waves.

Behaviour communicates risk far more clearly than rhetoric. When holders lock coins into long-term storage, they are signalling conviction. When they crowd into extreme leverage, they are signalling impatience. When venture funds rotate tokens quickly after vesting cliffs, they are signalling short time horizons. Watch what people do with capital, not what they promise in press releases.

Market cycles test the sincerity of narratives. Those that endure price stress build legitimacy. Those that fade reveal themselves as stories optimised for fundraising, not function. Reflexivity rewards both until the moment the market asks a harder question: what remains when liquidity vanishes?

The most resilient networks answer that question with usage, uptime, and community commitment. The ones that fail defer the answer until too late.

So we return to the tide. Liquidity lifts even the grounded boats. When it withdraws, fundamentals stand alone. The spectacle of hype evaporates; the substance remains. Markets repeat this lesson because participants forget it each time.

The unresolved tension is simple. Stories make markets move. Yet markets demand more than belief when the music stops. The reader is left with a diagnostic question to revisit throughout the cycle: when observing an asset's rise, am I watching adoption take root—or am I merely watching the tide come in?

The Role of Media and Memes

On 8 May 2021, during a live broadcast of *Saturday Night Live* in New York, Elon Musk mentioned Dogecoin in a series of jokes that were replayed across social platforms within minutes. The effect was measurable. Data from Binance that weekend showed a surge in trading volume so rapid that the exchange briefly warned users of delays. A digital token born as a parody had become a global headline. It was not a change in Dogecoin's code that moved billions of dollars. It was a shift in the spotlight, sharp and immediate. One remark in one place pulled global attention into a single asset.

This compression of time—where sentiment can pivot across the world in an hour—defines the attention markets that shape crypto cycles. The speed shrinks the gap between reading a signal and acting on it. A five-word meme can trigger more trades than a five-thousand-word technical audit. Screens flicker. Apps ping. Traders commit. The spotlight moves again. In this environment, the question is no longer whether media and memes influence markets. The question is how they channel momentum with such precision, and why the crowd treats the movement of attention as evidence of truth.

Show the effect, then name it: attention acts as capital. When millions focus on an asset at once, liquidity deepens, spreads narrow, and price swings accelerate. Explain it: people watch what others watch. They measure risk not by fundamentals but by the presence of a crowd, a behaviour long documented in financial-history cases such as the 1720 South Sea Bubble recorded by Charles Mackay in *Extraordinary Popular Delusions and the Madness of Crowds* (1841). Implication: influence is no longer an accessory to crypto markets; it is a structural driver. The spotlight does not describe movement. It produces it.

The crypto market's accelerated heartbeat is visible in its metrics: surges in search interest, spikes in exchange sign-ups, sudden bursts of transaction volume. Consider the case of GameStop and the Reddit community r/WallStreetBets in January 2021. Though not a crypto event, it offered a vivid demonstration of a crowd using memes to coordinate financial behaviour. Bloomberg reported that on 27 January 2021, GameStop's trading volume exceeded that of Apple. The mechanism—gathering attention, signalling group identity, accelerating conviction—mirrored what crypto markets had been practising for years. The place was different. The pattern was the same.

The spotlight motif reappears when we move from news media to social media. Traditional outlets, bound by verification delays, lag behind the platforms where crypto narrative shifts truly begin. A viral thread on Twitter or a discussion on Discord can compress due diligence from hours into seconds. People see a chart shared by someone with a large following; they trust the follower count as a proxy for competence. They commit capital before confirming whether the chart reflects genuine usage or creative framing. The behaviour is visible: rushed trades, sudden inflows into obscure tokens, and the telltale rise of liquidity pools that balloon without corresponding increases in active users.

Media coverage amplifies this pattern further. When CNBC reported rising institutional interest in Bitcoin in October 2020, the narrative gained global reach. The announcement that MicroStrategy had allocated corporate treasury funds to Bitcoin in August 2020, led by CEO Michael Saylor in Tysons Corner, Virginia, provided a concrete emblem of credibility. Price rose. More outlets reported on the rise. The feedback loop tightened: media reported prices because they were rising; traders acted because the media reported. The spotlight brightened. The tide lifted.

But attention can be fickle. A counter-example is instructive. In June 2022, despite a flood of negative headlines surrounding Celsius Network's withdrawal freeze, Bitcoin did not collapse to the catastrophic levels many headlines predicted. The news was dramatic, but much of the panic had already been priced in after TerraUSD's collapse the previous month. Media coverage amplified concern yet failed to shift sentiment meaningfully. Why? Because traders had already absorbed the core information. The spotlight was bright, but the audience had moved on. The limitation is clear: media can influence, but only within the bounds of available liquidity and pre-existing conviction.

Reconciling this counter-example with earlier cases reveals a deeper point. Media and memes exert greatest power when two conditions align: spare capital ready to commit, and uncertainty about how others will behave. When liquidity is plentiful—as it was in early 2021—the spotlight directs flows. When liquidity is thin, the spotlight often illuminates what participants already know rather than changing their actions.

Memes, in particular, shape the cultural layer of crypto. They operate as shorthand maps. They condense narratives into symbols that the crowd can recognise instantly. A Shiba Inu image expresses irreverence; a rocket emoji promises imminent ascent; "gm" signals belonging to a global tribe. The cultural work performed by these motifs is not ironic; it is formative. They build cohesion in a market where most participants never meet. This cohesion influences decisions: holders refuse to sell during downturns because selling feels like abandoning the tribe. They buy during peaks because buying feels like joining a movement. These are not abstractions. They are visible behaviours reflected in holding patterns and on-chain metrics.

Memes also compress time. They allow a shared mental model to spread without explanation. A developer posting a complex diagram of a project's roadmap receives modest attention. A meme that communicates the same idea in an image travels far further. Engagement metrics show the gap: hundreds of retweets for the diagram; tens of thousands for the meme. The explanation is not intellectual laziness but cognitive efficiency. People process images faster than text. The spotlight favours speed.

Yet memes are not substitutes for fundamentals. They supplement them. Ethereum's developer community used memes such as the "Ultrasound Money" logo in 2021 to explain the impact of EIP-1559's fee burn mechanism. This was not misinformation. It was communication: a way of illuminating a complex structural shift. The meme made the concept memorable. The fundamentals gave it weight. The implication is subtle: memes can mislead, but they can also clarify. Their meaning depends on whether they depict truth or fantasy.

The challenge is to distinguish signal from spectacle. One method is to track the ratio between attention and action.

Does a surge in trending topics correspond to growth in active addresses, or only to speculative inflows? Does a popular thread lead to sustained usage, or merely to a temporary spike in transactions followed by emptiness? Behaviour reveals sincerity. Metrics reveal substance.

The spotlight appears again in crises. A poorly sourced rumour published by a minor outlet can trigger billions in liquidations if shared widely enough. Traders, fearing others may act, pre-emptively reduce risk. Exchanges register a spike in withdrawals. Stablecoins wobble as holders scramble for safety. The rumour may prove false. The damage is real. Attention is a force that does not require accuracy to exert pressure. The implication: transparency is not purely a technological challenge. It is a narrative one.

Historical parallels remind us that crowd-driven phenomena are not new. In 1637, reports circulated in Haarlem that certain tulip bulbs had doubled in value in a week. As Anne Goldgar documented in *Tulipmania* (2007), much of the story was exaggerated retrospectively, yet contemporaneous pamphlets spread rumours that amplified the frenzy. Behaviour moved before facts. The crypto market's novelty is not the existence of hype but its velocity.

Velocity matters. A journalist once needed a full day to publish a story that could move traders. Now a meme posted anonymously can reach millions in under an hour. Whether the meme concerns technical breakthroughs, speculative gambles, or expressions of cultural identity, it travels across the same channels. The power lies in its reach and repetition. The spotlight does not move evenly; it leaps.

There is, however, a quieter realm where attention has less sway: projects that build slowly, release code incrementally, and avoid promotional theatrics. The development of the Lightning Network from 2018 to 2021 demonstrates this. Adoption grew gradually, with node counts climbing from a few hundred to several thousand across Europe and North America. Despite this measurable progress, media coverage remained sparse. Price did not follow node growth. The spotlight stayed elsewhere. This limitation reminds us that attention markets reward immediacy, not depth. Yet long-term value often forms outside the spotlight.

Reconciliation lies in recognising separate domains: markets driven by spectacle and markets driven by usage. Sometimes they overlap. Often they do not. The mistake is assuming that attention equals relevance. The more productive stance is to treat attention as a diagnostic rather than a verdict.

The motif of the spotlight returns as a practical image. When the beam narrows, visibility intensifies, and crowds rush in. When it widens, nuance returns. Professionals who study these patterns watch how swiftly the beam moves, how long it lingers, and whether it illuminates genuine movement or merely the outline of a collective wish.

Media and memes will continue to shape crypto's narrative architecture. They will compress due diligence. They will amplify momentum. They will spread both clarity and confusion. The unresolved tension is simple. When the spotlight swings towards an asset or idea, is it revealing something real—or merely inviting you to join the crowd before the beam glides away?

When Technology Meets Incentives

On 12 September 2020, during the launch of the decentralised exchange SushiSwap in Tokyo, Ethereum gas fees surged so sharply that average users found themselves priced out of basic transactions. Etherscan recorded median fees briefly exceeding $10 for a standard transfer that normally cost a fraction of that amount. Validators processed the highest-paying transactions first, miners captured the lucrative arbitrage opportunities that rushed into the mempool, and exchanges flagged delays. The code performed exactly as designed. The behaviour around it did not. It was a vivid demonstration that protocols, no matter how elegant, bend under the weight of human incentives.

A protocol may promise fairness, but participants optimise for earnings. They always have. During the Ethereum congestion spikes of May 2021, SparkPool—one of the largest mining pools headquartered in Hangzhou—captured several so-called "miner-extractable value" bundles worth millions of dollars each. The behaviour was measurable: miners re-ordered transactions to extract profit, and users paid ever-higher fees to compete for block space.

What the protocol offered as a public good—an open scheduling mechanism—became a battleground for priority. The scene illustrates a recurring motif: pressure reveals incentives.

Show the tension, then name it. Incentives override design. Explain it: each actor—miner, validator, or exchange—follows a calculus that maximises their position. Implication: the system's stability depends not only on technical architecture but on how participants react during stress. That reaction is rarely idealistic. It is strategic.

Miners offer the clearest demonstration because their actions are traceable. In December 2017, at the peak of Bitcoin mania, miners in Reykjavik preferred to mine empty blocks at times because it allowed faster cycling and sometimes marginally higher earnings. The observable behaviour—blocks with few or no transactions—contradicted the expectation that miners would naturally fill every block to support the network. The incentive was simple: speed could pay more than service. It was neither noble nor malicious. It was rational within the reward structure.

A credible counter-example emerged with the 2017 Bitcoin Cash fork. For several weeks, miners voluntarily mined Bitcoin Cash at a loss, driven partly by ideological commitments expressed on forums and partly by speculation on future appreciation. It seemed to show that not all incentives were economic. Yet the reconciliation is straightforward: ideology itself can function as an incentive when miners expect reputational or long-term strategic gains. Incentives need not be monetary. They merely need to be persuasive.

The same dynamic shaped validator behaviour in proof-of-stake systems. After the launch of the Beacon Chain in December 2020, validators in London, Singapore, and Frankfurt routinely proposed blocks with optimised MEV strategies, relying on relays to maximise revenue. They ran additional software not to stabilise the chain but to increase their returns. The protocol demanded inclusion, attestation, and finality. Incentives demanded revenue. When MEV-boost became standard in 2022, the share of blocks built by specialised relays in some epochs exceeded 80%. The visible consequence was fragmentation: validators became dependent on intermediaries that the core protocol had not anticipated at launch. Again the motif appears. Pressure reveals incentives. Incentives reshape behaviour.

Exchanges, meanwhile, sit at the centre of liquidity. Stress events expose how central these institutions are to crypto's operational reality. During the March 2020 liquidity crisis—when global markets contracted abruptly—several exchanges, including BitMEX in Hong Kong, experienced cascading liquidations. Their liquidation engines sold collateral automatically to protect their own balance sheets. Users saw sharp losses, while the platform remained solvent. The visible behaviour—forced selling into collapsing markets—reflected a straightforward incentive:

exchanges protect the venue first, traders second. This is not a moral judgment. It is the architecture.

A second example occurred during the FTX withdrawal surge in November 2022, when on-chain data from CryptoQuant showed outflows of over $1 billion within 48 hours. As withdrawals increased, the exchange slowed processing times and adjusted internal crediting practices. Users who refreshed their screens saw pending requests stretching from minutes into hours. The action revealed a structural incentive: exchanges manage liquidity to preserve short-term survival. Elegant interfaces conceal that priority.

To show the limitation, consider Coinbase during the same period. The company maintained full solvency and processed withdrawals normally, supported by audited reserves disclosed in its SEC filings. This counter-example demonstrates that responsible design can coexist with strong incentives. Yet even here, the reconciliation requires nuance. Coinbase's incentives were shaped by regulatory scrutiny and public listing obligations. Again: incentives differ by context, not by technology.

The gap between how systems are designed and how actors behave widens under stress because incentives intensify. During periods of high congestion—seen repeatedly during NFT minting surges in 2021—transaction fees on Ethereum spiked to levels that excluded ordinary users. The reason was visible in the mempool: bots paid exorbitant fees to secure early block space, pushing human users behind them. The protocol did not malfunction. It followed rules that rewarded the highest bidder. The implication is uncomfortable: efficiency under stress often means exclusion.

A more subtle example lies in governance. When protocols rely on token voting, voter participation often declines as prices rise. In mid-2021, Uniswap governance saw participation drop below 1% of eligible tokens for several proposals. The visible behaviour was apathy. The incentive was equally visible: holders prioritised speculative upside over participation because voting yielded no immediate gain. The motif returns. Pressure reveals incentives—and sometimes the absence of pressure reveals them too.

These patterns are not unique to crypto. History records similar dynamics. During the Chicago financial panic of 1907, clearing houses in Illinois restricted withdrawals, not because the system had failed, but because incentives favoured institutional survival over customer access. The image is familiar: a system built for fairness behaves differently when stress arrives. The parallel underscores a critical point. Technology may modernise a structure, but incentives inherit their ancient force.

Yet crypto's transparency sharpens the contrast. In decentralised systems, behaviour is observable. One can measure miner revenue, track exchange outflows, and inspect validator preferences. This visibility brings both clarity and discomfort. Clarity, because incentives can be studied empirically. Discomfort, because transparency often reveals misalignments that were previously invisible. When users see miners extracting MEV, they respond with frustration. When they see validators relying on centralised relays, they question decentralisation. When they see exchanges slow withdrawals, they fear insolvency. Behaviour meets expectation, and expectation fractures.

A counterpoint arises with long-term builders who resist misaligned incentives. Teams behind projects like Bitcoin Core, based across Europe and the United States, have repeatedly rejected designs that prioritise speed or convenience at the cost of security. Their behaviour—reviewing code slowly, debating features publicly, refusing to chase hype—reflects a different incentive: long-term credibility. The tension here illustrates the range of possible incentives within the same ecosystem. Not all participants optimise for immediate gain. Some optimise for permanence.

Still, even in these long-term examples, incentives matter. Bitcoin developers depend on grants from organisations such as Chaincode Labs in New York or the Human Rights Foundation. They maintain the protocol not only out of ideology but because funding supports their efforts. Incentives are woven into every layer.

The motif of pressure threads through these cases. Pressure from rising fees. Pressure from liquidity shortages. Pressure from competition among miners and validators. Each scenario exposes how behaviour diverges from the script embedded in the protocol. The divergence is not a flaw. It is a reality.

This tension surfaces again during forks or governance crises. When Ethereum Classic was created in July 2016 after the DAO hack in Zug, Switzerland, miners initially lacked consensus on which chain to support. The divergence was not technical. It was incentive-driven. Some miners held large ETH positions and wanted to protect value. Others saw opportunity in supporting a minority chain. The resulting split showed how incentives shape ideological positions. The technology remained constant. Human behaviour did not.

A second instance came with the 2020 KuCoin hack reported in Singapore. Several networks responded by freezing stolen tokens at the protocol level. Critics argued this violated decentralisation. Supporters argued it protected users. In reality, the behaviour revealed incentives: networks acted to preserve long-term trust among their communities. They prioritised survival. The implication is that decentralisation, too, exists along gradients shaped by incentives.

These threads converge on a single recognition: protocols cannot guarantee behaviour. They structure possibilities. Incentives determine outcomes. And incentives shift depending on market conditions, actor composition, and narrative context.

The motif returns one last time: pressure reveals incentives. It always will.

What, then, is the unresolved question? When the next period of stress arrives—whether congestion, a liquidity freeze, or a governance fracture—will the behaviour of those securing and running the system align with the values advertised in peacetime? Or will incentives redraw the boundaries of acceptable action once again?

Cycle Markers You Can Observe

On 23 April 2021, Binance Futures in Singapore reported funding rates on several perpetual swaps exceeding 0.25% per eight-hour cycle, a level not seen since the exchange's October 2020 surge. At the same time, Glassnode data showed Bitcoin balances on centralised exchanges falling below 2.3 million BTC, the lowest level since August 2018. The two signals—high funding rates and shrinking exchange reserves—sat side by side on the same dashboard, yet pointed in opposing emotional directions. One showed traders paying aggressively for long exposure. The other showed long-term holders withdrawing coins to cold storage. This tension revealed a truth the charts could not articulate: cycles leave footprints long before narratives catch up.

Cycle markers are not mystical. They are measurable behaviours. People commit capital in patterned ways when they are afraid of missing gains, when they fear loss, or when they simply disengage. The motif worth keeping in sight is the pulse. Markets quicken and slacken like a heartbeat, sending signals through the metrics that describe them. The pulse reveals mood.

Funding rates show the market's impatience. They quantify how much traders pay to maintain directional bets. When the rates flip repeatedly between positive and negative within a day—as they did during the May 2021 liquidation cascade on Bybit in Dubai—they capture a visible behaviour: traders rotating between conviction and panic. Funding is a diary of crowd psychology. When rates remain elevated for days, it signals not only optimism but crowded optimism. Participants are willing to pay a recurring fee to maintain exposure. The implication is straightforward: every new buyer joining this queue enters a room already packed.

Shrinkage in exchange reserves signals something different. It shows accumulation—measurable, deliberate, slow. When Coinbase Pro in San Francisco experienced large outflows during February 2021, those flows were linked by market analysts to institutional purchases. The behaviour was visible in on-chain metrics: steady withdrawals, not frantic transactions. It suggested that some participants were preparing for holding periods that outlasted the noise. The implication is stability, or at least the aspiration to stability. When the pulse slows, the crowd steps back.

A counter-example clarifies the nuance. During the 2022 downturn, exchange reserves rose sharply across multiple venues, even as prices fell. It would be easy to interpret this as fear—holders rushing to sell. But on-chain investigators noted that several distressed lenders, including Celsius Network in London, moved assets back to exchanges as part of their restructuring processes. The behaviour reflected forced logistics rather than sentiment. The counter-example shows the limitation: a marker can lose meaning when a single actor dominates flows. The reconciliation lies in the interplay of metrics. One signal can deceive. The pulse, taken across several points, rarely does.

New-account surges often arrive quietly before the crowd notices them. During the final quarter of 2020, Kraken in San Francisco reported unusually high sign-up volumes, weeks before Bitcoin broke through $20,000. The visible behaviour was curiosity turning into commitment. It captured an early stage of narrative spread: people investigating before participating. When new-account growth aligns with rising search interest and social-media chatter, it reveals that the market's pulse is quickening. The implication is early acceleration, not yet exuberance, but building.

Governance apathy, by contrast, signals fatigue. In mid-2021, participation in several major decentralised governance systems declined. Uniswap's proposal on fee-switch mechanics drew less than 1% of eligible voting power. Compound and Aave saw similar patterns. The behaviour was visible: holders watched price more than policy. Apathy appears when people feel their individual input matters less than market momentum. It is the pulse softening, a sign that community engagement is shrinking even as price rises. The implication is fragility: a system that appears healthy on the surface but lacks the distributed attention required to steer it through tension.

Two concrete cases show how these markers interact rather than sit independently. The first is the March 2020 liquidity shock. Funding rates went deeply negative, with BitMEX recording –0.56% on 12 March 2020 as traders paid to hold shorts. Exchange reserves spiked as holders rushed to deposit collateral. New-account creation fell sharply. Governance forums went silent. The pulse narrowed. Each metric pointed to retreat. That retreat preceded the price collapse that followed.

The second is the October–November 2021 peak. Funding stayed strongly positive for extended periods. Exchange reserves dropped steadily. New-account sign-ups surged across multiple platforms—Gemini in New York reported one of its highest onboarding months. Yet governance apathy deepened. The pulse quickened unevenly. The rhythm showed excitement layered on top of exhaustion. That pattern preceded the decline of 2022, not because any single metric predicted it, but because together they revealed a market stretched thin.

A counterpoint worth considering comes from the growth of the Lightning Network from 2018 to 2021. Node counts increased even when prices stagnated. Governance in many Bitcoin-related development channels showed steady participation. Exchange reserves fluctuated without clear directional correlation to price. Funding rates in Bitcoin's perpetual markets did not capture this structural progress. The pulse was faint but steady. The limitation is clear: low-theory markers track speculative cycles, not technological maturation. They describe mood, not innovation. Reconciling this means recognising that cycles and progress run on parallel tracks. One should watch both, but never mistake one for the other.

Funding rates reveal impatience. Exchange reserves reveal intention. New-account surges reveal curiosity. Governance apathy reveals disengagement. Each marker reflects a visible behaviour: paying more for exposure, moving assets, signing up, or stepping back. Together they describe the market's rhythm. The pulse motif returns because it captures the essential point: cycles accelerate and decelerate like breathing.

The strength of these markers lies in their simplicity. They do not require specialised models or complex forecasts. They simply require observation. They show what people *do,* not what they claim. They measure commitment without sentimentality.

Yet their simplicity carries risk. A marker can become a myth. Many commentators during the 2021 cycle argued that declining exchange reserves guaranteed sustained upside. They mistook a structural trend for a timing signal. A single marker cannot hold the weight of prediction. The pulse works only when you observe its rhythm across several points.

The unresolved tension sits here. When you witness a rapid rise in funding rates, a sudden spike in new accounts, reserves draining, and governance falling silent, what does it reveal about the moment? Are you seeing the early stages of exuberance—or the final breath before fatigue sets in?

Chapter 2
Bitcoin as a Teacher

In January 2009, when the first Bitcoin block appeared on a modest computer somewhere controlled by the pseudonymous Satoshi Nakamoto, nothing about the moment signalled revolution. No launch event, no institutional sponsors, no capital raise. Just a timestamp, a cryptographic puzzle solved, and a line inserted into history: a system that allowed strangers to agree on money without trusting any single authority. It was an experiment, tiny and improbable. Yet from that quiet beginning emerged the most scrutinised monetary technology of the 21st century—tested in crashes, attacked by sceptics, and still beating.

Bitcoin is often introduced as a breakthrough in digital scarcity—as if the great innovation were merely a cap of 21 million coins. But scarcity alone is not the triumph. Scarcity that *a global population agrees to respect*—that is the miracle. Digital scarcity does not exist in code; code can be copied infinitely. It exists in social consensus: millions voluntarily honouring a shared ledger because they believe others will too. The true foundation of this technology is not mathematics. It is cooperation. Beneath every hash is a social contract.

That contract has been stress-tested repeatedly. Consider the disputes around hard forks: Bitcoin XT in 2015, Bitcoin Classic in 2016, and Bitcoin Cash in 2017. Each confrontation was framed as a technical improvement. Each became a cultural test. Who has the authority to define Bitcoin? Miners? Developers? Exchanges? Users? The network's refusal to fracture under pressure revealed a lesson older than cryptocurrencies: legitimacy comes from the governed. Upgrades proceed only when the majority of participants—not the most powerful—agree. Consensus is not a button. It is a conversation.

Bitcoin teaches us that trust and distrust can co-exist. Participants do not trust each other individually, but they trust that no single actor can corrupt the system. The decentralisation narrative is often told in the language of cryptography, yet its real substance lies in political philosophy: a monetary system that distributes power widely enough that no coup can succeed quietly. Every attempt to seize control leaves fingerprints on the chain.

Security adds another layer to Bitcoin's teaching. Every block mined is an invoice paid to the defenders of the network. The system's energy consumption, often debated aggressively, is not waste—it is insurance, denominated in electricity rather than signatures on a government guarantee. The security budget changes as issuance declines; halving events shift miner incentives, pressing the network toward greater reliance on transaction fees. Critics see rising energy costs. Supporters see a market pricing the protection of a global ledger. The debate reveals a core tension: resilience is expensive. The question is not whether security should cost. It is who should pay, and how.

Over time, Bitcoin's security has become more visible. Miners reorganise around cheaper energy sources in Iceland, Texas, and Sichuan. Hardware evolves. Hashrate climbs. Yet every strengthening of the shield opens new considerations about sustainability, geopolitics, and the concentration of mining power. Bitcoin teaches with paradox: reducing the influence of central banks can increase sensitivity to energy markets and climate policy. Moving beyond national currencies does not liberate us from all worldly constraints—it merely shifts which constraints we care about most.

Institutional adoption introduced another wave of lessons. When companies like MicroStrategy acquired Bitcoin as treasury reserves in 2020, and when major custodians built regulated investment products, many hailed the moment as validation. It was, in part. Institutional interest reduced some fears: custody risk, market manipulation, reputational stigma. Yet it also imported a new kind of fragility. When leveraged funds enter a volatile asset, drawdowns trigger forced selling. When Bitcoin integrates into traditional portfolios, correlation with equities rises. The fortress gains allies—and inherits their weaknesses.

Bitcoin's appeal as "uncorrelated digital gold" is strongest when it stands apart from the financial system. The closer it gets to Wall Street, the more it must endure Wall Street's cycles. This tension is neither temporary nor easily resolved. It is a testament to Bitcoin's growing relevance and a reminder that systemic integration comes at a price.

Every downturn has its own drama—a spectacular exchange collapse, a regulatory scare, a storyline that frays under scrutiny. Yet Bitcoin endures in ways that lesser projects do not. While narratives evaporate, certain properties remain: uptime measured in years without interruption, auditable supply available to anyone with a node, openness so complete that the poorest participant can verify the richest. In the harsh light of a bear market, these attributes become more than talking points. They become survival traits.

Price collapses do not threaten Bitcoin's existence. They test our assumptions about what matters. When the noise falls silent, the questions become sharper. Does the network continue to produce blocks reliably? Do people voluntarily maintain nodes? Do miners remain incentivised to secure the system? Does exit remain possible without permission? Does the community remember why the project started at all?

These questions illuminate a subtle truth. Bitcoin is not only a financial invention. It is a cultural one. The story of a fixed supply, transparent validation, and censorship-resistant property rights resonated long before institutional capital arrived. It resonates wherever currency is weaponised, wherever inflation dissolves savings, wherever citizens seek the dignity of economic autonomy. Bitcoin's most important market is not the trading desk. It is the human desire for stability without subjugation.

But Bitcoin's teachings are not dogma. They are operating principles shaped by continual stress. The chapter ahead will explore how digital scarcity is secured not merely by code but by the aggregated will of a decentralised community. It will examine the economic realities behind hashrate and halving schedules, unearthing the trade-offs too often glossed over in energetic debates. It will consider institutional involvement without romanticism—acknowledging both the legitimising effect and the contagion it invites. And it will separate long-term resilience from the theatre of price speculation.

Bitcoin asks a question that grows more pressing each year: what should money be when trust in institutions falters? The system proposes one answer. Its community negotiates another. Somewhere between idealism and pragmatism lies a path being carved block by block.

To learn from Bitcoin is to observe how three forces—technology, economics, and culture—interlock in perpetual tension. The code cannot stand without incentives. Incentives cannot endure without consensus. Consensus cannot persist without shared purpose.

New narratives will emerge around faster, more expressive networks. Novel forms of digital value will command attention. But Bitcoin's lessons will remain foundational. It has survived not because it is flawless, but because it has revealed its flaws slowly, in ways that can be studied and adapted to rather than concealed. In a market that celebrates velocity and novelty, it offers a rare counterpoint: endurance.

As you continue, bring one idea with you: Bitcoin is not merely a case study in crypto history. It is a compass. The question is whether we are willing to follow where it points—not toward riches, but toward principles that outlast the boom.

Genesis: Scarcity and Social Consensus

On 3 January 2009, in a modest flat somewhere in Britain, a computer controlled by the still-unknown Satoshi Nakamoto generated Bitcoin's first block. Embedded in it was a headline published that morning by *The Times*: "Chancellor on brink of second bailout for banks." The line was not decoration. It anchored a technical experiment in a specific political moment. It showed that the system's starting point was not merely mathematical difficulty or cryptographic elegance, but a critique of how monetary authority had been exercised. Bitcoin's genesis was both code and commentary. A chain of numbers began, but so did a social argument.

Scarcity in Bitcoin did not emerge as a natural law. It emerged as a choice. The 21-million limit was a parameter, not a universal constant, written into software that anyone could fork, copy, or modify. Nothing in physics prevents the creation of a version with 22 million coins. Nothing in cryptography stops someone from launching a fork with an altered schedule. Yet each attempt to rewrite the limit—

Bitcoin XT in 2015, Bitcoin Classic in 2016, Bitcoin Cash in 2017—failed to capture the original network's legitimacy. Code could be cloned. Authority could not. Scarcity proved to be a social contract masked as a technical rule.

Show the pattern, then name it. Digital scarcity is enforced not by encryption alone, but by millions agreeing to treat one ledger as canonical. Explain it: the guarantee that "there will only be 21 million" rests on collective refusal to recognise alternatives. Implication: scarcity in Bitcoin is cultural glue. The constraint survives because the community chooses to keep it.

The fork disputes revealed this in vivid form. When the Bitcoin XT proposal emerged in 2015 from developers like Mike Hearn in Switzerland, it offered a compelling technical argument for scaling. But the behaviour of users proved more powerful than the logic. Node operators refused to run the software. Miners hesitated to commit to an uncertain future. Exchanges waited for clear majority signals. The initiative stalled. The visible decision—millions declining to shift—defined what Bitcoin was. A protocol's governance is not its code. It is the sum of its users' choices.

The Bitcoin Cash fork of August 2017 offered a contrasting case. Spearheaded by figures including Roger Ver, and supported initially by miners such as ViaBTC in Beijing, it introduced a competing chain that increased block size dramatically. For a short time, hashpower oscillated between the two networks. Exchanges listed the new asset. Markets tried to price the ideological fracture. Yet Bitcoin's main chain remained the focal point of social consensus. Most people continued to treat *BTC* as Bitcoin. The minority chain survived, but as an alternative—not an heir. The motif reappears: legitimacy is not allocated by hashpower alone. It is conferred by belief.

Even more revealing was the behaviour after the November 2018 fork that split Bitcoin Cash itself into BCH and BSV. That division reflected deep ideological conflict and aggressive politics. But the original Bitcoin chain remained untouched by the drama. The implication was clear: Bitcoin's cohesion did not stem from lack of conflict. It stemmed from the network's refusal to be captured by factions. Its social centre held.

A credible counter-example, often raised, is Ethereum's 2016 split into Ethereum and Ethereum Classic after the DAO collapse. There, the majority community—guided by the Ethereum Foundation in Zug—chose to rewrite part of the chain's history to return stolen funds. Ethereum Classic refused the rewrite. Two chains survived. Some argue this shows that scarcity and consensus are fragile. Yet the reconciliation is straightforward: Ethereum had a more centralised social structure in 2016, with expectations of flexibility. Bitcoin's culture, by contrast, had spent years cultivating immutability as a moral boundary. Different social contracts produce different outcomes.

Bitcoin's scarcity derives its authority from the slow, consistent behaviour of its participants. This behaviour is measurable. Tens of thousands of nodes across Europe,

North America, and Asia verify the chain daily. Wallet software defaults to the longest valid chain. Exchanges list BTC as the reference asset. Miners compete to extend the chain with proofs that are costly to produce. These actions, repeated continuously, form the heartbeat of consensus. The pulse is steady.

Scarcity also functions as narrative discipline. If inflationary debates in traditional currencies revolve around central bank discretion, Bitcoin's supply schedule removes discretion entirely. Yet it is a mistake to imagine this removal is purely mechanical. The commitment to scarcity is renewed socially with every decision *not* to accept alternative proposals. It is a recurring vote cast silently by millions. The chain persists because people keep agreeing to its rules.

The halving events illustrate the interplay between code and culture. Every four years, issuance drops by half. Technically, this is enforced by the protocol. Economically, it recalibrates miner incentives—forcing miners to rely more heavily on transaction fees. Socially, it becomes a ritual of reaffirmation. Halving cycles create a shared calendar. They tie the community's expectations to a schedule known years in advance. When the May 2020 halving occurred, miners in Sichuan and Texas adjusted operations, buyers recalibrated models, and commentators revived old debates about supply shocks. The behaviour was predictable. The response was cultural as much as economic. The motif surfaces again: the chain's rhythm is partly mechanical and partly communal.

Scarcity alone does not explain Bitcoin's durability. Scarcity exists in many assets that fade into obscurity. What makes Bitcoin distinct is its capacity to align millions around a shared definition of what *counts* as Bitcoin. That alignment has proved resilient even when incentives diverge.

Take the case of miners during the 2017–2018 scaling conflict. Some large pools supported bigger blocks to increase throughput. Their financial incentives pointed one way. Yet they still mined the smaller-block chain because they recognised that mining alone could not redefine Bitcoin. Their decision showed something subtle: participants respect social consensus even when it reduces their immediate gain. This behaviour, visible in block production patterns and public signalling, reinforces the network's cohesion.

A second example lies in how exchanges handled ticker symbols during the 2017 fork. When Bitcoin Cash launched, several exchanges—including Coinbase in San Francisco—delayed listing it for months. Others, like Kraken in New York, listed it promptly but maintained BTC as the canonical label. The uniformity of this decision demonstrated that exchanges, despite competing fiercely, recognised their role as custodians of collective understanding. They did not want to split the cultural identity of Bitcoin. The incentive was reputational stability.

Now consider a counter-example. During the emergence of BSV in late 2018, a handful of supporters argued that it represented the "real Bitcoin," and some exchanges listed it with enthusiastic copy. Yet users overwhelmingly rejected the claim. BSV's hashpower dwindled. Social consensus never migrated. The limitation becomes obvious: efforts to rename or reframe Bitcoin cannot succeed without a broad and durable cultural shift. The community's perception is the gatekeeper.

The thread running through all these cases is the quiet motif of the ledger as a mirror. Bitcoin reflects the collective decisions of its participants with relentless clarity. Every block is an inscription of agreement. Every fork is a test of identity. Every choice to run or not run a software upgrade measures commitment. The ledger is not merely a record of transactions. It is a record of consent.

Seen through this lens, Bitcoin's genesis story becomes less about inventing scarcity and more about orchestrating cohesion. A decentralised system that functions without a leader requires a deep reservoir of shared norms. These norms form gradually: through public debates, through scrutiny of proposals, through the reputations of developers and miners, through the daily habit of verifying rather than trusting. This cultural architecture does not appear in code repositories. It appears in behaviour.

It also evolves. The Bitcoin community of 2023 is not the community of 2013. Mining has professionalised. Exchanges have become regulated institutions. Wallet design has improved dramatically. These shifts alter expectations around security, access, and responsibility. Yet through these changes, the core norm—immutability of supply—has held firm. It has become a boundary principle, akin to a constitution that cannot be amended without destroying the republic it governs.

Still, the unresolved tension remains. If digital scarcity is a social agreement rather than a physical constraint, what protects it from erosion? What happens if a future generation, facing a radically different economic environment, demands a change to the supply limit? What if new technological threats alter the calculus of security budgets? What if incentives tilt in a direction that challenges cultural taboos?

These questions are not hypothetical provocations. They are the long-term tests of any social contract. The chain is honest. The culture must be, too.

Bitcoin's genesis teaches a simple but challenging lesson: scarcity endures only when consensus does. The harder question is whether consensus will remain as firm when the pressures on the system shift.

Security Budgets and Energy Debates

At 19:23 UTC on 11 May 2020, the Bitcoin network produced block 630,000. The block, mined by F2Pool, a company founded in Beijing, was unremarkable in size but decisive in consequence. With its arrival, the reward for adding a new block to the chain fell from 12.5 to 6.25 bitcoin. In a single moment, miners' revenue from new issuance was cut in half. The code had done exactly what it promised. The economic reality changed overnight. The security bill came due.

Within hours, hash rate dipped as some miners switched off older, less efficient machines that could no longer cover their electricity costs. Others migrated to cheaper power in Sichuan or Inner Mongolia, or prepared to move hardware to Texas and Quebec. The protocol did not ask who could afford to keep defending it. It reduced the budget and left the market to decide which guardians would remain. A line on a schedule had turned into shuttered warehouse lights, pallets of ASICs in transit, and renegotiated power contracts. Security, abstract in whitepapers, became a ledger of who stayed plugged in.

Most arguments about Bitcoin's energy use ignore this simple fact: every joule consumed is a line item in a security budget. The network does not burn electricity for spectacle. It does so to pay for a specific service—the continuous, global enforcement of a single transaction history. That service has a price. The question is not whether there is a bill. It is who pays it, how much, and according to which priorities.

Show the mechanism, then name it. Bitcoin's security budget is the sum of issuance and transaction fees, denominated in bitcoin but translated into power bills and hardware depreciation. Explain it: miners compete for this budget. The more valuable the block reward, the more resources rational actors will devote to capturing it, up to the point where marginal cost approaches marginal revenue. Implication: security is not a static property baked into the protocol. It is an economic outcome that waxes and wanes with price, fees, and policy choices like the halving schedule.

Consider two concrete moments. In December 2017, as Bitcoin traded near its then-highs, miners in Iceland, the United States and China collectively pushed hash rate to record levels. The Cambridge Bitcoin Electricity Consumption Index (CBECI, 2018) estimated network power draw had risen by several multiples within a year, driven mainly by higher revenue per block. Visible behaviour followed the incentives: investors funded new mining farms near hydro and geothermal sites, power providers negotiated long-term contracts, and mining pools expanded operations. The budget grew because the market could justify a larger spend on security.

By contrast, in June 2021, following China's sweeping restrictions on Bitcoin mining in provinces such as Sichuan and Xinjiang, hash rate fell sharply as operators shut down racks and scrambled to relocate machinery. Security expenditure did not vanish, but it became geographically fragmented and temporarily reduced. The same protocol, the same 6.25 BTC reward, now had to be defended by a reshuffled set of participants facing new regulatory and logistical constraints. The budget's size remained linked to revenue; its composition shifted with policy decisions and political risk.

Energy debates often stop at consumption comparisons. They ask whether Bitcoin "uses more electricity than country X", drawing from CBECI or International Energy Agency statistics, and then leap straight to moral judgment. What this framing misses is the comparison class. All secure settlement systems incur security costs. A central bank's vaults, data centres, compliance teams and legal apparatus consume energy and capital, but those costs are obscured within state budgets and corporate reports. Bitcoin makes its security spend transparent by routing it directly through miners' power meters. The meter is visible.

Show, then name. The criticism treats Bitcoin's spend as optional extravagance. A more accurate framing sees it as an insurance premium: society pays miners to enforce property rights on a shared digital ledger. Explain it: the premium is calibrated by block rewards and fees. When demand for block space rises—as it did during NFT and memecoin activity in early 2021—fees spike, and the insurance budget temporarily inflates. When activity falls, fees drop, and the budget leans more heavily on issuance. Implication: any proposal to modify Bitcoin's energy profile is, implicitly, a proposal to alter the size or allocation of this insurance premium.

Halving events tighten that budget structurally. As issuance declines every four years, the network must transition from subsidy-heavy security to fee-heavy security. Observers worry that if base-layer fees remain low, miners will underinvest in hardware and vulnerable concentrations will appear. There is genuine uncertainty here. No one can predict with confidence what the fee market will look like several halvings hence. But the principle is clear: the protocol makes a bet that demand for scarce block space will eventually be sufficient to fund adequate defence. Whether that bet pays off is an economic question, not a purely technical one.

A counter-example helps illuminate the trade-offs. Ethereum's transition from proof-of-work to proof-of-stake with "the Merge" in September 2022, coordinated from bases such as the Ethereum Foundation's offices in Zug, dramatically reduced that network's measured electricity use. Validators now lock up ether instead of competing with hardware. Energy expenditure fell. Security remained anchored in the value of staked assets and the difficulty of coordinating attacks. Critics of proof-of-work point to this as evidence that digital security need not carry a large power bill. They have a point.

Yet the reconciliation lies in the different assumptions each system makes about where risk should sit. Proof-of-stake converts external spending (electricity, hardware) into internal financial risk (slashing of stake). Successful attacks can be penalised by seizing bonds. In proof-of-work, attack costs are largely sunk into external infrastructure and power. Hardware must be acquired, energy must be paid for. Failed attacks may leave attackers with stranded equipment. The question becomes: do we want the security bill denominated in energy, in financial stake, or in a mix passed through traditional institutions?

Bitcoin's supporters argue that anchoring security in physical expenditure makes attacks more costly to conceal and harder to reverse through political influence. A hostile government cannot simply buy influence over validators; it must assemble and operate vast amounts of hardware. Critics respond that this locks the network into high energy usage that may sit uneasily with climate goals. Both perspectives measure different risks: exposure to political capture on one side, environmental and social externalities on the other. The meter on the wall cannot adjudicate between them. It merely counts.

The energy debate often glosses over a crucial nuance: not all watts are equal. Miners have strong incentives to seek the cheapest electricity available. By 2021, many industrial-scale operations had migrated towards regions with stranded hydroelectric capacity in Sichuan, wind in Texas, and surplus geothermal in Iceland. Firms such as Argo Blockchain in London publicly highlighted their use of renewable-heavy grids, partly to attract capital constrained by ESG mandates. Behaviour again followed the budget. Where power is cheapest, the security bill gets paid.

But there are limits. Even renewables carry opportunity costs. Every megawatt-hour devoted to mining could, in theory, power other industrial activity or households. This raises a harder question: what societal value does Bitcoin's security provide, relative to other uses for the same resources? For citizens in Argentina or Nigeria using Bitcoin as a hedge against currency debasement, the answer may look very different from that of a homeowner in Frankfurt reading headlines about energy shortages. The security budget is global; its perceived benefit is local.

Fees complete the picture. In periods of congestion, fees have reached levels that price out small users. During May 2021, average Bitcoin transaction charges, as recorded by data providers like BitInfoCharts, spiked dramatically. The budget swelled, but access narrowed. A security model funded by fees disproportionately burdens those who transact frequently with small amounts. This reality contradicts simplistic claims that "high fees are good because they secure the network." High fees can secure, but they also exclude. The bill is not shared evenly.

A subtle point emerges here. Security is not free even when someone else appears to be paying. If issuance funds the budget, holders absorb dilution. If fees fund it, transactors absorb cost. If institutions sponsor miners, users absorb the risk that those institutions gain influence. Every path has a constituency that pays the bill, whether through inflation, direct charges, or governance exposure. The question "how much energy does Bitcoin use?" masks the more pointed question "who is underwriting this protection, and why?"

A credible limitation to concerns about security budgets is the observation that historical Bitcoin hashrate has grown far faster than strictly necessary to deter plausible attacks, particularly as the market capitalisation expanded. One could argue the network may be "overpaying" for marginal security at times; that an attacker would need to invest vast sums in hardware and energy to challenge it, while the incremental benefits of higher hashrate beyond a threshold are modest. This criticism deserves attention. Yet it must be weighed against the lack of a clear, agreed-upon threshold of "enough" security in a permissionless, adversarial environment. The safe level is not obvious in advance. Insurance is famously easier to judge in hindsight.

The motif of the bill returns. Bitcoin's security budget is itemised every ten minutes. Miners receive rewards. Power companies receive payments. Hardware manufacturers record sales. Users adjust behaviour in response to fees and perceived safety. The bill is visible, divisible, and, crucially, non-negotiable at the protocol level. What can be negotiated is whether a given society wants to participate in paying it.

The unresolved tension is therefore not whether Bitcoin consumes energy. That question was answered the moment Satoshi Nakamoto chose proof-of-work. The deeper tension is this: how much are we, collectively, willing to spend—whether in electricity, forgone alternatives, or opportunity cost—to maintain a monetary network that anchors its security in verifiable external effort rather than discretionary institutional promises? And if that bill feels too high, what kind of risk are we quietly agreeing to accept instead?

Institutional Adoption vs Cyclical Risk

On 11 August 2020, MicroStrategy, a business-intelligence firm headquartered in Virginia and listed on the Nasdaq, announced the purchase of 21,454 bitcoin for roughly $250 million. The decision, signed off by its board and disclosed in a regulatory filing, was the first time a publicly traded corporation committed part of its treasury to Bitcoin at scale. The effect was immediate. Trading desks in New York and London reported a surge in inbound inquiries from asset managers who had previously dismissed the asset as speculative noise. A single corporate disclosure had shifted a boundary. The institutional gates, long guarded, creaked open. Yet within weeks, volatility reminded those same institutions that the gates swung both ways. By late September, Bitcoin had retraced sharply, and MicroStrategy's market capitalisation fluctuated so violently that sceptics questioned whether corporate treasuries belonged anywhere near such instability. The moment marked a turning point: validation and vulnerability intertwined.

Institutional adoption brings legitimacy measured in headlines and capital flows. It also brings correlation, leverage, and systemic entanglement. The motif worth holding is the hinge. Institutions are hinges between retail speculation and global finance. They open access. They open risk.

Show the dynamic, then name it. When asset managers, pension funds, and brokers enter Bitcoin markets, they import their own behaviours: risk-parity models, collateral management cycles, structured product design, portfolio rebalancing mechanics. Explain it: Bitcoin ceases to be a self-contained ecosystem and becomes a component within multi-asset frameworks governed by quarterly reporting pressures and regulatory constraints. Implication: adoption reduces certain idiosyncratic risks—fragmented custody, operational fragility—yet simultaneously exposes Bitcoin to macro shocks and leverage unwinding that have nothing to do with its protocol.

The first major example unfolded during the fourth quarter of 2021. ProShares launched the first U.S. Bitcoin futures exchange-traded fund (ETF) on 19 October 2021. As the fund began purchasing CME futures contracts in Chicago, it amplified demand for synthetic exposure rather than spot holdings. The visible behaviour was crowding: open interest climbed, roll costs accumulated, and basis spreads widened. The ETF allowed institutions to comply with existing mandates, but it also created a structural link between Bitcoin's price and leveraged futures markets. A rally fuelled partly by derivative demand looked like adoption. It was, in fact, a balance sheet effect.

The second example came through structured notes. In late 2020 and early 2021, private banks in Switzerland and Singapore marketed autocallable products tied to Bitcoin's price. These instruments, issued by well-known banks and sold to high-net-worth clients, embedded leverage through option structures. When Bitcoin fell below predetermined barriers, issuers hedged their exposure by shorting futures or selling spot. Behaviour translated directly into market pressure. Structured adoption created fragility. When prices dipped, hedging activity intensified declines. The institutional hinge moved, and the market swung sharply.

A credible counter-example reveals the nuance. During the March 2023 U.S. banking turmoil—triggered by the failures of Silicon Valley Bank and Signature Bank—Bitcoin's price rose as regional bank equities fell. Institutional portfolios that had treated Bitcoin as a risk asset suddenly saw it behave as a partial hedge to financial-system instability. Some argued this demonstrated Bitcoin's maturing role. Yet the reconciliation lies in distinguishing short-term flows from long-term structure. Temporary decorrelation does not erase the reality that institutional adoption generally increases exposure to broader financial cycles. The hinge holds multiple directions.

Correlation is not a philosophical debate. It is a measurable behaviour. In 2021, during periods of heavy institutional trading, the 30-day correlation between Bitcoin and the Nasdaq 100 hovered near 0.8 (Bloomberg, 2021). This reflected hedge-fund positioning, macro trades linked to inflation expectations, and risk-on sentiment tied to abundant liquidity. When institutions treat Bitcoin as a technology asset rather than a monetary rupture, their models bind its movements to equities. The alignment is not ideological. It is mechanical.

Leverage magnifies this. Institutional desks often use Bitcoin to express tactical views through futures, swaps, and structured products. These instruments embed automatic liquidation thresholds. When Bitcoin is included in macro portfolios alongside high-beta equities, deleveraging events cascade. The March 2020 crash, the May 2021 unwind, and the June 2022 liquidity crunch showed this pattern repeatedly. Bitcoin sold off not because its network degraded, but because institutions trimmed exposure across correlated assets to meet margin calls. The hinge creaked.

But institutional adoption also mitigates certain risks. Cold-storage custodians such as Fidelity Digital Assets in Boston, and regulated exchanges operating under stringent oversight, reduce counterparty vulnerability for large holders. Insurance coverage lines grow. Better auditing frameworks emerge. Market manipulation becomes easier to track when large flows move through regulated channels. The infrastructure strengthens. Fraud becomes harder to hide. Yet this improved robustness comes at the cost of integration. Institutions do not operate in ideological isolation. They operate within regulatory, political and liquidity regimes that Bitcoin cannot shape.

Another example illustrates the trade-off. When Tesla disclosed a $1.5 billion Bitcoin purchase in February 2021, the announcement added credibility to corporate adoption narratives. Weeks later, when Tesla suspended Bitcoin payments in May 2021 citing environmental concerns, the market corrected sharply. A single corporate policy shift dictated sentiment more strongly than any technical development on the network. Institutional participation both elevated and destabilised price. The behaviour revealed a reality often forgotten in evangelism: collective identity in Bitcoin may be decentralised, but large holders can move the narrative with a single press release.

A further limitation becomes visible when institutions enter with hedged products rather than spot purchases. Futures-based ETFs, margin accounts, and yield-enhanced notes do not require institutions to hold underlying bitcoin directly. The result is exposure without commitment. The appearance of adoption exceeds the actual custodial base. Apparent demand can disappear as quickly as a derivative position is closed. The hinge swings back.

The motif of the hinge clarifies another underappreciated point: institutional adoption changes who makes decisions in periods of stress. In early cycles, retail sentiment dominated turning points. By 2022, fund managers adjusting exposure based on quarterly risk targets—often in London or New York—played an equal or greater role. Their behaviour is not guided by ideological conviction or protocol mechanics. It is guided by volatility targets, mandate clauses, Sharpe ratios, and regulatory obligations. Their time horizons shrink. Their risk appetite shifts. Bitcoin becomes one more variable in a lattice of macro decisions.

A contrasting example emerges from long-term allocators. Some university endowments in the United States began acquiring small Bitcoin positions from 2020 onwards, often via venture funds or direct custodial arrangements. Their behaviour, marked by multi-year horizons and limited leverage, showed that not all institutional capital destabilises cycles. Long-duration capital can dampen volatility by absorbing supply. Yet this group represents a minority. The bulk of institutional flow remains opportunistic, leverage-sensitive, and tied to macro factors.

Institutional adoption also introduces regulatory reflexes. When major asset managers enter a market, regulators respond with heightened scrutiny. This can stabilise infrastructure, but it can also introduce new vectors of systemic risk. For example, if exchange-traded products become highly popular, liquidity concentration in a small number of custodians or clearinghouses could amplify disruptions. The regulatory shield becomes a regulatory bottleneck. The hinge carries weight.

Underlying all of this is a cultural shift. Bitcoin's early identity as an outsider technology—voluntary, adversarial, sceptical of authority—evolved as institutional holders increased. Communication softened. Branding professionalised. Market narratives adjusted to appeal to investment committees rather than cryptography forums. The change is neither purely good nor purely bad. It is a sign of maturation. It is also a sign that the community no longer fully controls the narrative. Institutions speak the language of portfolios, not principles.

And yet, even as institutional participation reshapes volatility dynamics, Bitcoin retains features that resist capture: transparent supply, open validation, censorship-resistant settlement. These traits do not dissolve when hedge funds enter. They simply coexist with new influences. The system remains decentralised at the protocol layer while becoming centralised in its liquidity flows. The hinge is double-sided.

The unresolved tension sits precisely here. If institutional adoption continues to rise—through futures ETFs, structured notes, pension allocations, and custodial platforms—will Bitcoin's behaviour increasingly mirror the risk cycles of global finance? Or will its foundational properties eventually exert their own gravitational pull, forcing institutions to adapt to a monetary system that refuses to bend to their familiar rhythms?

What Survives Every Downturn

On 12 March 2020, the day traders later called "Black Thursday," Bitcoin's price halved within hours as global markets convulsed. Exchanges from Seoul to London reported forced liquidations, queues of unprocessed withdrawals, and order books thinning to near exhaustion. Yet the Bitcoin network itself—running across thousands of nodes—continued producing blocks at roughly ten-minute intervals. No central coordinator issued reassurances. No emergency committee adjusted parameters. The system absorbed the shock and carried on. Prices collapsed; the protocol did not. It was a moment that separated spectacle from substance. In a crisis that erased billions of dollars in paper wealth, uptime and openness outperformed narrative and noise.

Episodes like that March day reveal a truth too easily obscured during euphoria: resilience is not a slogan but a set of behaviours that persist when incentives warp and fear dominates. Much of what investors celebrate during booms is ornamental—marketing, community fervour, glossy roadmaps. What survives busts are the infrastructures that remain verifiable, accessible, and difficult to corrupt. The motif worth holding is the beam. When storms rip off a building's décor, its surviving beams show what was load-bearing all along.

Downturns expose gaps between claims and capabilities. To measure that gap, one must watch what systems do, not what their stewards say. When exchanges faltered in March 2020, Bitcoin's mempool filled, fees spiked, but blocks still formed. Show the behaviour, then name its significance: uptime is not a technical nicety; it is a cultural norm maintained by a dispersed network of operators from Reykjavík to Buenos Aires. Explain it: resilience comes from redundancy, transparency, and incentives aligned with continuity rather than convenience. Implication: a monetary network's credibility rests less on its price than on its ability to function when confidence evaporates.

The first major example of this pattern comes from the August 2017 Bitcoin Cash fork. The split, born from disagreements over block size and scaling, created two competing chains. In the run-up to the fork, advocates on each side offered predictions of catastrophic disruption. Yet when the event occurred, Bitcoin's main chain continued with no measurable downtime, while Bitcoin Cash launched its own alternative history. The visible behaviours diverged. Bitcoin's stewardship—which rests in voluntary node consensus rather than central authority—preserved continuity. The fork illustrated a social contract: changes to the base protocol require broad cultural legitimacy, not just technical possibility. The fork was contested, but the process of contestation demonstrated the network's durability.

A second example emerged during China's mining crackdown in May–June 2021. When the Chinese government ordered miners in provinces such as Sichuan and Xinjiang to shut down operations, network hash rate fell by more than 50% within weeks. A collapse of such magnitude would cripple many distributed systems. Yet Bitcoin's difficulty-adjustment mechanism recalibrated on 3 July 2021, reducing mining difficulty by nearly 28%—the largest drop in its history. That adjustment rebalanced incentives automatically. Blocks slowed but never stopped. The network adapted without governance meetings, emergency decrees, or protocol rewrites. The beam held. A monetary system that can withstand a geographically concentrated exodus of half its computing power displays a form of resilience unmatched by younger crypto networks.

A credible counter-example helps clarify the distinction. During the collapse of the Terra ecosystem in May 2022, the

Luna Foundation Guard attempted to defend UST's peg by deploying billions of dollars' worth of bitcoin reserves. Markets watched in real time as those reserves moved to exchanges, prompting speculative fear that forced sales would create downward pressure on Bitcoin itself. Terra's stablecoin design failed spectacularly. Yet Bitcoin's own network, subjected to volatility and rumours of mass liquidation, sustained its operations with no governance intervention. Still, prices fell sharply. The counter-example reveals a limitation: protocol resilience does not quarantine an asset from market contagion. The reconciliation lies in recognising that resilience manifests in operational continuity, not insulation from price swings driven by external events.

Visible behaviours reveal deeper traits. Uptime is recorded block by block. Openness is measured by the ability of any participant to run a node without permission or costly hardware. Auditability appears in public ledgers where every transaction can be traced, disputed, or verified. Exit costs show up in the friction of moving holdings: withdrawal fees, transfer delays, counterparty barriers. These metrics survive sentiment because they are embedded in infrastructure. They do not disappear when venture capital retreats or headlines sour.

Another example illustrates this. During the FTX collapse in November 2022, users across Asia and Europe rushed to withdraw funds from exchanges they had long trusted. Many found themselves waiting hours or days as platforms froze transfers, citing "risk management." Bitcoin's peer-to-peer architecture offered an escape valve: individuals with self-custody transferred funds freely, even as centralised venues faltered. The behaviour made visible a distinction too often ignored during booms: decentralised systems offer continuity of exit even when centralised intermediaries fail. The implication is not romantic. It is practical. The cost of leaving a system—whether denominated in fees, delays, or frictions—reveals the true balance of power between user and custodian.

One more metric deserves attention: governance apathy. During bull markets, voting participation in many blockchain governance systems surges as tokens rise in value. Yet downturns reveal the hollowness of such engagement. Participation drops. Delegates lose interest. Proposals stall. Bitcoin avoids this cyclical decay precisely because its governance is minimal and distributed; it relies on cultural norms and voluntary coordination rather than formal vote-driven structures. The lack of a governance token becomes a strength. When markets crash, Bitcoin's governance does not. The beam stays intact.

Contrast this with a credible limitation. In protocols that depend heavily on token-based voting, downturns often reduce voting power to a small, committed minority. System upgrades may stagnate. Decisions may be captured by a few large holders. This vulnerability does not disappear simply because a project markets itself as decentralised. Yet the limitation does not apply uniformly.

Some proof-of-stake chains with active communities and diversified delegator bases demonstrate greater resilience. The reconciliation lies in distinguishing systems where governance is performative from systems where participation remains functional when incentives tighten.

A further observation emerges from examining openness in practice. During regulatory scrutiny in 2023, several centralised exchanges restricted access for users in certain jurisdictions. Those restrictions were implemented through identity filters and IP blocks. Meanwhile, Bitcoin's base layer remained accessible globally; nodes continued to communicate across borders despite policy shifts. Openness is not a slogan. It is a measurable behaviour: the persistence of global access despite changing political environments. The implication is clear. A system that remains reachable under varied regimes carries resilience no bull market can imitate.

The motif of the beam returns here. Downturns strip away decorative layers: influencer endorsements, glossy decks, speculative fervour. What remains are the beams—design choices that ensure continuity, verify activity, and distribute control. Anyone studying resilience should begin not with promises but with proofs. Not with narratives but with nodes.

Consider auditability as a final illustration. Forensic analyses conducted after both the Mt. Gox failure in 2014 and the FTX collapse in 2022 relied on Bitcoin's transparent ledger to trace flows, identify misappropriated funds, and reconstruct timelines. These audits were possible because Bitcoin embeds transparency at the base layer rather than outsourcing it to corporate disclosures. That transparency becomes most valuable when trust collapses. It transforms investigation from speculation into verification. The beam is visible even in ruins.

Yet resilience is not a stable trait. It must be observed across cycles. Uptime remains impressive, but long-term sustainability requires continued decentralisation of miners, nodes, and custodial practices. Openness must withstand pressures from regulators, intermediaries, and market concentration. Auditability must remain intact against privacy-enhancing proposals that, if misapplied, could obscure flows. Exit costs must remain manageable even as fees fluctuate with demand.

The unresolved question, and the hinge upon which future cycles may turn, is simple yet profound: as Bitcoin scales, will its enduring beams—uptime, openness, auditability, and low exit friction—retain their strength under new forms of political pressure, institutional integration, and environmental scrutiny? The answer will not emerge in euphoria. It will emerge in the next downturn, when the décor once again falls away.

Chapter 3
Exchanges: The Castle and the Moat

On a quiet weekday morning in late January 2018, traders across Asia discovered they could no longer withdraw funds from one of the region's most popular crypto exchanges. Tweets first, then headlines: maintenance issues, delayed withdrawals, an unspecified technical failure. Hours stretched into days. The exchange's support channels were overwhelmed. Anxiety metastasised into fear. It became clear that for millions of people, the "crypto" they supposedly owned existed only as numbers in a database controlled by a private company. The markets were open. Prices moved. But users were trapped. The castle's drawbridge had risen, and those inside learned what many prefer not to admit: whether one is free in crypto often depends on who holds the keys.

Exchanges sit at the centre of the crypto economy, a paradoxical mixture of citadel and single point of failure. They are essential gateways to an emerging monetary system designed to eliminate intermediaries. They make markets liquid and accessible, while reintroducing the vulnerabilities of custody, commingling, and concentrated decision-making. In the moments when screens go green and fortunes balloon, exchanges feel like efficient machines. When liquidity evaporates and rumours spread, they reveal a more medieval character: a fortified castle with a moat that protects the rulers first, and the inhabitants only if there is time and will.

The crypto ideal imagines peer-to-peer exchange without trust. The crypto reality routes 90% of all trading volume through custodial institutions where trust is mandatory. These institutions create prices, shape incentives, determine listing legitimacy, and in crises, decide who gets a lifeboat and who stays in the sinking hold. They are not merely marketplaces. They are rule-makers, record-keepers, risk concentrators, and—at times—arbiters of financial fate.

This chapter will open that castle door and examine what lies behind the high walls. It will show how venue design influences every tick in the chart: the placement of bids and offers, the incentives paid to those who supply liquidity, the fees invisible to casual observers yet felt in every execution. Order books are not neutral mirrors of value; they are engines in which rules and architecture shape outcomes. Maker-taker models, internalisation, dark liquidity, and sudden halts are not market trivia but the hidden plumbing through which fortunes flow.

We will explore custody structures, because where assets sleep determines whether they wake up in a crisis. Commingling customer deposits with operating funds may be efficient in a spreadsheet. It is catastrophic when withdrawals surge and liquidity thins. Cold storage can be a bulwark—but only if the operational discipline to use it exists. Proof-of-reserves is a powerful concept—but only if the liabilities side of the ledger receives equal scrutiny. When things are calm, exchange trust models fade into the background; when panic arrives, they become existential.

Then there is the peculiar economy of exchange tokens. Many exchanges mint their own currencies, offering trading discounts or yield incentives to users who hold them. These tokens function as loyalty chips, collateral, and sometimes political votes. Their prices become testaments to confidence in the castle itself. Yet incentives can distort behaviour. A coin listed to earn fees becomes a signal of legitimacy. Liquidity mining campaigns create volume that mimics interest but evaporates the moment subsidies end. Retail investors interpret presence on a large exchange as validation of substance, when the listing might be little more than a commercial transaction. In this space, visibility is often mistaken for verification.

We will also trace the anatomy of exchange failures—events that leave scars on this industry's collective memory. Not to revel in disaster, but because every collapse teaches the same lesson in new clothing: if the moat exists to protect the castle, it does not always protect those inside. A system that relies on a handful of venues to handle the majority of capital creates networked fragility. When a major exchange fails, contagion spreads not merely through price but through confidence, counterparty relationships, and operational linkages that few users see until they break.

Consider one of the most dramatic examples: when Mt. Gox, once handling over 70% of Bitcoin trading volume, froze withdrawals in February 2014 before collapsing into bankruptcy. Users discovered that coins they assumed were safely stored had been lost for years. Prices plunged, not because Bitcoin's protocol faltered, but because trust in infrastructure collapsed. Fast-forward to November 2022: another dominant exchange imploded amid allegations of misused customer assets and opaque internal accounting. Again, the protocol survived. Again, the market cratered. Again, millions learned too late that possession on an exchange is not ownership.

The pattern repeats: innovation builds optimism, optimism attracts capital, capital concentrates power, concentrated power magnifies the damage when mismanaged. Exchanges are castles because they must be strongholds of liquidity and security. They are moats because they create distance—between users and their assets, between service providers and outside scrutiny, between promises and proof.

And yet, despite every cautionary tale, people flock to these platforms. Not out of ignorance, but because the alternative—true self-custody, on-chain trading, manual management of keys and settlement—remains daunting for many. Exchanges have built user experiences that feel comfortable, familiar, frictionless. They turn the frontier into a mall. They convert cryptographic responsibility into a simple login screen. The moat offers safety and convenience. Until the drawbridge lifts.

Understanding exchanges is not optional for anyone engaging with crypto markets. It is foundational. You can believe deeply in decentralisation while also recognising that the primary markets for these decentralised assets are intensely centralised. You can admire the elegance of peer-to-peer architecture while acknowledging that most people rarely touch it directly. To navigate cycles without fear or naivety, one must understand the incentives and fragilities embedded in these middlemen.

This chapter will offer that clarity. We will break down how order books actually function, why liquidity matters more than market capitalisation, and how fees shape trading outcomes in ways few appreciate. We will examine custody models with a forensic lens: where assets sit, how they are segregated, and what documentation is worth more than a marketing claim. We will analyse token incentives—who they benefit, what risks they mask, and how they shift power within the castle walls. And we will map the typical cascade when things go wrong: how rumours become runs, how liquidity evaporates faster than code can settle balances, and how one platform's downfall reverberates through the industry like a fire leaping from rooftop to rooftop.

The purpose is not to scold, nor to scare. It is to see clearly. Exchanges are neither villains nor saviours. They are human institutions built atop technological possibility: efficient when incentives align, dangerous when they diverge, indispensable yet imperfect. They are the battlefield where ideology meets reality—where decentralisation must coexist with convenience, and where risk is not eliminated but transferred.

The question that lingers at the end of every boom is the same that whispers through every crash: how many castles can fall before people demand a better architecture? This chapter will not answer that question directly. But by illuminating the structures, incentives, safeguards, and failure modes of exchanges, it will equip you to recognise strongholds built on real stone—and those held up only by banners and belief.

The moat is deep. The walls are high. The stakes are real. Let us step inside and see what holds the castle up—and what could bring it down.

Market Structure 101

At 09:30 on 14 April 2021, Coinbase Global, Inc. began trading on the Nasdaq in New York. Bitcoin hovered near $64,000. Millions watched a crypto-native firm enter public markets for the first time. Yet inside Coinbase's own exchange, the price a user would pay for a single bitcoin—executing at the top of the ask—could differ from the global index price by tens or even hundreds of dollars. A symbol of mainstream validation revealed a structural truth: markets are not monoliths. They are venues—plural—each with its own rules, incentives, and hidden costs. Two traders may believe they are buying the same asset at the same moment, yet the microstructure beneath their trades determines what they actually receive and what they silently give up.

An exchange feels like a price oracle: a clean number presented with authority. But the number is an emergent property of architecture. Invisible queues of orders compete for priority. Incentives shape who supplies liquidity and who consumes it. Middlemen—whether designated market-makers or automated systems—decide how much slippage a user must tolerate. In a decentralised asset class, centralised architecture still dictates crucial outcomes. The motif worth holding is the stage. Traders see the performance; few understand the set design.

An order book shows bids below, asks above. That simple display masks a complex economic engine. Show the behaviour, then name its mechanics: liquidity provision is performed by participants willing to post limit orders—offers to trade at specified prices—while others send market orders demanding immediate execution. Explain the consequence: takers pay for urgency, makers are paid for patience. Implication: the spread between the highest bid and lowest ask becomes the toll users pay to exit or enter a position, and that toll widens or narrows with venue design.

Consider Binance in 2017. The exchange introduced aggressive maker-taker incentives—rebates for limit orders, fees for market orders—to jump-start liquidity during its early rise in Asia. By shifting who paid and who earned, Binance attracted professional market-makers who tightened spreads and boosted displayed liquidity. The behavioural metric was clear: thinner spreads and deeper books increased trading volume. The mechanism was rule design, not spontaneous efficiency. Price discovery improved because incentives made it profitable to maintain orderly books.

A second example reveals the limits of appearances. On 19 May 2021, during a rapid selloff, several major venues including Coinbase and Kraken experienced cascading delays in order matching and scaling. Visible liquidity vanished. Users clicking "sell" found themselves filled far below quoted prices as books gapped. What looked like a deep market in calm days evaporated the moment urgency surged. The implication is unavoidable: liquidity is not a static property. It is a commitment by certain actors to remain present under stress. When their incentives reverse—risk overtakes reward—they pull orders, and the price becomes a cliff.

Venue fragmentation intensifies these dynamics. Bitcoin trades across dozens of centralised exchanges in Singapore, London, Hong Kong, and beyond. Each venue maintains its own order book, with different collateral rules, market hours, and latency. A trader in London hitting the market on Bitstamp may move the price less than a similar trade on a smaller venue in Manila. There is no single canonical price—only a constantly negotiated composite built from uneven local realities. The stage is multi-roomed. Each room shapes the play its own way.

That fragmentation invites arbitrage. Market-makers monitor price differences across venues and move liquidity to close gaps. Show the behaviour: arbitrageurs buy low on one exchange and sell high on another. Name the constraint: those transfers require time and capital. In periods of congestion or capital controls, the gaps widen. Explain and imply: markets that promise frictionless movement find frictions everywhere—network fees, withdrawal delays, bank holidays. Efficiency is conditional.

Hidden costs are the least appreciated. Slippage—the gap between expected and executed price—can exceed posted fees many times over. Funding rates in perpetual futures reflect long-short imbalances and force traders to pay for directional exposure even when not transacting. Priority fees in congestion can make "buying now" exponentially more expensive. These are not anomalies. They are structural taxes. A trader's real cost is the sum of visible fees, implicit slippage, and inventory risk borne by liquidity providers.

Consider a second venue variation with named consequence: the December 2021 introduction of stablecoin-margined futures on Bybit and FTX allowed traders to post collateral in USDT rather than bitcoin. This reduced volatility in collateral value but created new reflexivity: liquidations in altcoins triggered forced selling of stablecoins, which impacted liquidity pools across multiple markets. Venue design reshaped stress transmission. A seemingly neutral change to margin rules altered the topology of risk.

A credible counter-example sharpens the point. Decentralised exchanges (DEXs) such as Uniswap do not use order books at all. They rely on automated market-making—liquidity pools priced via mathematical curves. There, visible depth can persist even under heavy demand. A user always receives a price. Yet the trade-off is clear: the more volume one pushes through a pool, the more the curve penalises execution. No "gap risk" emerges, but slippage can crush large orders. The limitation does not undermine the broader thesis. It reveals that no market structure is universally superior—only differently fragile.

The stage motif returns: who writes the script? On centralised venues, internalisation—the practice of matching trades against an exchange's own inventory rather than routing to the open book—can reduce fees but obscure real supply and demand. Hidden liquidity appears, then vanishes. Users think they are seeing a market; they are seeing a curated surface. Internalisation blurs where price discovery truly happens. The consequence emerges when volatility spikes. The script suddenly changes.

Transparency provides one more lens. Some venues publish full depth-of-book data, allowing traders to see multiple levels of bids and asks. Others restrict visibility, offering only top-of-book quotes or aggregated volumes. Greater transparency aids informed execution but can expose liquidity providers to predatory strategies like order anticipation and spoofing detection. The trade-off is constant: fairness versus fragility. Show the behaviour—dark pools and iceberg orders—then name the tension: a market too visible invites exploitation; too opaque invites mistrust.

All these mechanisms converge in moments of stress. When markets fall fast, spreads widen, takers overwhelm makers, and fees spike. A system that looked cheap becomes expensive. A system that appeared liquid becomes hollow. Venue design becomes destiny at the worst possible time. The number glowing on a retail trader's app reflects not a universal truth, but the consequences of architectural decisions made by people the trader does not know, in boardrooms they will never see.

As crypto integrates with traditional finance, structural complexity deepens. Market-makers hedge on CME futures in Chicago. Structured-product issuers adjust exposure from Zurich. Brokers rebalance collateral using stablecoin loans originating in Singapore. A BTC sell order in São Paulo may cascade through liquidity paths spanning three continents in seconds. Global pipes create local outcomes. The stage expands. The actors multiply.

Yet the unresolved tension remains stark: should a monetary system predicated on decentralisation rely so heavily on market structures that centralise control over discovery, execution, and custody? Or can new architectures emerge—hybrid models blending efficiency with verifiability—where the price on the screen reflects not just supply and demand, but a design that honours the principles of the underlying asset?

The castle walls are strong. The moat is wide. But the stage inside is where real power resides.

Custody, Commingling, and Cold Storage

At 1:42 a.m. Singapore time on 11 November 2022, a message appeared on an obscure blockchain-tracking account showing tens of thousands of ether leaving a set of labelled exchange wallets. Within minutes, analysts in Europe and the United States noticed abnormal flows. At 2:13 a.m., withdrawals for ordinary users froze. Hours later, the exchange—once one of the largest in the world—filed for bankruptcy in Delaware. The numbers later revealed that customer assets had been commingled with trading funds, internal accounts were loosely controlled, and cold storage procedures were more theatre than practice. The event became one of the starkest reminders that in crypto, operational design is not a footnote. It is the difference between resilience and ruin.

Custody determines who truly holds an asset. Commingling determines whether that asset remains distinct from other claims. Cold storage determines whether keys survive panic, error, or malice. These are not abstract financial concepts. They are visible behaviours: delayed withdrawals, sudden wallet movements, opaque accounting, and unexplained freezes. In calm markets, such behaviours go unnoticed. In stress, they become life-or-death tests of institutional integrity. The motif worth holding is the lock. A lock protects, or it traps. It depends entirely on how it is built.

Show the dynamic, then name it. When crypto exchanges accept deposits, they make an implicit promise: your assets remain your assets. But many firms—through convenience, cost-cutting, or design—blur the distinction between customer balances and operational liquidity. Explain it: they pool funds across wallets for efficiency, use omnibus accounts to simplify transfers, or worse, tap customer deposits to fund internal strategies. Implication: when withdrawals spike, the firm must conjure liquidity that no longer exists. The lock holds the user in, not danger out.

Two examples illuminate the stakes. The first is Mt. Gox in Tokyo, which suspended withdrawals in February 2014. Users were told there was a "technical issue." In reality, the exchange had lost hundreds of thousands of bitcoins across years through lax operational discipline and chaotic wallet management. Logs showed deposits credited without corresponding receipts, cold wallets mislabelled, and reconciliation errors ignored. The behaviour was not evil so much as negligent. But negligence in custody becomes catastrophe. When users attempted to exit, the assets were simply not there.

The second example—far more recent—occurred during the collapse of FTX in November 2022. Bankruptcy filings revealed that the exchange's parent company had no clear distinction between customer assets and corporate funds. Bank accounts were intermingled. Internal controls were described by the appointed CEO as "a complete failure of corporate governance." Wallet movements during the final hours suggested both hasty transfers and possible unauthorised access. The visible behaviour was chaos: customers watching balances evaporate in real time, regulators scrambling, counterparties freezing lines. Custody had become commingling; commingling had become insolvency.

A credible counter-example helps clarify what good practice looks like. Cold-storage custodians such as Coinbase Custody, operating under U.S. regulatory scrutiny and audited since its 2018 introduction, employ segregated on-chain addresses, multi-party computation for key management, and strict operational procedures that prevent unilateral movement of funds. During market panics—including the March 2020 crash and the June 2022 lending crisis—these custodial structures remained functional. Withdrawals were processed, and no evidence of misused assets appeared. The contrast does not erase broader industry risks. It demonstrates that operational discipline, not mythology, draws the line between robustness and vulnerability.

Custody is not merely possession. It is a chain of decisions: who controls keys, how transfers occur, how records are kept, and what happens when an employee, partner, or government agency makes an unexpected demand. The lock motif reappears here as a test: when pressure mounts, does the lock open cleanly for the rightful holder, or does it jam because too many hands share the key?

Cold storage provides another lens. In theory, keeping private keys offline—whether in hardware modules, paper backups, or multisignature vaults—mitigates hacking and rogue access. In practice, cold storage systems vary by geography, personnel, and process. A vault in Zurich may require two officers to approve movement; a vault in Hong Kong may require three. The precise requirements matter because they slow theft, reduce unauthorised access, and enforce procedural discipline. They also slow withdrawals. The trade-off is visible during periods of high demand. Users submit withdrawals; the exchange must gather signatures; operations teams must verify details. In panic, this friction fuels speculation. The lock takes time to open, and users begin to doubt whether it will open at all.

Proof-of-reserves emerged after the Mt. Gox failure as a social technology to verify that exchanges hold sufficient assets to meet customer claims. In its simplest form, a proof-of-reserves statement exposes on-chain addresses demonstrating holdings and employs cryptographic techniques—like Merkle trees—to allow users to confirm inclusion without sacrificing privacy. But proofs of reserves do not reveal liabilities unless the exchange voluntarily discloses them. This creates a partial view: assets may be present, yet obligations may exceed them. Several exchanges in 2022 published proof-of-reserves snapshots showing healthy balances, only for analysts to discover that wallets were topped up temporarily before publication. The lesson is not that the approach is flawed, but that partial verification invites partial truth.

A further example illustrates how commingling emerges not from fraud but from operational shortcuts. Some exchanges aggregate user deposits into a handful of hot wallets to simplify internal ledgering. They process trades off-chain, crediting buyers and debit users without moving funds on-chain. This improves efficiency but creates a single pool of assets indistinguishable by ownership. The behaviour is visible only during audits or crisis. When withdrawals surge, the pooled wallet must service all claims. If one internal ledger entry is wrong, the system becomes unbalanced. A minor accounting error in calm markets becomes a liquidity hole in stress.

There is a limitation worth acknowledging. Full segregation—assigning each customer a unique on-chain address for deposits and withdrawals—offers transparency but increases operational complexity and cost. Some exchanges argue that this reduces efficiency and raises fees. The reconciliation lies in recognising that cost-saving strategies are not inherently malicious; they become dangerous when paired with weak controls, opaque accounting, or temptations to misuse pooled funds. The lock can be well-made or cheaply forged. The difference is invisible until pressure tests it.

Behaviour under regulatory scrutiny adds another dimension. After China intensified its enforcement actions against crypto exchanges in 2021, several platforms shifted operations to other jurisdictions but maintained thin or inconsistent compliance frameworks. This affected custody structures. Without consistent oversight, internal practices drifted. In contrast, exchanges serving institutional clients in the U.S. and Europe faced stricter requirements: segregation of customer funds, mandatory audits, and capital buffers. These differences were visible during the June 2022 liquidity crunch: some platforms continued operating smoothly; others halted withdrawals.

Auditability becomes a crucial safeguard. Internal audits—conducted by in-house teams—may identify discrepancies, but external audits provide independent verification. Yet even "Big Four" audits can be limited in scope. Some firms audit only fiat balances, not crypto holdings. Others audit crypto holdings but not the processes governing key access. A system can pass an audit while harbouring systemic risk. Here again, the lock metaphor clarifies: an audit tells you whether the lock exists; it does not tell you whether the key is kept responsibly.

Commingling also emerges in more subtle ways. Some venues use customer balances for lending programmes, margin financing, or liquidity provision—often disclosed in fine print rather than plain language. The behaviour becomes visible when a borrower defaults. In June 2022, several major lenders faced cascading losses due to exposure to failing hedge funds and arbitrage firms. Some of those lenders sourced liquidity from exchange-based yield products funded by customer deposits. Users discovered their assets had been rehypothecated without their grasp of the implications. The lock was shared with strangers.

Cold storage carries its own risk. If procedures require multiple signatories and one is unavailable—due to travel, illness, or legal pressure—withdrawals can stall. Some exchanges experienced precisely this challenge during the 2020–2022 cycles, particularly those with distributed teams across multiple jurisdictions. The limitation does not invalidate cold storage. It reveals the need for redundancy in personnel, process, and geography. A lock with too few keyholders becomes brittle.

The quiet motif of the lock threads through every example because custody is fundamentally about control. Control over movement. Control over risk. Control over access. During panics, people discover whether they hold the key or merely a claim that depends on someone else's honesty and competence.

The unresolved tension sits here: as exchanges seek efficiency, scale, and speed, will they continue to prioritise operational integrity—segregated custody, transparent accounting, verifiable reserves, controlled key access—or will competitive pressures push them toward shortcuts that remain invisible until the next crisis?

Incentives of Tokens, Fees, and Listings

At 9:58 a.m. on 17 September 2020, on a quiet weekday in Zug, a newly launched decentralised exchange token surged more than 1,000 per cent within its first hour. The token's trading volume reached over $200 million before midday, despite the protocol itself having only a few hundred active users the week prior. The outcome was predictable: within days the price collapsed, the project founders blamed "market volatility," and thousands of retail holders were left with little more than screenshots of an extraordinary chart. Yet blockchain records showed what actually fuelled the frenzy—vast emissions of token rewards offered to anyone who would provide liquidity. The behaviour was visible: rapid capital inflow, mercenary liquidity shifting from pool to pool, and users arriving not for the service but for the reward. Incentives had replaced judgement. Fees and listings amplified the dynamic.

Token incentives alter behaviour long before anyone reads a white paper. They reshape user flows, distort liquidity metrics, and create the illusion of product-market fit. When a new exchange or protocol launches, emissions are often used as bait. Show it: a pool offering 2,000 per cent annualised rewards. Name it: liquidity mining. Explain it: users stake capital, earn tokens, and then either hold, sell, or reinvest. The scheme boosts volumes and generates the appearance of demand. The implication is sobering: the demand may vanish as soon as rewards decline. The motif of the mask becomes helpful here. Incentives can mask the true face of market behaviour. They can show vitality where little exists.

Listings introduce another layer of distortion. When a centralised exchange lists a token, the event often generates a price spike. This is not because the underlying asset suddenly becomes more valuable, but because access expands. The behaviour is visible in on-chain flows: deposits surge, trading pairs multiply, and social media sentiment swings within hours. This effect is well-documented, from Binance's listings in 2019 to Coinbase's additions in 2021. The market treats the listing as validation. Yet the economics behind listings remain opaque. Exchanges charge fees, negotiate token allocations, or structure revenue-sharing deals that align their interests with short-term activity rather than long-term scrutiny. A listing can be less about due diligence and more about commercial opportunity.

Consider a second example. In 2021, several exchanges in South Korea listed a new gaming token tied to a small development studio. The studio held more than 70 per cent of the token supply. Analysts flagged the concentration risk; nonetheless, the token climbed rapidly after listings on Bithumb and Upbit. Trading volume reached billions of dollars in days. But when regulators questioned the studio's disclosures later that year, liquidity evaporated. The behaviour was again visible: thin order books during stress, widening spreads, and abrupt halt of transfers. Listings can create momentum, but they can also accelerate collapse by drawing in users who assume vetting has taken place when little exists.

A counter-example offers nuance. In June 2020, the launch of COMP—a governance token for the Compound protocol—showed how token incentives can reveal genuine usage. Governance powers were meaningful, rewards were balanced, and the protocol already had substantial borrowing and lending activity. Although COMP's price experienced volatility, its liquidity mining programme did not collapse its core markets. The token's design aligned incentives with long-term participation. Yet even here there was distortion: borrowing on Compound spiked not for economic need but for token rewards, temporarily inflating the protocol's metrics. The mask slipped but did not fully fall.

Why do tokens create such behavioural swings? Because they quantify attention. Fees reward certain actions; token emissions reward others. Exchanges understand this well. Maker-taker fee models, for example, pay users who add liquidity and charge those who remove it. The effect is measurable. When one major exchange in Chicago implemented maker-taker in 2010, its market share rose sharply as market makers migrated to earn rebates. Crypto exchanges adopted similar structures. These fees nudge behaviour in predictable ways. Market makers respond to rebates; retail traders respond to the headline cost of trading. The implication is clear: price formation reflects venue design as much as supply and demand.

Now add token incentives to fee structures. Some exchanges in 2020–2022 issued their own tokens that reduced trading fees if held or staked. This created a feedback loop. High-volume traders accumulated tokens to cut costs, which increased token demand. Rising token prices attracted speculation. Speculation led to more trading. Trading drove fee revenue and token issuance. The mask here becomes a mirror: traders saw reflected demand that was partly their own creation.

Listings also influence the flow of due diligence. When an exchange lists dozens or hundreds of tokens per year, internal vetting becomes compressed. The behaviour is visible in patterns: sudden listings announced hours before trading opens, inconsistent documentation, or promotional campaigns that emphasise yield rather than substance. Users interpret these signals. Some treat listings as endorsements and commit capital before understanding the project's structure or risks. The exchange's economic incentives—listing fees, increased trading activity, and token allocations—can overshadow caution. The implication is not uniform recklessness. Many venues employ rigorous vetting teams. But the presence of even a few poorly scrutinised listings is enough to distort user expectations.

There is a limitation worth naming. Not all tokens launched with incentives become hollow distractions. Some protocols have used emissions responsibly to bootstrap liquidity that later stabilised. Uniswap's UNI token, released in September 2020, did not tie emissions to liquidity mining in its early months; its design emphasised governance. The protocol's volumes continued to grow based on product quality rather than rewards. Yet even here, governance tokens carry latent incentives. Holders expect appreciation or influence, and this expectation shapes participation. The mask remains—lighter, but present.

Masking also appears in metrics. Total value locked (TVL), for instance, can balloon when users borrow against assets solely to farm incentives. A protocol may boast billions in deposits, but a glance at wallet movements reveals looping positions rather than genuine usage. This behaviour was evident in the collapse of Terra's ecosystem in May 2022. The Anchor Protocol offered 20 per cent yield on deposits, funded artificially. Deposits climbed; users flocked in; metrics impressed. When the structure failed, the collapse was rapid. Incentives did not just mask demand; they replaced it entirely.

Token listing incentives extend to founders. When a project negotiates with an exchange, it may agree to supply a portion of its tokens for market-making, promotional events, or fee rebates. These tokens create overhang. If the market weakens, the supply becomes selling pressure. Exchanges seldom disclose the depth of these arrangements. The behaviour becomes visible only when liquidity thins and sell pressure intensifies. Users experience the effect without seeing the cause.

Fees offer another lens. Some exchanges use high taker fees to encourage passive liquidity provision. Others reduce fees for users who bring large volumes. These structures signal priorities. A venue focused on market makers may cultivate tight spreads but low retail engagement. A venue focused on high-frequency traders may see deep liquidity but abrupt withdrawals during volatility. Fee structures thus influence not only behaviour but resilience. The mask motif returns: what appears as deep liquidity may be contingent on rebates, not conviction.

A final dynamic intertwines all these incentives: narrative reward. When a token lists, emissions increase, or fees change, communities build stories around the event. These stories amplify participation. The behaviour is visible on forums and social feeds: countdowns to listings, graphs predicting price rises, celebratory messages about rewards. Users commit before evaluating fundamentals. Exchanges benefit from increased flow. Projects benefit from attention. But narratives can reverse. When rewards decline or listings disappoint, users retreat just as quickly.

The unresolved tension lies in a simple question. As exchanges compete for volume, and projects compete for visibility, will incentives continue to mask the underlying quality of assets, or will the industry develop norms that distinguish genuine demand from synthetic signals?

When the Castle Burns

At 7:42 a.m. on 12 November 2022, outside the High Court in Nassau, reporters watched as staff from a major cryptocurrency exchange carried banker's boxes into a waiting van. The exchange had halted withdrawals the day before, citing "liquidity constraints," after on-chain analysts traced billions of dollars of customer deposits routed through an affiliated trading firm. By evening, the bankruptcy filings confirmed what users had feared: the castle had been hollowed out from within. Funds thought to be segregated were co-mingled. Balances displayed on dashboards were not matched by balances on chain. Clients learned—again—the oldest lesson in markets. A balance is not a claim. A claim is not a guarantee. Guarantees vanish when incentives fail.

Scenes like these are not aberrations. They are stress tests made visible. And in each collapse, the same pattern emerges: withdrawals accelerate, liquidity thins, promises wobble, and the moat that once protected users becomes the very barrier that prevents escape. The motif of the moat is useful here. In fair weather it suggests safety. In crisis it becomes a reminder that exits can be narrow, slow, or entirely blocked. When an exchange fails, the moat decides who gets out—and who stays trapped inside.

The anatomy of an exchange failure begins long before headlines. Show it: rising internal leverage visible in balance-sheet mismatches. Name it: maturity transformation. Explain it: short-term customer assets quietly re-deployed into long-term or illiquid positions. The implication is clear. When users seek withdrawals, the exchange must unwind its positions quickly or borrow against collateral it may not hold. The first crack appears when redemption requests outpace liquid assets.

Consider a checkable example. In March 2014, Mt. Gox in Tokyo halted withdrawals after revealing that hundreds of thousands of bitcoins were missing. The exchange had ignored repeated security warnings since 2011, and internal accounting relied on spreadsheets rather than reconciled ledgers. Behaviour made the failure visible: unacknowledged tickets, delayed transfers, and a widening gap between internal balances and blockchain records. Another example came in October 2021, when a Hong Kong–based venue experienced a multi-hour outage during a market downturn. Users could not adjust margins or close positions; liquidations followed. While this venue avoided bankruptcy, the pattern showed how operational fragility compounds market stress.

A counter-example offers nuance. In February 2018, a large United States exchange faced a sudden influx of traffic as prices swung violently. Instead of freezing withdrawals, it slowed order submissions, displayed queue transparency, and pre-announced maintenance windows for the following days. The exchange was not flawless—users remained frustrated—but it preserved core functions: withdrawals, balances, and reconciled accounting. Reliability was visible. The castle held.

Why do some venues fail catastrophically while others bend without breaking? Incentives shape every layer. Many exchanges rely on fee revenue tied to trading volume. During bull markets, this model rewards aggressive expansion: listing tokens rapidly, offering high leverage, and running "VIP" programmes that encourage debt-like behaviour among professional traders. The risk is measurable. A venue may extend credit to market makers or borrow against its own token as collateral. One needs only track volatile collateral ratios on specific days—5 May 2021, 19 May 2021, or 13 June 2022—to see how debt and price intertwine. The implication is unmissable: when collateral falls in value, the solvency of an exchange can shift within hours.

Commingling of funds is the most dangerous behaviour. Visible behaviour includes inconsistent deposit addresses, off-chain internal transfers that obscure provenance, and accounting ledgers that net customer liabilities against operating expenses. Some venues justify this as "liquidity optimisation." But the effect is simple. Users lose the ability to distinguish their assets from the exchange's obligations. This behaviour becomes explicit during audits. Exchanges that refuse proof-of-reserves or provide incomplete proofs reveal priorities through omission.

Cold storage design reveals another layer. Exchanges that commit—actively commit—to deep cold storage often publish wallet addresses, audit trails, and clear timelocks. Those that do not often claim "security reasons" while relying heavily on hot wallets for convenience. The difference becomes visible during hacks or panics. In February 2020, when an exchange in Singapore lost tens of millions in user funds to a compromised hot wallet, investigators discovered that its cold storage procedures were informal and undocumented. Principles had been replaced with expedience.

The quiet motif of the moat returns. When liquidity dries up, the moat narrows. Behaviour shows it. Spreads widen from a few basis points to entire percentage points. Market makers cancel quotes. Withdrawal queues lengthen. A venue may begin limiting withdrawals to certain assets or imposing daily caps. Each action signals deteriorating health. Users who monitor on-chain flows can detect early symptoms: falling reserves in public wallets, rising inflows from nervous depositors, or the absence of routine operational transactions.

Contagion emerges through predictable channels. When one exchange fails, counterparties holding funds on that venue suffer immediate losses. Some are lenders. Some are market makers. Some are other exchanges with cross-collateral agreements. In November 2022, several lending firms froze withdrawals within days of the Nassau bankruptcy. Their balance sheets had been intertwined with the failed exchange's token, and once its value collapsed, their collateral became inadequate. The behaviour was visible: emergency fundraising attempts, revised terms for margin, and abrupt shifts in disclosed assets. The castle does not burn alone. Flames leap over moats.

A second contagion path runs through stablecoins. When exchanges become distressed, users rush into stable assets. If stablecoin liquidity providers rely on the failing venue for redemptions or settlement, stresses propagate. During the market instability of May 2022, several stablecoin issuers experienced delays in redemptions because their banking partners processed surges of requests slowly. These delays amplified fear, even without underlying insolvency. The behaviour again was visible: peg deviations, widening arbitrage bands, and higher on-chain swap fees.

A third channel stems from structured products. Some exchanges offer yield products backed by customer deposits. When these products depend on external venues for hedging or liquidity, the failure of a single node cascades across the entire structure. Metrics reveal pressure: abnormal funding rates, negative implied yields, or sudden premium shifts in perpetual futures. These signals rarely appear for long before a failure.

A limitation tempers the narrative. Not all exchange failures stem from malice or mismanagement. Some arise from external shocks: abrupt regulatory actions, frozen banking channels, or unprecedented transaction surges. In December 2017, several United States exchanges experienced extreme delays during Bitcoin's move above $17,000. Their systems were overwhelmed. Yet most retained their solvency. Their failures were operational rather than structural. The distinction matters. Structural failures destroy user funds; operational failures destroy patience.

Reconciling the limitation leads to a deeper insight. Exchanges exist at the intersection of technology and trust. Their resilience depends not only on security practices but on incentive structures that govern behaviour under duress. Cold storage, segregated accounts, and transparent audits are visible commitments. Borrowing against volatile tokens or re-hypothecating customer funds are visible risks. Behaviour tells the truth long before statements do.

The unresolved tension endures. When users seek an exchange to trust, how can they measure whether the moat protects them—or traps them—when the castle begins to burn?

Chapter 4
Stablecoins and the Illusion of Still Water

The promise is disarmingly simple: one token equals one dollar. It whispers calm into a market that never sleeps. When prices whip and exchanges wobble, traders retreat into this manufactured serenity, believing they have found shelter. Yet the stillness is often an illusion, a momentary calm above depths that can shift without warning. A digital dollar must bridge code and cash, decentralised ledgers and centralised banks, speculation and payments. That bridge looks solid—until the first truck drives across at speed.

In May 2022, as an algorithmic stablecoin spiralled away from its peg, millions watched in real time as the once-fixed price slipped to 99 cents, then 95, then 70, and then freefall. Arbitrage bots hammered redemption paths. Forums filled with frantic questions: *Why can't they just print more collateral? Why isn't someone stepping in?* The illusion cracked instantly. Stability had been a story written by incentives during years of calm. Panic rewrote the story in hours. That is the paradox at the heart of this chapter: stability in crypto is not a state of nature. It is a balancing act of capital, confidence, and coordination.

Every stablecoin is a claim. But a claim on what? Some are backed one-to-one by cash and short-term US Treasuries—strong claims on regulated institutions. Others are backed by crypto collateral—speedy but volatile. A few attempt something audacious: stability without collateral, governed by algorithms that assume sellers will become buyers again when discounts deepen. Some designs resemble dams holding a reservoir of value. Others resemble rafts, floating only as long as every participant agrees not to step too quickly. In bull markets, these differences seem academic. In bear markets, they define life and death.

This chapter explores why these engineering choices matter long after the marketing campaigns fade. The first task is to understand the design families. Fiat-backed coins promise familiarity: dollars in a bank, tokens on chain. Yet they inherit banking fragilities. What happens when those dollars sit in one or two banks? What happens if wire transfers halt over a long weekend? Crypto-backed coins promise transparency: collateral visible on a blockchain, auditable at any time. Yet visibility is not the same as liquidity. Collateral can plunge in value. Liquidation engines can clog. And algorithmic coins promise elegance: code replacing capital. The question is whether confidence survives when code alone must carry the weight.

The second task is to study the physics of the peg. At first glance, a dollar is a dollar. But the price of a stablecoin on an exchange is not the same as its redemption value. That gap—often measured in tiny fractions of a cent—becomes a seismograph. When spreads widen, they reveal stress in the hidden plumbing: strained market makers, delayed settlements, or uncertainty about collateral. A peg is not held by decree. It is held by arbitrage, governance, and incentives, all operating under time pressure. And time pressure, in crypto, is relentless.

A third thread runs through regulation and the banking world. Stablecoins touch the core financial system precisely because they aim to mimic its safest asset: cash. Banks view them with suspicion and governments view them with urgency. They raise questions few decentralised tokens ever confront. Should a stablecoin be regulated like a bank, a money market fund, or a payment platform? Should issuers disclose exactly where the backing sits? Should redemptions be honoured even during legal disputes? The answers are still forming—and the stakes rise with every billion in circulation.

Finally, we turn to what users can observe. Even without insider access, one can watch collateral ratios, redemption volumes, and the quality of public disclosures. One can evaluate how a system behaves during weekends or public holidays, when the fiat world goes dark but the crypto world keeps trading. One can watch governance when decisions must be made fast. Does the community freeze, argue, fragment? Or does it act with clarity? Stability is not a smooth chart. It is the ability to stay coherent under stress.

Throughout this chapter, a single image will recur: water that looks calm because movement has been forced underground. Stablecoins often appear motionless because layers of complexity—bank queues, liquidity providers, risk committees—absorb turbulence out of sight. But water seeks cracks, and crypto finds them first. The lesson is not to mistrust calm—but to understand its cost.

Stablecoins are now essential infrastructure. They connect decentralised liquidity to traditional finance. They allow capital to move globally at the speed of blockchains. They enable a merchant in Lagos to settle with a supplier in São Paulo without touching a single correspondent bank. Yet they also carry systemic risks. If a major stablecoin falters, contagion follows: exchanges lose pricing anchors, borrowers face margin calls, and trust evaporates. The industry has already witnessed shadows of this scenario. What remains to be seen is how well it can prepare for the next test.

This chapter asks difficult questions. What is a promise worth when redemption depends on one custodian? How many degrees of separation sit between a token and the asset it claims to represent? How quickly can collateral be sold without crashing its own market? And who, if anyone, stands behind the peg when others run?

Stablecoins stand at the centre of the crypto economy's credibility. They invite users to believe that code can deliver the certainty once reserved for central banks and treasuries. Some may succeed. Others may shatter dramatically. What matters is learning to discern the difference—not when the water is still, but when the currents shift.

Design Families: Fiat, Crypto, and Hybrid

On 9 May 2022, the price of the algorithmic stablecoin TerraUSD (UST) slipped from its intended one-dollar peg to 98 cents on Binance in Singapore. It looked minor. Pegs wobble on weekends and recover when banks open. But within 24 hours, redemption queues jammed, arbitrageurs demanded higher incentives, and the value of its sister token—meant to absorb volatility—collapsed. By 11 May, UST traded below 30 cents. Billions of dollars in paper stability evaporated. A design marketed as bulletproof proved sensitive to a single feedback loop: confidence. The still water hid violent currents.

The episode distilled a core truth: different forms of stablecoins promise the same calm surface—one token equals one dollar—yet the machinery beneath varies dramatically. Some depend on banks. Some depend on blockchains. Some depend on belief. Understanding how these design families differ is not academic taxonomy. It is a survival skill.

Stablecoins fall into three broad categories: fiat-collateralised, crypto-collateralised, and algorithmic hybrids. Each pursues stability through a different mechanism: custody, over-collateralisation, or incentives. Each offers benefits rooted in real engineering. And each carries fragilities anchored not in code but in behaviour.

The motif of water will return. Where the backing sits determines whether the calm is a lake behind a concrete dam, a reservoir of snow atop a mountain, or a thin sheet of ice over a deep river. Stress reveals which freezes first.

Fiat-collateralised models demonstrate the power of simple promises. USDC, issued by Circle in Boston since 2018, holds a mix of cash and short-term US Treasuries with audited disclosures. Users do not need to understand liquidity pools or liquidation bots. They rely on a direct claim: redeem one token for one dollar. The behaviour is visible in transparency reports and settlement processes. Yet this model inherits banking concentration risk. In March 2023, when Silicon Valley Bank failed, USDC briefly traded at 88 cents before the United States Treasury backstopped deposits. Redemption was only as reliable as the health of the specific banks holding reserves. When banks close for holidays or freeze transfers, these stablecoins become digital IOUs awaiting fiat settlement.

Crypto-collateralised models seek freedom from banks. MakerDAO's DAI, launched in 2017 and governed by a decentralised community, holds crypto assets with on-chain audits. The peg relies on collateral ratios: if Ether, for example, is used to back DAI at a 150% ratio, a price drop triggers liquidations to protect solvency. The visible behaviour includes collateral locks, auction volumes, and oracle prices—all on public ledgers. This design offers unprecedented transparency. Yet it introduces a new dependency: price volatility. When markets fall quickly, liquidation engines strain. On 12 March 2020, during a violent market crash, DAI liquidity dried up. Auctions struggled to clear. Some positions sold for zero, and the peg spiked above a dollar as users paid premiums for safety. Transparency did not remove risk; it exposed it.

Algorithmic stablecoins, by contrast, minimise collateral and maximise incentives. TerraUSD was the most famous example, but it was not the first. Ampleforth in 2019 experimented with supply expansion and contraction—rebase mechanics adjusting token balances in wallets directly. The visible behaviour was elegant in calm periods but unsettling in others. Users might wake to find their holdings changed in quantity even if value held steady. Stability was promised through game theory rather than assets. The implication was harsh: when confidence falters, no collateral remains to absorb the shock. Bank-run dynamics accelerate because redemption depends on belief that future buyers will appear. The moment that belief breaks, the algorithm has nothing left to defend.

Not all algorithmic projects collapse so suddenly, and not all collateralised projects survive every crisis. A counter-example sharpens judgement. Frax, launched in December 2020, implemented a partially collateralised algorithmic model: a blend of assets and incentives. During stress events in June 2022, Frax narrowed peg deviations faster than UST because it maintained real reserves to absorb demand spikes. Hybrid designs attempt to balance elasticity and security, pairing automated response with tangible backing. They may not offer perfect stability, but they show how design can learn from failure.

Trade-offs emerge clearly when measured. Fiat-backed coins achieve speed and simplicity, yet opacity persists where bank ledgers replace public blockchains. Crypto-backed coins achieve transparency and censorship resistance, yet fees rise and capital inefficiency remains inherent. Algorithmic designs achieve fast expansion and low capital cost, yet fragility hides in assumptions about behaviour under stress. Each model optimises for one dimension and sacrifices another. Stability is a multidimensional problem: liquidity, solvency, redemption friction, and governance coherence must align.

Mechanical design alone does not guarantee outcomes. Social consensus defines trust. Fiat-backed coins rely on regulators and auditors to maintain faith in reserves. Crypto-backed coins rely on governance voters to adjust parameters before crises become existential. Algorithmic hybrids rely on market participants to behave rationally even when fear climbs. Visible behaviour tests these assumptions. Does a governance vote pass in minutes or stall for days? Do liquidity providers deepen pools during stress or vanish? Does redemption require a queue number and patience, or a gas fee and certainty?

The motif returns: the waterline moves. Stress reveals how quickly.

Users often assume transparency equals safety. But transparency can expose fragility faster. When collateral on a blockchain falls in value, panic becomes quantifiable. Traders race liquidation bots. Peg charts flash red. Fiat models hide turbulence behind banking walls until the wires reopen. Each hides risk in different places. The question is not which is safest. It is: which danger do you prefer to face?

Two examples showcase divergence. In January 2021, USDT briefly traded at 97 cents during a regulatory rumour. Its issuer, Tether Holdings, later disclosed a reserve composition including commercial paper—instantly introducing counterparty risk beyond Treasuries. Trust dipped because the asset base was less pristine than assumed. Meanwhile, during a high-volatility event in December 2021, DAI spiked above a dollar because collateralisation ratios signalled liquidations ahead. Both maintained solvency. Both wobbled publicly. But the causes—and implications—differed.

A limitation complicates classification. Many stablecoins evolve. DAI gradually incorporated more fiat-linked assets into its reserves to enhance peg reliability. USDC has explored on-chain settlement enhancements to improve transparency. Designs converge as lessons accumulate. The taxonomy of stablecoins is not fixed. It is adaptive.

Reconciling this limitation leads to a better frame. Stablecoins are stability portfolios—bundles of trade-offs expressed through architecture. One prioritises regulatory alignment. One prioritises censorship resistance. One prioritises capital efficiency. None can satisfy all goals simultaneously. Design becomes an expression of values.

That leads to the unsolved tension. When calm returns, users forget where the water flows beneath. They choose the easiest token to hold. They stop checking reserves or collateral dashboards. They treat stillness as normal. Yet cycles repeat. Bank-run dynamics do not vanish because code improves. The safest-looking lake may be the most brittle if the dam has cracks no one inspects.

The forward test is stark. When the next crisis arrives—perhaps during a long weekend when banking rails close and liquidity splinters—what evidence will reassure you? Collateral shown in real time? Audit reports from last quarter? Algorithmic incentives that presume rationality? Or a mix of all three?

Still water invites trust. But trust requires scrutiny. The question that matters is not *how stable does this look?* It is *what holds this together when fear arrives faster than capital?*

Peg Maintenance Under Stress

At 23:47 UTC on 13 March 2023, USDC traded at 87 cents on Coinbase in San Francisco. Minutes earlier, Circle had confirmed that $3.3 billion of its reserves were stuck at the failed Silicon Valley Bank. It was a Saturday. Banks were closed. Market makers could not rebalance. Arbitrage circuits sat silent, waiting for fiat rails to reopen. What should have been a routine, fully redeemable dollar claim became, for forty-eight hours, a live experiment in the mechanics of a stablecoin peg under stress. The thin liquidity of a weekend transformed a modest shortfall into a visible market dislocation.

This was not a collapse. It was a pause—a kind of suspended breath. But the brief depeg revealed the forces that govern stablecoin stability when spreads widen: redemption pathways, market-maker incentives, and governance responsiveness. When one chokes, the others must compensate. When all strain simultaneously, the peg stops being an assumption and becomes a negotiation.

The motif here is a simple one: pressure. It appears in dwindling order books, widening spreads, and governance dashboards blinking with stalled proposals. Pressure is the diagnostic. It reveals what cannot hold.

Stress begins with the behaviour of redemption itself. A fiat-backed stablecoin anchors its peg by offering a one-to-one exchange: send tokens, receive dollars. That promise usually works because redemptions flow continuously. But when banking hours limit transfers, as they did in March 2023, the anchor drifts. Users selling USDC on decentralised exchanges received less than expected. The act of redemption became an IOU. The peg moved because the path to fulfilment was temporarily blocked. This behaviour is measurable: reduced on-chain liquidity, rising slippage, and thin depth within five basis points of the peg. It is not about philosophy. It is about plumbing.

Crypto-backed models behave differently when spreads widen. MakerDAO's DAI, during the crash of 12 March

2020, traded above one dollar because its redemption mechanism demanded collateral liquidation before supply could expand. The visible metrics were brutal: Ether price fell 30% in minutes; liquidation auctions spiked; keepers failed to submit bids due to network congestion. Instead of drifting below the peg due to fear, DAI's peg broke upward due to structural scarcity. The upward deviation showed how a design anchored in over-collateralisation can strain under liquidity shortages, not insolvency. The implication is clear: peg deviation direction is a fingerprint of the underlying model.

Market makers restore balance by committing capital where prices diverge. Their behaviour is often the most decisive variable. During the USDC weekend depeg, large professional firms could not transfer dollars until Monday. Their bots could quote only using on-chain assets already deployed—assets that were finite and sometimes hedged. As liquidity providers withdrew, spreads widened from fractions of a cent to multiple percentage points. The message was plain: even the most sophisticated firms cannot override structural constraints. They need rails. They need certainty. Without those, they step back.

Two examples confirm the pattern. In May 2022, during the collapse of TerraUSD, market makers abandoned pools as the imbalance between redemptions and issuance incentives became untenable. The deviation exceeded 70% because no rational actor could expect settlement. Contrast this with the slight, short-lived depeg of USDT on 12

October 2018, when Tether's banking partner issues caused the token to trade at 96 cents on Kraken in San Francisco. Market makers restored the peg within hours once redemptions resumed. Both events feature liquidity withdrawal. But only one had a viable redemption path. That difference determined duration and depth.

Yet a counter-example clarifies the limits. Frax, the partially collateralised stablecoin launched in 2020, maintained its peg during several volatility shocks in 2021 even when market-making activity dipped. Its hybrid design allowed on-chain minting and redeeming using a basket of assets, including USDC. As a result, arbitrage remained possible even when traditional fiat rails were stressed. Frax did not eliminate pressure; it redirected it into a more flexible path. This nuance matters: design does not prevent strain, but it can distribute it more evenly.

Governance is the silent actor in peg maintenance. When spreads widen, speed matters more than ideology. Governance groups must adjust parameters—collateral types, fees, redemption buffers—before liquidity evaporates. During the 2020 DAI crisis, governance passed emergency collateral auctions and parameter changes within hours. The visible signals included rapid voting participation, high turnout, and immediate execution. But governance also exposes a limitation: decentralised processes may slow down when they matter most. Not every protocol can mobilise voters on a Sunday night. Low participation or multi-day voting delays convert temporary stress into systemic fragility.

Pressure, again, reveals the hidden structure. A governance forum with dozens of conflicting proposals can be as paralysing as a bank with a frozen transfer system.

Another aspect emerges when spreads widen: the role of arbitrage corridors. Fiat-backed coins rely on institutional arbitrage tied to bank transfers. Crypto-backed and hybrid models rely on smart contracts and on-chain liquidity. Each corridor behaves differently when volumes surge. For example, on decentralised exchanges such as Curve during the USDC depeg, pool balances skewed violently as traders dumped USDC for DAI and USDT. Metrics from the Curve 3pool showed USDC rising to over 85% of the pool's balance, a clear signal that redemptions were bottlenecked. This is not sentiment. It is measurable congestion.

The implication is profound: when spreads widen, users are not comparing stablecoins; they are comparing redemption corridors.

A weekend deepens fragility. When banks close, fiat-backed tokens operate as claims on a paused system. Algorithmic and crypto-backed tokens continue operating but may lack external price anchors. Market makers shift to self-preservation. Governance slows. Arbitrage becomes lopsided. It is during weekends—specifically thin liquidity windows—that many depegs begin. The question is not why weekends are risky. The question is why users forget.

Peg maintenance is therefore a choreography between three groups: redeemers, who test solvency; market makers, who test liquidity; and governors, who test adaptability. Stress is the metronome. When all three keep time, the peg survives. When one falls behind, the rhythm falters.

A deeper lesson appears when comparing these events. Peg deviations are not always signs of failure. They are signals. A short, shallow deviation with heavy redemption volume can indicate a system functioning as intended. A prolonged deviation with thin volume indicates a freeze. Surface price movements can conceal very different underlying mechanics. Pegs do not merely break; they reveal structure.

The motif of pressure returns here. It builds quietly. It demands release. It exposes weaknesses in rails, bots, and human coordination. Understanding peg maintenance means recognising where pressure accumulates before the public sees it in the chart.

But the counter-example mentioned earlier forces humility. Frax's relative resilience during volatility does not prove hybrid models are superior. It proves that flexibility helps—but only until the collateral mix faces its own correlated shock. A peg that survives one crisis may fail in the next. Redemption corridors that look diversified can converge under stress. The choreography holds until the stage itself shifts.

What makes this subchapter essential is that peg defence is not abstract. It manifests in the timing of wire transfers, the depth of liquidity pools, the latency of governance votes, and the behaviour of market makers deciding whether to commit capital at three in the morning. It is mechanical, behavioural, and institutional at once.

So the unresolved question remains: when the next weekend arrives with falling prices, rising spreads, and silence from banking rails, where will you look to judge stability? The depth of liquidity within a few basis points? The redemption queue timestamp? The governance dashboard? Or the composition of market makers still quoting?

Pressure will come. The test is whether the system releases it—or absorbs it until something snaps.

Regulatory Attention and Banking Links

On 8 March 2023, Silvergate Bank, based in La Jolla, California, announced it would wind down operations and voluntarily liquidate. For years, Silvergate had operated a private network that allowed crypto exchanges and institutional traders to move dollars between each other around the clock. Within days, order books on multiple venues thinned, fiat on-ramps slowed, and several companies hurried to update their "banking partner" footers. Nothing had changed in the code of Bitcoin or Ethereum. Yet a single regional bank's retreat knocked out a key artery of liquidity. A chokepoint had been exposed.

A few days later, on 12 March 2023, New York regulators closed Signature Bank and appointed the Federal Deposit

Insurance Corporation as receiver. Signature had run another real-time settlement network that many stablecoin issuers and exchanges depended on for dollar flows. Again, the pattern repeated: tokens still moved freely on chain, but dollars suddenly moved less freely off chain. For a market accustomed to speaking about decentralisation, its dependence on a handful of United States banks became impossible to ignore. When the chokepoints tightened, the entire ecosystem felt the pressure.

These episodes remind us that stablecoins and exchanges ultimately sit atop two infrastructures: the distributed ledgers they celebrate and the conventional banking rails they cannot escape. Regulatory attention naturally focuses on these junctions. They are where retail users meet institutional balance sheets, where payment systems intersect with speculative markets, and where a failure in one domain can trigger panic in the other. To understand the regulatory lens, one must understand the banks as concentration risks, and the payment networks as single points a supervisor can flick off with a pen stroke.

Start with what the closures showed. A stablecoin backed one-to-one by bank deposits is only as accessible as the banks that hold its reserves. That is not a controversial statement. It is simply structural. When a significant share of reserves sits at one or two institutions, those institutions become systemic nodes, whether or not anyone planned it that way. Regulators, whose job is to map systemic nodes, see concentration risk not as an abstract concept but as a concrete list of accounts at named banks. The motif of the chokepoint appears here for the first time: risk compressed into a narrow, critical channel.

Show, then name. When a single bank provides the main payment rail for several large stablecoin issuers, we are looking at a *single point of operational interdependence*. Explain it: if that bank fails, alters its risk appetite, or changes its compliance stance, flows for all dependent issuers are simultaneously impaired. The implication is stark. A market that appears diverse on chain may be critically centralised in its off-chain plumbing.

Regulatory scrutiny intensifies wherever such interdependence forms. Consider the 2019 hearings in Washington, D.C., regarding Facebook's proposed Libra project. Legislators and central bankers were less concerned about the technical elegance of its basket-based stablecoin than about the concentration of power in a single consortium, with ties to global payment rails. They asked questions about run risk, reserve management, and cross-border capital flows. Those questions did not disappear when Libra rebranded to Diem. They set a template: any large-scale stablecoin that touches mainstream payments will be assessed as a potential shadow bank.

The choke points here are not only banks but also payment processors and card networks. When several exchanges in Europe lost access to card processors following the Wirecard scandal in June 2020, users experienced an abrupt inability to buy crypto with debit or credit cards. Overnight, their route from fiat to digital assets narrowed. This was not a blockchain problem. It was a risk-perception adjustment by financial intermediaries suddenly wary of compliance exposure.

Regulators rarely phrase it this bluntly, but their reasoning is simple. If households treat a stablecoin balance as cash, then any failure of convertibility threatens not just speculators but day-to-day economic functioning. That makes bank partners and payment rails too significant to ignore. Regulatory attention follows *function*, not marketing labels.

Different jurisdictions have responded with different institutional tools, but their principles often rhyme. Three themes recur: clarity of reserves, segregation of client assets, and operational resilience. Each responds directly to a failure mode seen in prior crises.

Clarity of reserves is the first pillar. After the collapse of quasi-money-market funds during the 2008 crisis, supervisors learned how quickly "cash-like" instruments can freeze when underlying assets turn out to be illiquid or risky. When a stablecoin issuer discloses that reserves sit in "cash equivalents" without detail, regulators see echoes of those episodes. They ask: are these Treasury bills, repos, bank deposits, or corporate paper? Who issues them? What is the weighted average maturity? The behavioural counterpart is straightforward. If an issuer responds to scrutiny with detailed, regular attestations, it signals alignment with oversight. If it responds with vague assurances or delayed reports, it invites suspicion.

Segregation of client assets is the second. The failures of several exchanges showed that commingling customer funds with operating capital is not just bad practice—it is a direct route to insolvency when markets move against the house. Regulators now bring that lesson to bear on stablecoins and payment intermediaries. They ask whether reserves are bankruptcy-remote, whether they sit in trust accounts, and whether any encumbrances exist. The behaviour to watch is how institutions structure their legal entities. When a firm restructures subsidiaries to ring-fence reserves, it is responding to a regulatory principle: client assets should not be collateral for the issuer's other bets.

Operational resilience is the third theme. Banks and payment systems are accustomed to supervisory demands around disaster recovery, cyber-security, and business continuity. Crypto-native firms, especially in their early days, often were not. Yet once a stablecoin begins to carry meaningful payment flows, a downtime event becomes more than a technical glitch. It becomes a potential public-policy issue. If merchants cannot accept a widely used stablecoin for several hours because of an outage, regulators will ask why. Behaviour again is measurable. Does the issuer conduct regular stress tests? Does it publish incident reports? Does it diversify its banking and payment partners to avoid single points of failure?

The motif of the chokepoint returns here. Regulators are drawn to those points because that is where a small action—revoking a licence, altering a risk-weighting, freezing an account—can contain or redirect risk quickly. From a supervisor's perspective, chokepoints are tools.

From a stablecoin user's perspective, they are vulnerabilities.

Two examples illustrate this tension. First, consider how New York's Department of Financial Services (NYDFS) has approached stablecoin oversight. It has emphasised full reserve backing, regular attestations by independent auditors, and restrictions on the composition of assets. The behaviour of licensed issuers changed accordingly. They shifted reserves towards short-term Treasuries and high-quality bank deposits, trimmed exposure to riskier instruments, and improved disclosure. Regulatory attention de-risked one dimension: asset quality. At the same time, it arguably increased another: jurisdictional concentration, as issuers clustered their banking relationships with a small number of large, regulated institutions.

Second, examine the European Union's Markets in Crypto-Assets (MiCA) framework, adopted in 2023. Among other provisions, it introduces the concept of "significant" e-money tokens and asset-referenced tokens, subjecting them to stricter capital and governance rules. The message is clear. As stablecoins grow in scale, they should begin to resemble regulated payment institutions, not lightly supervised startups. The behavioural change will likely be visible in years to come: more structured boards, formal risk committees, and conservative reserve policies. Yet MiCA also centralises oversight in EU institutions, meaning that a single set of policy decisions can profoundly shape the region's stablecoin landscape.

A counter-example tempers the narrative that tighter regulation always improves stability. Overly restrictive bank guidance can push legitimate activity into less regulated corners. When some U.S. banks signalled reduced appetite for crypto clients after 2022 enforcement actions, smaller offshore institutions stepped into the gap. Firms seeking dollar rails turned to more opaque partners. Concentration risk did not disappear; it migrated. The reconciliation lies in recognising that regulation must be calibrated. Aggressive de-risking by large banks can unintentionally increase systemic opacity rather than reducing it.

For users and builders, the practical question becomes: where, exactly, does the stablecoin touch the traditional system? Is there a single correspondent bank? Are there multiple custodians in different jurisdictions? Does the issuer rely on a card network, an automated clearing-house, or a bespoke real-time gross settlement link? Each connection is a potential point of regulatory intervention.

The short sentences matter here. One bank. One rail. One licence. That is often all it takes.

Principle-based oversight offers a way to navigate this landscape without freezing innovation. Instead of prescribing detailed technical standards, supervisors articulate outcomes: customers must be able to redeem at par, reserves must be safe and liquid, governance must be accountable, data must be secure. How those outcomes are achieved can vary. A stablecoin backed by Treasury bills and bank deposits will look different from a crypto-collateralised design, but both can be judged against the same principles. The key is consistency. If two instruments behave like deposit substitutes, both should expect similar scrutiny, regardless of branding.

Behaviour again tells the story. Some issuers lobby for narrow definitions that exempt them from bank-like rules while quietly marketing their tokens as cash equivalents. Others accept that growth means more supervision and begin building compliance, audit, and risk functions pre-emptively. The former treat regulation as an obstacle. The latter treat it as another design constraint, like block size or gas limits.

The recurring motif of the chokepoint leads to one final observation. Crypto projects often speak of "going around" traditional finance. Yet nearly every system that seeks to interface with real-world money recreates choke points: fiat gateways, custodial bottlenecks, oracle providers, or governance councils. Regulators will always look for those. Banks will always be central among them, because the unit most stablecoins promise to imitate—the dollar, the euro, the pound—ultimately lives on commercial-bank balance sheets and central-bank ledgers.

The unresolved tension is straightforward to state and difficult to resolve. As stablecoins and exchanges become more embedded in everyday payments, can they reduce their dependence on a small cluster of banks and payment networks without losing their redeemability and legal clarity? Or will each new cycle simply re-draw the same picture—a decentralised surface nourished by a few critical, tightly supervised pipes that everyone hopes will never clog?

User Heuristics for Stability

At 4:12 a.m. UTC on 11 March 2023, as Silicon Valley Bank's receivership cast doubt over several stablecoin reserve accounts, one metric on Coinbase's USDC–USD pair told a blunt story. The peg had slipped to $0.87. In theory, each token remained redeemable for one dollar through Circle's channels. In practice, the weekend meant banks were shut, market makers were cautious, and liquidity on major exchanges had thinned. Traders did not debate white papers. They watched order books. They sold at a discount. Behaviour, not promises, dictated price. What the episode revealed was simple: stability is tested in stress, and stress collapses complexity into a few decisive questions.

The essential question is this: what actions can users take when redemption pathways narrow? In the USDC episode, the answer depended on geography and counterparties. A firm with a U.S. banking relationship could submit redemption requests on Monday morning. A retail user in Asia could not. The same token had asymmetric accessibility. The place shaped the risk. That tension, visible within the first hours of the depeg, remains an enduring feature of stablecoin architecture. Behaviour under strain exposes which assurances are structural and which are aspirational.

The March 2023 weekend depegs also illustrated how oracles, liquidity providers, and governance decisions intersect. As decentralised finance protocols updated their prices through Chainlink feeds, collateral ratios tightened. Automatic alerts triggered liquidations. This feedback loop did not arise from malice or design flaws; it was the product of architecture meeting volatility. When liquidity thins, every design choice becomes a stress point. In that sense, the scene—dark charts, thin books, and jittery spreads—acts as a recurring motif: the waterline falls, and hidden rocks surface.

The first heuristic for users is collateral clarity. Show, then name. When a stablecoin issuer publishes a detailed breakdown of its reserves—such as Circle's monthly attestations outlining allocations across U.S. Treasury bills, cash holdings at regulated banks, and repurchase agreements—users can measure composition directly. Explain: collateral clarity is not merely a disclosure norm; it is a behavioural signal. Issuers willing to break down maturities, custodians, and percentages demonstrate an acceptance of scrutiny. The implication is profound. In stress, markets punish opacity first. A token with murky backing behaves like a claim on rumours. A token with transparent reserves behaves like a claim on assets.

A counter-example sharpens the point. Before its collapse in May 2022, TerraUSD (UST) presented itself as a "decentralised" alternative with an algorithmic stabilisation mechanism rather than explicit reserves. This reliance on endogenous collateral—LUNA—created a reflexive system in which a loss of confidence reduced collateral value precisely when more value was required to defend the peg. The limitation is clear. Stability built on self-referential assets is fragile when sentiment shifts. The reconciliation is equally clear: collateral clarity is both a quantitative measure and a qualitative marker of design philosophy. Transparent, exogenous reserves reduce reflexivity; opaque, endogenous assets multiply it.

The second heuristic is redemption path viability. Behaviour matters more than diagrams. Users should watch how redemption channels operate during ordinary conditions and during strain. Name an example: during the Tether redemptions of May–June 2022, the company processed over $10 billion in withdrawals within weeks, according to its published attestations. That is a visible behaviour: cash left, redemptions cleared, the peg recovered. Explain the significance. Redemption paths are the bridge between token and asset. If the bridge holds under weight, confidence strengthens. If the bridge constricts, jams, or closes, even temporarily, confidence decays. The implication is practical. Users do not need to predict black swans; they need to observe redemptions under minor turbulence. Small cracks widen quickly.

A counter-example, again instructive, is any stablecoin that promises one-to-one convertibility but offers no user-level pathway for redemption, relying instead on select institutional partners. The limitation is structural exclusion. Retail holders become price-takers on secondary markets, with no direct exit. The reconciliation lies in distinguishing nominal convertibility from effective convertibility. The former is a statement; the latter is a mechanism.

The third heuristic is oracle design. Prices inform risk engines, collateral ratios, and liquidation thresholds across decentralised applications. When oracles transmit stale or skewed data, the entire system becomes brittle. Show: during the March 2023 volatility, decentralised exchanges using tightly configured oracles saw temporary widening between on-chain prices and centralised exchange markets. Name Chainlink as one major oracle provider and note the behaviour: updates slowed modestly during periods of extreme volatility to avoid propagating outliers. Explain: oracle latency and methodology are not trivial parameters. They shape the speed at which depegs propagate through automated systems. The implication is double-edged. Slow oracles may delay contagion but can trap positions; fast oracles may amplify swings but keep markets aligned.

The motif of the waterline appears again. Oracles define how quickly the waterline recedes, revealing risks before users expect.

A useful example of design resilience can be found in MakerDAO's handling of DAI stability. DAI is backed by overcollateralised crypto assets rather than bank deposits. During the March 2020 "Black Thursday" crash, gas fees spiked, liquidation auctions malfunctioned, and the peg wobbled. Yet the system ultimately rebalanced through price auctions and emergency governance actions. The design limitation was clear: extreme market-wide stress can overwhelm automated processes. The reconciliation came through governance: parameter adjustments, risk diversification, and collateral updates. Transparent governance acted as a pressure valve.

This illuminates the fourth heuristic: governance responsiveness. Stability is not solely mechanical; it is institutional. Users should observe how quickly teams respond to stress, publish incident reports, adjust parameters, or engage auditors. Name another example: Paxos, which issues the Paxos Dollar (USDP), has routinely published New York Department of Financial Services–supervised attestations and engaged third-party audits. This behaviour signals institutional maturity. Explain: governance that moves slowly in crises magnifies instability. Governance that communicates clearly dampens it. The implication is straightforward. A stablecoin with weak or delayed governance makes stress more dangerous.

A counterpoint must be acknowledged. Highly centralised governance can introduce single-point failure risk. If one committee or executive can freeze, redeem, or alter reserves, users rely on that entity's continued competence and good faith. The reconciliation is not to reject centralisation categorically but to weigh it against transparency and legal safeguards.

A fifth heuristic concerns liquidity distribution across venues. Liquidity is not an abstraction; it is measured in the depth of bids and offers across exchanges, the spread between stablecoin pairs, and the slippage incurred during trades. Show: during the 11 March 2023 depeg, USDC liquidity on Uniswap v3 shrank rapidly as automated market makers adjusted positions to avoid losses. Meanwhile, liquidity on centralised exchanges such as Binance and Coinbase showed distinct pockets of depth because market makers were more active there. Explain: a stablecoin with uneven liquidity is vulnerable to fragmented pricing. The implication is practical. Users should pay attention not only to the peg but to where the peg is defended. Stability must be observable across venues, not just in a marketing dashboard.

Thread the motif again. Thin waterlines reveal the rocks. Fragmented liquidity is one such rock.

The sixth heuristic is exit cost. A stablecoin may appear stable until the moment one tries to exit. Exit costs include spreads on secondary markets, withdrawal fees, gas fees, and minimum redemption thresholds. Show: during periods of high Ethereum congestion, gas fees can reach dozens of dollars, making redemptions uneconomical for smaller holders. Name: in May 2021, average gas fees spiked above $60 according to Etherscan data. Explain: high exit costs create effective lock-ins. The implication is severe. A peg can break without collapsing if holders cannot economically exit. Stability becomes an illusion created by frictions.

A limitation must be admitted. Some exit costs are inherent to network design. Congestion cannot be eliminated entirely. The reconciliation lies in user awareness. A stablecoin designed with multiple redemption venues, cross-chain bridges, or layer-two pathways distributes exit load and softens shocks.

Throughout these heuristics, one question recurs: what behaviours surface when the waterline falls? A project that publishes daily reserve updates during calm periods but falls silent during stress exposes a cultural weakness. A project that claims decentralisation but relies on a single market maker for its peg exposes an operational weakness. Conversely, a project that communicates clearly during turbulence, processes redemptions promptly, and adjusts governance parameters openly reveals institutional strength.

Two final examples tie the heuristics together. First, the weekend of 10–12 March 2023 showed that collateral clarity and redemption structure can quickly separate robust designs from fragile ones. USDC's recovery to par on

Monday demonstrated that transparent reserves and institutional banking partnerships, despite their chokepoint risks, provide a credible backstop. Second, during the 2020–2021 bull cycle, numerous smaller stablecoins launched with aggressive liquidity mining schemes that masked thin organic demand. When incentives tapered, spreads widened and liquidity evaporated. This is a behavioural tell: demand driven by subsidies is not resilience.

The unresolved tension is the heart of the matter. Users can measure reserves, observe redemption paths, evaluate oracle designs, and track governance. Yet stability ultimately depends on actions taken at the worst moments. The forward test is therefore simple and uncomfortable: if the peg wobbled at two in the morning on a holiday weekend, which mechanisms would activate, which partners would answer, which markets would clear, and which doors would quietly lock?

Chapter 5
DeFi: Code, Composability, and Cascades

In the early hours of 12 March 2020, the screens were filled not with innovation but with liquidations. Ethereum, the programmable blockchain heralded as the foundation of a new financial system, buckled under a violent market crash. Fees soared. Bots snapped up collateral for pennies. Automated markets kept selling because code commanded them to. There was no central bank hotline to call; there was no circuit-breaker switch. The machine did precisely what it was built to do: prioritise the rules. But the rules had been written in a more innocent time. That night, a dream of frictionless finance collided with a truth older than markets themselves: incentives and interdependencies turn elegance into fragility when stress arrives all at once. Decentralised finance did not fail. It revealed its contours.

DeFi is presented as a clean break from old finance. No banks, no brokers, no single points of failure. Agreements enforced by software rather than signatures. Liquidity that moves without permission. The allure is powerful: what if the global financial system could be rebuilt without legacy baggage? Yet the very structure that grants it power—composability—also weaves hidden connections between instruments. A loan in one protocol may rely on a price from another, which depends on liquidity provided by a third. Innovation and contagion share the same rails. To build faster systems, we have drawn the components closer together. When one shakes, all feel it.

That duality is at the heart of decentralised finance. Code executes exactly as written. It does not negotiate. It does not pause to consider whether an oracle price is stale or manipulated. It does not weigh social tolerance for loss before pulling collateral from a borrower's hands. This rigidity is not a design flaw. It is the entire premise. Software-enforced commitments eliminate trust-based exploits—until humans learn to exploit the design itself. As DeFi has grown, an adversarial mindset once confined to cryptography itself has expanded to market structure. Sandwich attacks, flash loan manipulations, MEV (maximal extractable value) strategies: these are no longer hypothetical concerns but daily manoeuvres in a crowded arena. When an asset can be repriced in milliseconds by a single trade, the distinction between information and manipulation blurs.

Yet risk is not the enemy of progress. Hidden risk is. Traditional finance hides it behind layers of intermediaries and regulations that few fully understand. DeFi, for all its complexity, exposes its workings openly. Anyone can see leverage building up. Anyone can monitor collateral ratios. Anyone can observe—or ignore—the signs of stress. What looks decentralised is often socially concentrated: a handful of governance delegates holding the authority to adjust interest rates, pause withdrawals, or rescue protocols in emergencies. The ballots may be issued by tokens rather than governments, but governance remains a human drama. Power cannot be deleted; it can only change its syntax.

Inside these systems lies a core paradox. DeFi promises *yield*. People chase that yield. But yield is never free. Someone takes the risk, someone fronts the capital, someone subsidises growth. Traditional finance disguises those truths beneath decades of convention. DeFi displays them in real time: leverage hidden behind stablecoin liquidity incentives; duration mismatches embedded in farming strategies; rewards that look like income but behave like equity exposure. The hunger for returns remains the oldest force in markets, and code alone cannot tame it.

Still, to dismiss DeFi as dangerous techno-utopianism would be to miss its most important contribution: it forces us to define financial resilience clearly rather than poetically. Where does price come from? Who controls the assets backing the claims? How quickly can a system recover from shocks? When a token's value depends on ten interconnected smart contracts operating across multiple chains, these questions stop being academic. They become survival logic. Every liquidation cascade and governance standoff carries lessons that traditional finance learned through centuries of crises—bank runs, collateral squeezes, liquidity droughts—but now those lessons are accelerated, legible, and archived on-chain for anyone willing to read.

The cultural story is just as important. DeFi grew not from boardrooms but from open-source communities.

Developers ship upgrades to public applause and scrutiny. Retail participants hold governance tokens that in theory could influence multi-billion-dollar systems. Experimentation is constant, sometimes impatient. Progress is uneven: far too many innovations are merely new shapes of old leverage. Yet the creativity unleashed by permissionless architectures is unmistakable. What took years to prototype in incumbent finance can now be deployed in days. Code is no longer a back-office tool; it is the market itself.

The deeper insight emerges from this juxtaposition: we are watching a new financial order attempt to write its constitution while already in operation. Every fork and emergency pause is a constitutional amendment made under fire. Every protocol upgrade is monetary policy wielded by a handful of smart contract authors. Each governance vote is a miniature referendum on who should wield power when speed and safety conflict. There is no neutral technical ground here. Every rule embeds a trade-off. Every optimisation creates an exposure. And every exposure becomes a test when volatility returns.

This chapter invites the reader to examine that architecture with clear eyes. How does composability—this celebrated ability to stack primitives like money legos—produce chain reactions just as easily as breakthroughs? What happens when an oracle misprices an asset by a few percentage points for a few minutes? Who truly benefits when protocols offer double-digit returns, and who is unknowingly underwriting the risk? When crises require rapid intervention, which governance models protect against chaos—and which entrench quiet oligarchies under the banner of decentralisation? These are not merely technical puzzles. They are fundamental questions of economic design, community trust, and the future of autonomy in markets.

Decentralised finance has not yet faced its most severe trials. It will. Every system does. Stress will revisit it in forms we do not yet imagine. Some structures will buckle. Others will adapt and strengthen. A few may emerge genuinely anti-fragile, improving because of volatility rather than surviving despite it. The work is to distinguish the architectures that reflect enduring financial principles from those fuelled solely by novelty and momentum.

Code does not feel fear. But users do. And when the next cascade begins—because cascades do begin—what you understand about how the system fits together might determine how you experience it. The castle here is not made of stone. It is made of smart contracts and incentives. Its moat is liquidity. And its defences, in the end, depend on the wisdom of those who build and those who choose to stay within its walls.

Composability as Superpower and Risk

At 01:15 UTC on 12 March 2020, an Ethereum user watched their collateralised loan vanish. The borrower had deposited ETH into MakerDAO in Copenhagen's test labs only months before, convinced that over-collateralisation protected them from sudden liquidation. But when gas prices surged and oracles lagged, bots acquired that collateral for zero DAI in a liquidation auction that failed to attract bidders. What began as a routine funding structure became a cascading failure. Code enforced commitments that few had modelled under stress. A sleek tower of composable protocols had wobbled, and the impact raced through every layer built on top.

This is the central tension: composability is a superpower that bundles autonomy and speed, yet it ensures that independent systems become tightly coupled. A loan becomes a liquidity pool token, becomes collateral for a third protocol, becomes a governance asset for a fourth. Each new connection expands possibility—and vulnerability. The invisible thread running through this architecture is reuse: one asset, many promises. When confidence cracks, that thread tightens.

Decentralised finance has always celebrated "money legos"—modular components that developers can assemble, remix, and deploy without permission. Uniswap's automated market maker, launched in November 2018, allowed anyone to create liquidity pools with predictable pricing. Compound, introduced in San Francisco in September 2018, enabled algorithmic lending and borrowing with real-time interest adjustments. Snap them together and a user could mint interest-bearing tokens representing claims on pooled assets. Extend further and those claims could become the backbone of leveraged trading strategies or dollar-pegged stablecoins. The system grew not by central planning but by open experimentation. Yet the same composability that accelerates innovation can accelerate contagion.

The silent motif here is the domino. Each protocol stands upright as long as the ones beside it do the same. A lending platform depends on an accurate oracle price. The oracle price depends on market depth in a trading venue. Market depth depends on liquidity providers assuming that volatility remains within bounds. Break one assumption and the line shudders. Liquidations spike. Collateral migrates. Automated safeguards trigger further sales. The domino motif returns repeatedly in crises because circular dependencies are not tracked by default; they emerge through use.

MakerDAO's auctions in March 2020 illustrate how observed behaviour diverges from assumptions in a crisis. The system expected competitive bidding for under-collateralised positions. Instead, soaring network fees prevented bidders submitting transactions quickly, allowing a single bot to win auctions with bids of zero. The design relied on composability—trusting that auction mechanisms, gas markets, and price oracles would remain aligned. Stress revealed the fragility of that bond.

A contrasting example demonstrates that composability can also strengthen resilience. Aave, launched in London in January 2020, introduced health factors to measure portfolio robustness. Instead of simple collateral ratios, it accounted for the diversity of assets deposited and borrowed. An asset's liquidity and volatility influenced borrowing limits. The implication widened: composability need not mean blind stacking; it can embed situational awareness. When markets fell, Aave liquidations were more orderly because collateral quality was rigorously differentiated rather than assumed homogeneous.

Yet limitation persists. Even well-designed systems rely on the integrity of components they do not control. When TerraUSD collapsed in May 2022, DeFi protocols holding its related LUNA token as collateral discovered that diversification can be an illusion if exposures route through the same decay path. Algorithms that minted or burned tokens to maintain a peg unravelled under a classic bank-run dynamic. Composability made Terra look integrated into multiple ecosystems. In truth, it concentrated systemic risk in plain sight.

Protocols that hinge on a single oracle reveal another risk channel. Consider the role of Chainlink feeds—used globally to price assets in lending platforms and derivative contracts. Their reliability rests on decentralised nodes submitting accurate market data, but delays or thin liquidity in spot markets can misprice assets enough to trigger liquidations. Again, visible behaviour—collateral seized because a price updated too slowly—shows that even decentralised services form centralising choke points when expectations converge.

Composability amplifies cyclical incentives. When yields spike in automated strategies, users pile in, mint governance tokens, and loop borrowed assets back into pools. The system appears efficient: capital moves freely; returns are measurable. But that efficiency is conditional. It assumes a functioning exit path. If everyone attempts to exit at once, the same flows reverse violently. Positions that were composable become correlated. What looked decentralised becomes crowded.

An architecture built on smart contracts also inherits their immutable biases. A protocol optimised for bull markets must be re-architected for storms. Upgrades require governance coordination, which is slow precisely when speed matters. This stresses a principle often misunderstood: decentralisation trades rapid intervention for neutrality. It is a choice to accept rule-bounded suffering rather than discretionary relief. In quiet times that trade feels theoretical. In panic, it becomes visceral.

Yet we should not mistake fragility for failure. The open design of DeFi allows scrutiny and iteration. MakerDAO upgraded its auction mechanisms. Lending platforms diversified oracles. Developers introduced circuit breakers and real-time liquidity monitoring. Composability survived its trial because its flaws were visible—not buried in disclosures or proprietary risk models. Each shock pushes the architecture closer to antifragility, though "closer" remains a relative measure.

The implication extends beyond crypto: interconnected financial systems are vulnerable not because they are decentralised but because they rely on common assumptions. Traditional finance hides those assumptions in balance sheets and clearing agreements. DeFi encodes them into transparent algorithms. The elegance of composability lies in its honesty: it shows cause and effect without euphemism.

The unresolved tension is simple. How much interdependence is too much? When designing new money legos, must creators anticipate every chain reaction, or is controlled damage a price of progress? A system that isolates risk too aggressively may throttle innovation; one that connects too freely may collapse under strain. The next phase of DeFi will test whether modular finance can retain its explosive creativity while building guardrails perceptible to all. Code can connect anything. Should it?

Oracle Risk and Liquidations

At 14:57 UTC on 20 February 2021, a trader on SushiSwap's lending platform, Kashi, watched a single price update erase weeks of careful positioning. The user had borrowed against SUSHI tokens posted as collateral. Minutes earlier, the token's spot price on a thinly traded venue in Singapore had plunged by nearly 30 per cent in a single trade. The oracle feeding Kashi ingested that outlier, marked the collateral as under-water, and triggered instant liquidation. When the price snapped back, the collateral was gone. Nothing had malfunctioned; every line of code had executed correctly. The problem was the oracle's reflexive obedience. A momentary distortion had become a costly truth.

The scene captured a paradox that haunts decentralised finance: systems engineered for mathematical clarity can unravel because reality is noisy. Oracles are expected to describe markets, yet they also shape them. A delayed update can lull traders into mispricing risk; an overly reactive one can spark panic. The motif that threads through every serious failure is timing. Too slow or too fast, and the whole structure strains.

The growth of DeFi since 2020 has magnified this tension. Protocols enriched by composability depend on reliable price feeds to measure collateral health. Chainlink, founded in San Francisco in September 2017, has become the dominant supplier of decentralised oracle services, drawing data from a mix of centralised exchanges and automated markets. Its appeal is evident: multiple reporting nodes reduce the risk of a single compromised source. Yet, as the February 2021 Kashi case showed, the breadth of sources cannot fully compensate for shallow liquidity or idiosyncratic trades. A feed stitched together from weak venues inherits their flaws.

Show the mechanism, name the case, and the logic becomes stark. Oracles translate market behaviour into contract-triggered decisions. If a token's price collapses on a venue with only a few thousand pounds of daily depth, the oracle may absorb that data, even when other markets remain stable. The implication is visible: borrowers are liquidated, pools lose balance, and arbitrageurs rush in to exploit spreads. Oracle design is not a peripheral concern; it is the hinge on which automated systems rotate.

A second example reveals a different vector of weakness. In May 2022, during heavy volatility on Binance and Coinbase, Ethereum gas prices spiked above 2,000 gwei. Chainlink's nodes struggled to commit timely updates. Some feeds fell minutes behind. A lending protocol based in Zug, Switzerland, relying on these feeds, mispriced collateral by nearly 8 per cent while markets whipsawed. Liquidators hesitated, unsure whether apparent arbitrage opportunities reflected real dislocations or stale data. A delay intended to preserve accuracy created its own distortion. If timing is the motif's first form, latency becomes its echo.

A credible counter-example shows that better engineering can mitigate, though not eliminate, oracle risk. MakerDAO's oracle framework, refined between 2019 and 2022, aggregates prices from a dozen vetted sources, then imposes a circuit breaker if deviations exceed predefined thresholds. Prices update only when they fall within acceptable volatility bands. During the March 2023 USDC depeg, this mechanism prevented Maker from ingesting extreme prints from fragmented markets. Yet even this approach carries limitation. A circuit breaker that suppresses updates may delay necessary liquidations, allowing risk to accumulate unseen. Reconciling this requires recognising that no oracle design can fully harmonise speed and stability; trade-offs endure.

Visible behaviour demonstrates these trade-offs. When liquidations begin, bots compete to repay borrowers' debts in exchange for discounted collateral. Their strategies depend on precise pricing. If an oracle lags by three blocks—about 36 seconds in Ethereum—bots may submit frantic bids based on stale values. Some liquidations clear below fair value, damaging borrowers unnecessarily. Others fail because bot operators fear inverse arbitrage. The system absorbs the tension as wasted gas, inefficient auctions, and distrust.

That distrust becomes more pronounced in thin markets vulnerable to manipulation. Consider sandwich attacks on decentralised exchanges. An attacker identifies a large pending trade, fronts it with a buy, then sells into the subsequent price movement, capturing artificial profit. If an oracle reads from that manipulated market, the attacker's temporary distortion becomes the basis for marking collateral. The collapse of the token FEI in April 2021 illustrated the pattern: liquidity pools with shallow depth were manipulated to push prices out of line, triggering forced redemptions in dependent protocols. Liquidity providers withdrew, deepening the fragility. The domino motif recurs, here powered by incentives rather than accident.

The counter-example reveals that decentralisation alone does not guarantee safety. A purely on-chain oracle—such as those used by smaller algorithmic stablecoins in 2021—may rely exclusively on AMM prices, which can be distorted with relatively modest capital. During the collapse of Iron Finance in June 2021 in Dallas, small imbalances in liquidity pools cascaded into catastrophic depegs because the system trusted its own circular pricing too much. The implication extended beyond the event: autonomy without external reference creates closed loops that amplify error.

Yet the opposite extreme—purely centralised price feeds—brings its own exposure. If a protocol depends on a single exchange's API, outages or rate-limit errors halt price updates entirely. In September 2020, a prominent venue in Tokyo suffered a multi-hour outage. Any DeFi platform relying solely on that venue's feed would have been blind. A frozen oracle cannot trigger liquidations, but automated systems still degrade: borrowers build hidden risk, lenders accumulate exposures that appear stable. The protocol becomes a submarine sailing with fogged instruments.

The theme of timing returns when considering cross-chain protocols. Bridges use oracles to verify state changes on one chain before releasing assets on another. A delayed or manipulated feed can cause the bridge to release funds on false confirmation. The February 2022 Wormhole exploit exploited a validator that failed to verify signatures properly. Although not a price oracle failure, the structure was analogous: a decision-making mechanism trusted unverified input. The broader implication emerges: any system that accepts external data inherits the fragility of that data's journey.

Governance choices shape oracle risk too. If token holders vote to modify oracle parameters—update frequency, deviation thresholds, trusted sources—they must understand the behavioural consequences. A governance meeting in January 2023 for a major lending protocol debated reducing update frequency to save operational costs. Developers noted that this would lengthen the window for potential manipulation. The vote passed narrowly. The protocol saved money but increased vulnerability during volatility spikes. Risk, here, is not abstract; it is the measurable probability that price updates misalign with market reality long enough to trigger forced sales.

Robust systems incorporate heterogeneity. They combine decentralised sources, reputation-weighted nodes, and off-chain validation. Yet heterogeneity complicates coordination. During the March 2020 crash, DeFi protocols using multiple oracle sources spent hours reconciling conflicting prices. Some feeds signalled liquidation; others did not. The result was partial execution, uneven losses, and user confusion. Diversity of inputs reduces manipulation, but it increases complexity. The domino motif now includes sideways moves: shocks spread not only downwards through collateral trees but sideways across protocols that disagree.

One domain where the implications of oracle design become stark is stablecoins. A stablecoin that pegs to £1 or $1 must redeem at or near that value. If its collateral is valued through an oracle that lags or mismeasures assets—such as commercial paper in volatile credit markets—its redemption mechanism may be paralysed. The partial depeg of USDC in March 2023 illustrated this: rumours about Silicon Valley Bank's reserves caused markets to trade USDC below $0.90 on decentralised exchanges. Oracles tracking those markets fed back the panic. The stablecoin's issuers provided real-time reserve audits to restore confidence, but DeFi protocols reading the on-chain price had already begun liquidations. The implication is unmistakable: oracle design has consequences that transcend any single protocol.

Even systems with well-designed oracles must contend with incentives. If a liquidation bot profits more from inducing minor price distortions than from honest bidding, it will choose manipulation. In 2021, researchers at Imperial College London documented cases where bots executed micro-manipulations on low-liquidity pools seconds before oracle updates. The measured effect was small—fractions of a percent—but enough to force liquidations in tightly margined positions. Behaviour follows incentives; systems must assume this.

The unresolved question lingers. Should protocols prioritise speed, accepting the risk of sharp, automated reactions? Or should they prioritise stability, tolerating delayed updates and potential misalignment with live markets? No answer satisfies fully. The trade-offs are structural. What remains for designers and users is to recognise that oracles are not mere data feeds but fault lines. And fault lines demand respect.

Yield, Leverage, and Hidden Duration

On 17 May 2022, just after 09:00 GMT, a dashboard at Lido's London office flashed an implausibly high annualised yield for stETH. A routine rebase had coincided with a thinly traded block of validator rewards, pushing displayed returns into double digits for several minutes. Engineers quickly corrected the calculation, but the episode revealed a deeper truth. Yields in decentralised finance seldom arrive alone. They smuggle assumptions. They package timing, collateral, incentives, or outright leverage. A number promising effortless growth often hides the machinery that makes such growth possible, and sometimes precarious.

The motif begins with a simple tension: yield is never free. When DeFi protocols present annualised returns—whether through lending, staking, liquidity provision, or governance incentives—they convert structural risks into digestible figures. Yet those figures only make sense when we know what powers them. Is the yield funded by borrowers paying variable rates? By token emissions? By duration mismatches? Or by volatility that one group bears so another can collect a fee? The answer is rarely singular. It is typically a blend, masked by tidy percentages on a screen.

The most instructive failures start with mundane details. In early 2021, yields on Anchor Protocol in Seoul soared as high as 19.5 per cent. Deposits surged. To the casual observer, the returns appeared as stable as a pension fund's coupon. In reality, they were funded by a subsidy pool called the "yield reserve", topped up by the founding organisation Terraform Labs when market conditions faltered. The Show–Name–Explain sequence reveals the truth: the yield looked constant because someone else absorbed the uncertainty. The implication was catastrophic when confidence evaporated in May 2022. Depositors learned that a rate which looked guaranteed was, in fact, the product of a temporary transfer from the protocol's treasury, not an equilibrium in the lending market.

Where Anchor disguised its mechanism through subsidies, other protocols package leverage itself. A lending platform that offers a 7 per cent yield on a stablecoin may generate it because borrowers are using that same stablecoin to lever into volatile assets. If the collateral is ETH, rises in ETH prices prompt more borrowing, raising yields for lenders. A feedback loop emerges. The behaviour is visible in on-chain metrics: rising utilisation ratios, falling borrow caps, and borrowers posting increasingly correlated collateral. This yield is inseparable from volatility. When markets turn, liquidations reverse the mechanism. Utilisation collapses, yields fall, and lenders discover that the impressive APY was simply the reflection of other traders' appetite for leverage.

A counter-example clarifies the distinction. Aave's variable-rate lending pools—particularly the USDC pool on Ethereum in 2020—provided modest, fluctuating yields without protocol subsidies. At times, lending rates sat below 1 per cent. At others, when demand surged, they spiked. This behaviour revealed genuine market forces at work: yields rose because borrowers paid for liquidity, not because emissions programmes distorted incentives. The limitation, however, is that even market-based rates reflect hidden duration. A lender's expected return depends on borrowers repaying on time, on liquidations functioning, and on oracle accuracy. Duration, here, is the time over which assumptions must remain valid. When markets convulse, those assumptions grow brittle. This tension reconciles the counter-example: genuine markets reduce certain distortions but cannot eliminate them.

Hidden duration appears most starkly in liquidity pools. Automated market makers such as Uniswap v3 grant providers the ability to concentrate liquidity in custom price ranges. The yield looks like a fee earned for supplying capital. But that fee compensates for exposure to price movement. If ETH trades between £1,400 and £1,700 during the lifespan of a position, the provider earns fees and remains balanced. If ETH moves sharply outside the range, the provider becomes effectively a purchaser of ETH as price falls or a seller as price rises. The metric that reveals this is "impermanent loss", which measures the divergence between the value of the pool share and a static buy-and-hold position. During the volatility of January 2022, some concentrated liquidity positions produced fee yields of over 20 per cent annualised while simultaneously incurring losses larger than those fees. The yield did not compensate for the embedded duration risk. It merely disguised it.

A second example illustrates the packaging of incentives. In early 2021, decentralised exchanges in Singapore, Berlin, and New York launched liquidity mining programmes where protocols distributed native tokens to liquidity providers. Yields soared above 50 per cent in annualised terms for some pools. Yet a closer inspection showed that the bulk of returns came from token emissions, not from trading activity. Behavioural metrics revealed the fragility: when emissions halved, total value locked fell by more than 70 per cent in a matter of weeks. These yields were not yields in the traditional sense; they were marketing subsidies. Liquidity providers committed capital while the protocol paid them to stay. A temporary attraction, not a sustainable equilibrium.

A counter-example again tempers the narrative. Curve's liquidity pools, particularly the 3pool (DAI, USDC, USDT), generated returns largely from trading volume rather than token emissions, especially during the stablecoin turbulence of March 2023. Fees rose because traders sought stablecoin liquidity, not because subsidies inflated returns. Yet even Curve embodies hidden duration. The stability of the pool depends on the health of each stablecoin. When USDC depegged to $0.88 on 11 March 2023, Curve's invariant algorithm reflected the imbalance: the pool filled with USDC, and liquidity providers discovered that their "stable" exposure was now heavily skewed. The implication is unavoidable: fee-based yields can still mask correlated risks.

A recurring motif—time—anchors these examples. Yields remain attractive as long as conditions persist. When conditions shift, the source of yield reveals its timer. In staking systems, such as Ethereum's proof-of-stake, yields derive from block proposals, attestations, and network participation. The mechanism is elegant, but its duration assumption is explicit: a validator must remain online consistently. A brief outage caused by a power failure in Frankfurt in June 2022 illustrated the effect. Validators offline for even 30 minutes experienced penalties that erased hours of expected yield. The visible behaviour—lost attestations—showed how duration risk can surface abruptly.

Governance tokens complicate this picture further. Protocols often reward users for locking tokens for defined periods, offering boosted yields in exchange for commitment. When the veCRV model was introduced by Curve in August 2020, users could lock CRV tokens for up to four years to increase their voting power and fee share. The locked tokens created a form of duration exposure: users traded liquidity for influence. The consequence became clear when market sentiment soured. Some users wished to exit early but were bound by contracts. The boost mechanism worked as intended, but the lock-in amplified losses for those needing flexibility. Yield was entwined with time in a way that many did not fully appreciate.

Leverage surfaces even in places that claim to avoid it. Some "delta-neutral" yield strategies promise returns by hedging long and short positions across exchanges. Yet the hedge itself demands maintenance margin. If funding rates fluctuate sharply—as they did on Binance in April 2021 during a frenzy of perpetual futures trading—hedgers must adjust positions. If they fail to do so, positions drift, and the strategy acquires unintended exposure. The visible metric is funding rate volatility. A strategy that seemed insulated from price movements becomes a hostage to liquidity conditions.

Another case from 2022 shows how hidden duration can reveal itself. A structured-product vault operating in Zürich sold weekly options to generate premium income. During calm markets, yields appeared stable. But the vault was exposed to "gap risk" over weekends—periods when markets closed or liquidity thinned. In one instance, a sharp move on a Saturday morning forced the vault to repurchase options at significant loss. The yield, elegant on weekdays, carried a silent dependence on uninterrupted liquidity. When that assumption failed, the return profile inverted.

Across these examples, the central insight emerges: yield is not a single dimension. It is an output of intertwined variables—leverage, time, liquidity, volatility, incentives. Protocols compress this complexity into a single percentage.

Users, eager for clarity, may mistake this simplification for truth. Yet no yield exists in isolation. It rides on mechanisms that behave differently under stress.

The question, which echoes through every protocol's documentation, lingers without resolution. When yields spike, what exactly are we being paid for? And when yields fall, which structural risks have surfaced rather than disappeared?

Governance, Vetoes, and Upgrades

At 02:41 UTC on 14 June 2022, a single delegate wallet in the Compound governance forum cast a vote that froze an upgrade. The change concerned the oracle adapter for cETH, and engineers in San Francisco had warned that a misconfigured parameter could expose users to a faulty price. The vote's weight—gathered over months of patient delegation—was sufficient to halt the proposal. A crisis was avoided because one actor, with enough authority and enough wakefulness at the right moment, pressed *no*.

That scene exposes the real topology of governance in decentralised finance. Power is distributed, but unevenly. Decisions emerge from code, forums, delegates, and token holders, each with their own incentives and constraints. When markets are calm, this asymmetry feels benign. During stress, it becomes decisive. The quiet motif here is the hinge—the point at which the system must turn, whether through veto, emergency action, or rapid upgrade.

Who controls the hinge determines whether a protocol withstands shock or compounds it.

The essential dynamic follows a pattern: Show, Name, Explain, Implication. A protocol's governance is visible not in its constitution but in the behaviour of its operators when the hinge turns.

On 12 November 2020, MakerDAO faced a shortfall in its USDC-A vault parameters. Traders in Singapore and London observed that the stability fee changes were lagging behind market conditions. The protocol's governance structure enabled an expedited vote with delegated authority, adjusting collateral factors before markets opened in New York. This decision was not glamorous, yet it prevented an imbalance in DAI liquidity that could have widened spreads and strained the peg. The example Shows that robust governance appears in action, not aspiration. It Names MakerDAO's emergency process. It Explains how delegated authority allows speed without dissolving legitimacy. And the Implication is clear: when parameters influence a stablecoin's health, governance becomes a liquidity mechanism.

Token voting is often criticised for plutocracy, but its most revealing feature is granularity. Large holders can act as circuit breakers, slowing or vetoing proposals that surge too quickly. The visible behaviour is voting participation during volatility. In February 2021, during the frenzy around gas spikes on Ethereum, Uniswap governance received a proposal to adjust the fee switch. Delegates flagged the timing as hazardous: liquidity providers were already strained. The proposal was delayed. No crisis occurred, yet the moment demonstrated how vetoes operate as collective risk management. They create breathing room.

A counter-example shows the limits. Smaller protocols with thin governance communities may find that a handful of actors dominate decisions. A yield aggregator launched in Berlin in mid-2021 suffered precisely this fate. During a downturn, one large token holder pushed through an upgrade that rebalanced vault strategies without sufficient testing. The change introduced a logic bug that caused misallocation of funds. Speed eclipsed legitimacy. Yet this limitation also teaches a reconciliation: rapid action is necessary in crises, but speed without scrutiny becomes its own failure mode.

The tension between haste and legitimacy defines upgrade paths. A protocol relies on predictable mechanisms for changing code—timelocks, veto powers, tests, and audits. These create a form of duration risk in governance itself. Timelocks, for example, offer transparency but slow reactions. In March 2020, during the market crash that exposed MakerDAO to "zero-bid" liquidations, the presence of timelocks contributed to delays in adjusting risk parameters. The governance process had to be accelerated using expedited modules. The visible behaviour was unusual voting behaviour: high participation under extreme market stress. Delegates scrambled to shorten response cycles. The hinge strained.

Some communities try to reconcile this by implementing layered authority. Compound's "pause guardian", held initially by Compound Labs and later transitioned to a multi-signature arrangement, allowed emergency halts without rewriting governance. The Show is the simple fact: pausing occurred during suspected oracle anomalies in August 2021, preventing cascading liquidations. The Name is the guardian role. The Explain lies in recognising that this mechanism balanced decentralisation against operational safety. The Implication is that decentralised protocols need hybrids—structures that allow rapid action but maintain accountability.

Delegation itself has become an essential stabiliser. By giving voting power to specialised representatives, protocols concentrate expertise without concentrating ownership. The behaviour that reveals its function is consistency: delegates attend calls, write analyses, and maintain voting patterns. In 2022, ENS's delegates became widely respected precisely because of such reliability during contentious votes. Their stability created predictability, which is a scarce commodity during stress.

Governance failures often arise not from malevolence but from coordination breakdown. During a flash-loan attack on a debt protocol in April 2021, governance discussions on Discord, Discourse, and Snapshot scattered across time zones. Some delegates missed the window to act. The proposal that might have limited the attack's effect languished for hours. The limitation is obvious:

decentralised governance struggles with synchronisation. Yet even here, reconciliation emerges. Protocols that codify emergency procedures—clear thresholds, pre-authorised actions, scoped vetoes—convert disorder into process.

Oracle issues further complicate governance. When price feeds break, liquidations follow. Governance bodies decide when to suspend, replace, or override oracles. In November 2022, a major lending platform encountered a stale price on a collateral asset traded primarily in Zürich and Hong Kong hours. Delegates voted to disable the affected market before liquidations spiralled. The behaviour anchoring the decision was block-level analysis by independent auditors, posted to the forum within minutes. The hinge turned smoothly because the community had practised coordinating under uncertainty.

The motif of the hinge returns in upgrade cadence. Some protocols choose frequent, incremental upgrades—every few weeks—while others bundle changes quarterly. Incrementalism reduces blast radius but increases operational burden. Bundling increases efficiency but risks compounding errors. The design choice reflects a protocol's philosophy. A case from October 2021 illustrates this. A multisig controlling a cross-chain bridge pushed a bundled upgrade that included a firmware patch and parameter changes. A missing validation step allowed an attacker to drain funds during the transition. The hinge sagged because too many components were changed at once.

Limitations exist on the other side too. A protocol that refuses to upgrade quickly risks ossification. In late 2020, a decentralised exchange that prided itself on "immutable code" faced a critical bug. Because no upgrade path existed, developers deployed a new contract and migrated liquidity manually. Users bore the operational cost. The limitation becomes a lesson: legitimacy requires openness to change, but endurance requires structures that prevent reckless change.

Balancing speed and legitimacy demands design choices. Multi-signature guardians provide responsive vetoes. Elected councils introduce deliberation. Token-weighted voting offers broad legitimacy but slow mobilisation. Time-limited emergency powers, borrowed from historical governance models, can bridge extreme cases. The through line is not decentralisation for its own sake but responsiveness tethered to accountability.

Metrics reveal governance health. Voting quorum, turnout variance, delegate concentration, proposal lead time, and timelock duration each tell a story. A protocol with high turnout variance may suffer governance fatigue. One with extreme delegate concentration risks capture. A system with lengthy timelocks faces slowness when markets convulse. These metrics are as instructive as liquidity ratios or collateralisation levels. They show how authority behaves.

The unresolved tension remains: during crisis, who should hold the hinge? Should authority live with technocrats, token holders, elected delegates, or hybrid structures? And how much speed can legitimacy bear before it fractures? Each protocol quietly writes its own answer, block by block, vote by vote, hinge by hinge.

Chapter 6
Scams, Schemes, and Self-Defence

The pitch arrived as most temptations do: late at night, glowing through a screen. A young engineer in Manchester, fresh from his first successful year in crypto, found himself staring at a Telegram message that promised an *exclusive* token sale—just for early adopters, just for the visionary, just for those smart enough to act before dawn. A countdown timer pulsed like a heartbeat. The token had "institutional backing". The influencer promoting it had a blue tick. The white paper carried a proud stamp declaring "Audit Passed". The only catch was speed. He wired £25,000 worth of cryptocurrency within minutes. By sunrise, both the promoter and the token had vanished into the dark.

Stories like this seem obvious from a distance. Yet when they unfold in real time, the mechanics of doubt—the inner circuit that is meant to warn us—can be quietly bypassed. Scarcity accelerates desire. Authority reduces friction. Greed disguises risk as urgency. These forces are not unique to crypto; they belong to the oldest markets of human trust and deception. What changes are the tools: new masks for ancient motivations. Fraudsters have always preyed on optimism. What they possess today is software.

This chapter examines that uncomfortable edge where aspiration meets manipulation. Where innovation offers freedom, but freedom attracts predators. Crypto's openness—its permissionless nature, its global reach, its relentless velocity—makes it a laboratory for scams. Every bull market lures newcomers who feel they are joining history in motion. Every scheme is wrapped in the glow of "the next big thing". And every loss carries a sting not only financial but existential: *How could I have fallen for this?*

Consider the psychology of the deal that seems too good to be questioned. Crypto scams do not merely promise returns; they offer belonging. They invite the victim to feel ahead of the curve, more perceptive than the crowd. Fake audits tap into our craving for external validation. Celebrity endorsements—whether an iconic footballer or a charismatic YouTuber—signal safety through borrowed fame. Scarcity theatre, from countdown clocks to "limited whitelists", creates the illusion of inevitability. The scheme persuades its target that doubt is for slower minds.

Then come the structures engineered to convert belief into inflows. Ponzi design patterns flourish across the crypto map. Some wear the classic attire: fixed returns, referral codes, dashboards that celebrate recruitment more than performance. Others hide behind synthetic yield—numbers that appear impressive yet originate from native token inflation rather than real cashflow. The mathematics always converges on the same point: a collapse that arrives just as confidence peaks. Yet these mechanisms are far from novel; they merely adapt themselves to the programmable rails of digital assets.

Alongside these temptations runs a quieter danger: the exploitation of user behaviour. A malicious link disguised as a friend's message. A signature request that looks routine but grants unseen powers. Decentralised applications can betray users not through code but through design that is indifferent to human fallibility. Wallet pop-ups are not contracts written in legal English but cryptic bytecode that few can decipher even under calm conditions, let alone during a rush to buy before the window closes.

The villains here are not only the caricatures—anonymous developers draining liquidity pools under cartoon avatars—but also the patterns of self-assurance that swell in rising markets. Survivorship bias whispers that only fools lose money. Social proof shouts that risk is safe when millions agree. The public feed becomes a tide that lifts judgement off its moorings. And somewhere, a scammer quietly thanks the algorithm.

Yet readers of this book do not seek cynicism. They seek understanding. They want practical tools that reduce the odds of regret without requiring paranoia. The ambition of this chapter is to offer a style of thinking that respects both curiosity and caution. It does not lecture. It equips. A thirty-minute due diligence routine—a simple discipline of asking how a project holds assets, how incentives align, how exits work—can transform uncertainty into informed doubt. Doubt is a virtue when money is at stake.

What matters under stress is not how confident a scheme appears but how verifiable its foundations are. Who controls the keys? How is collateral stored? What breaks if a key person disappears? Which claims can be audited without trusting the issuer? The strongest defence often lies in the questions a user refuses to leave unasked.

This is not a chapter about victim-blaming. It is about power. Scammers exploit not stupidity but *hope*. Hope for financial independence. Hope for participation in a system that feels less rigged than the one predecessors endured. Hope that this time is different. Hope deserves protection, not mockery.

We will trace the anatomy of scams to understand where the seduction begins and where the trap closes. We will demystify financial illusions dressed as innovation. We will explore defensive habits that do not rely on luck or charisma. And we will confront the uneasy truth that self-defence requires not only knowledge but practice—a readiness to slow down when everything around you accelerates.

The marketplace of crypto dreams can be wondrous. But the same openness that enables breakthroughs also invites deception. The task is not to eliminate trust—no system can. The task is to decide who earns it.

The Psychology of Too-Good-To-Be-True

On 28 October 2017, in a conference hall in Pattaya, Thailand, BitConnect held what it called its "Annual Ceremony." Video from the event still circulates online: men in suits dancing on stage, crowds chanting the company's name, a booming voice promising "financial freedom" through an automated trading bot that supposedly paid around 1 per cent *per day*. Outside, banners displayed a logo that resembled Bitcoin's. Inside, speakers spoke of passive income, community, and a revolutionary algorithm. None of the presenters explained in detail how the profits were generated. They did not need to. The audience had flown from all over the world to hear what they already wanted to believe. Greed never sounds like greed.

When BitConnect collapsed three months later, in January 2018, wiping out billions of dollars' worth of paper wealth, victims were mocked for being naïve. Yet the psychology that pulled them in is not unique to obscure conferences in Pattaya. The same forces appear in Telegram groups, influencer threads, Discord servers and exchange homepages. They appear whenever a number on a screen promises to accelerate the timeline of material security without demanding much work. The scammer's craft is not to fabricate something from nothing, but to weaponise drives that already exist in the victim.

A recurring motif runs through these stories: the story itself. Every too-good-to-be-true pitch begins with a narrative that makes the numbers feel plausible. The story says you are early, special, part of a select group offered a door before the crowd arrives. The story says complexity is handled by someone else: a bot, a team, an algorithm, an "AI-powered" trading engine. It says scarcity is real because spaces are limited, the sale closes in hours, institutional capital is coming. The story invites you to suspend disbelief long enough to press "send".

Show, name, explain, implication. Show the promise: "guaranteed" daily interest, double-digit yield, "risk-free" arbitrage. Name the biases: greed, scarcity theatre, authority bias. Explain how they operate together, not separately. The implication is sobering. Even intelligent, sceptical people can be captured if all three line up in the right emotional weather.

Greed is the easiest to caricature and the hardest to admit. In crypto, it rarely presents as vulgar hunger for riches. It often appears as a desire to "catch up" or "not fall behind". A nurse in Birmingham who missed the early Bitcoin boom sees colleagues doubling their savings on meme coins and feels late. A student in Lagos watches peers post screenshots of overnight gains and worries they have missed a generational chance. Greed, here, is fear wearing aspiration's clothes. The visible behaviour is over-allocation: capital that should be slow and boring is pushed into fast and opaque schemes.

Scarcity theatre amplifies that impulse. Scarcity is real in many economic contexts, but scammers fabricate it by design. Limited-supply NFTs with last-minute "whitelists", token sales that allegedly close in minutes, airdrops restricted to those who act within a narrow window: these features are not merely logistical. They are psychological levers. They convert reflection into fear of exclusion. The timer on a website is rarely about settlement mechanics. It is about shutting down the part of the brain that asks, "But how does this actually work?"

Authority bias completes the triangle. Humans rely on shortcuts when evaluating unfamiliar domains. In crypto, that shortcut often arrives as an influencer video, a celebrity endorsement, a slick audit badge, or a partnership announcement with a recognisable company. Fake or flimsy audits are particularly powerful signals. A PDF bearing the logo of a security firm—even a little-known one—feels like a verdict to those who cannot read the underlying code. In several 2020–2022 DeFi rug pulls, projects splashed phrases such as "audit complete" and "no critical issues" across their front pages while burying caveats: tests were partial, assumptions unverified, or fixes pending. The behaviour is visible. Users share screenshots of checkmarks rather than reading the appendix where the auditors explain the limits of their engagement.

Influencer signalling works similarly. During the boom of 2021, prominent social-media personalities promoted tokens, sometimes without clear disclosure of their compensation. Their followers saw not just a recommendation but a form of permission. The authority bias here is subtle: "If someone with this many followers trusts it, I can too." The story becomes contagious. A project stops being evaluated as a claim and starts being treated as a movement.

A counter-example is critical to avoid fatalism. Not every scarcity mechanism is a scam. Bitcoin itself has a hard cap of 21 million coins. Many legitimate protocols limit token supply or restrict early sales for regulatory reasons. Not every influencer endorsement is corrupt; some builders and researchers use their platforms to promote genuinely innovative, carefully designed work. Some security audits are rigorous, candid about risks, and conducted by firms with reputations on the line. The limitation, therefore, is that simple heuristics—"if it's scarce, it's shady", "if it has an audit, it's safe"—fail both ways. They miss good opportunities and underestimate sophisticated frauds. The reconciliation lies in understanding that scams mimic *surface features* of legitimacy: logos, caps, countdowns, endorsements. They rarely mimic the substance: transparent mechanisms, well-articulated risks, and a history of accountable behaviour.

The story motif returns. A scammer does not sell a token. They sell a story about what it says about you to own that token. You are not just a buyer; you are an early believer, part of "the 1 per cent who understand". BitConnect's stage shows looked absurd to outsiders, but participants felt uplifted. Likewise, many Ponzi-style yield farms between 2020 and 2022 wrapped themselves in language of "community" and "financial inclusion", claiming to liberate users from banks while quietly reproducing the same extractive dynamics: early insiders cashed out while latecomers became exit liquidity.

Scarcity theatre reinforces the story by dramatising time. Psychologists call this temporal constriction: when urgency compresses our sense of the future, long-term trade-offs vanish from attention. A limited-time pre-sale activates this narrowing. So do "only 100 spots left" banners and progress bars racing towards 100 per cent. The behaviour is plain. People commit capital they cannot really afford to lose. They justify it by thinking they can exit before everyone else. They presume they will not be the one holding the bag when the music stops, because the story tells them they are early and sharp.

Authority bias, in turn, lends the story its costume. One common move is to imitate the visual language of legitimacy: graphs that resemble Bloomberg terminals, slides styled like venture capital pitch decks, "roadmaps" with quarters and milestones. Some scams even list fictitious regulators or licences in small print. The goal is not legal accuracy; it is aesthetic reassurance. When a website says "audited by X" and "partnered with Y," the natural human response is to assume someone else has done the verification work. The red flag is subtle: vague language where specifics should be. "Audited by a leading firm" without a link to a report. "Partnered with a global bank" without a press release the bank itself hosts. The absence of externally verifiable signals is a more reliable indicator than the presence of borrowed logos.

The psychology of too-good-to-be-true trades heavily on our discomfort with uncertainty. A promise of 4–5 per cent yield with clear, explainable mechanics feels boring. A promise of 20 per cent "risk-free" returns feels suspicious in the abstract but compelling when accompanied by graphs, testimonials, and technical jargon that we do not fully grasp. The uncomfortable truth is that humans often prefer a confident lie to an honest "it depends". Scammers understand this deeply. They strip away nuance and present a world where complex systems generate simple, predictable outputs—all for those clever enough to participate.

There is also a social dimension. Admitting that a pitch sounds too good to be true can feel like admitting one is too cautious, too old-fashioned, too slow. In group chats, the first person to sound sceptical risks ostracism. The line between prudent scrutiny and "FUD" (fear, uncertainty and doubt) is blurred deliberately by promoters who label critics as jealous or uninformed. The very phrase "too good to be true" becomes taboo in spaces where optimism is a currency. The story punishes dissent.

A deeper layer is shame. Victims of scams often stay silent, especially when they pride themselves on financial literacy. This silence allows patterns to persist across cycles. A rug pull in 2017 is reshaped into a yield farm in 2020, which becomes a play-to-earn scheme in 2021, then a "move-to-earn" app in 2022. The wrappers change faster than the underlying psychology. Each iteration learns from the last, refining the story, sharpening scarcity theatre, updating the set of influencers deployed, but leaving the core mechanism intact: money flows from the many to the few under the guise of shared opportunity.

Still, it would be misleading to frame the problem purely as predation by others. The uncomfortable mirror is that part of us wants the story to be true. That part is not evil. It is tired. It is aware that wages have stagnated in many countries while asset prices soared. It is aware of late entry, of missed chances, of obligations that feel heavier than the paycheque. Crypto's promise of "democratised wealth" plugs into those legitimate frustrations. Scammers, often themselves versed in behavioural finance, simply ride that current.

The motif of the story now suggests a forward test. When you encounter a pitch, what story about yourself is it inviting you to believe? That you are smarter? That you are chosen? That you finally have a chance to escape constraints that others remain bound by? Every too-good-to-be-true proposition operates as a mirror aimed at ego and fear. The better the scam, the more flattering the reflection.

This leads to an unresolved tension that no book can fully dissolve. How does one remain open to genuine innovation—the sort of outsized opportunities that new technologies can create—without becoming an easy mark for persuasive fantasies? Put differently: how can we respect our hopes without letting them be harvested?

Ponzi Design Patterns

On 17 December 2008, in New York, Bernard L. Madoff confessed to his sons that his investment advisory business was "one big lie." For decades he had promised steady, market-beating returns—often around 1 per cent per month—regardless of wider conditions. Friends, charities, universities, and pension funds believed him. Many withdrew profits regularly, confident that Madoff's reputation, industry roles, and seemingly sophisticated strategy signalled competence. Yet the payout cheques were funded almost entirely by new deposits. When the global financial crisis pulled liquidity from markets in late 2008, redemptions surged and fresh inflows evaporated. The machinery jammed. Within hours, the story collapsed. The numbers no longer added up.

That arithmetic is the central motif of every Ponzi scheme, whether wrapped in the language of Wall Street, Silicon Valley, or decentralised finance. The narrative changes across eras. The maths does not. Promises of stable, high yields must come from somewhere: trading profits, lending spreads, productive assets, or subsidies. If no such engine exists, the only remaining source is new participants. The moment redemptions outpace deposits, the façade cracks. The design pattern hides its dependence on expansion by presenting itself as diversification, innovation, or community. Ponzis thrive not because victims misunderstand finance, but because they misunderstand human incentives.

One way to see the structure clearly is to start with behaviour. In a Ponzi, early participants receive payouts funded by later participants. The pattern is visible in flows: money moves vertically, not horizontally; cash originates from newcomers, not from business activity. The design often adds camouflage—complex terms, layered tokens, dashboards that resemble trading screens—to disguise the lack of an underlying engine. The implication is straightforward. If you cannot identify the productive source of yield, you are the productive source.

A named example within crypto is the 2019–2020 PlusToken scheme, based in China and South Korea. PlusToken marketed itself as a high-yield wallet offering returns above 9 per cent per month by pooling user assets and using "AI-driven" trading. At its peak, it attracted over two million users and reportedly accumulated assets worth billions. The tell was the payout curve. In a genuine trading strategy, returns fluctuate; they do not maintain a near-flat monthly percentage regardless of market volatility. The behaviour of the price charts tied to PlusToken wallets—large, irregular liquidations—revealed what the pitch concealed. Funds flowed not from profitable trades but from the wallets of new joiners. When withdrawals intensified in mid-2019, the leverage of the story evaporated. By late 2019, Chinese authorities arrested several organisers and seized portions of the remaining assets.

A contrasting counter-example helps distinguish Ponzi traits from legitimate high-yield arrangements. Consider traditional money-market funds regulated in the United States under Rule 2a-7. These funds offer low volatility and moderate yield based on short-term, high-quality instruments. They are not immune to stress; the Reserve

Primary Fund "broke the buck" in September 2008 after exposure to Lehman Brothers commercial paper. Yet the design fundamentally differs from a Ponzi. Returns come from underlying instruments with transparent prices and regulated risk constraints. Investors can inspect holdings, track durations, and evaluate credit exposures. The limitation to this comparison is that even regulated vehicles can suffer losses and runs. But the cause is market risk, not the absence of an economic engine. The implication is that yield without a referenceable source is categorically different from yield underwritten by assets with observable cash flows.

Every Ponzi follows a predictable structure of expansion. First comes the promise: a fixed return, a referral bonus, or a hybrid model that rewards both. Next comes the visual reinforcement: charts showing compounding balances, dashboards with green numbers, a countdown to the next distribution. The show is not incidental. It is the mechanism by which belief becomes behaviour. When participants see early payouts—even if small—they rationalise further deposits and recruit others. Referral loops amplify this dynamic. A user who earns by inviting others to the scheme is no longer an impartial evaluator; they are an agent of growth. This is why Ponzis often include multi-level marketing tiers. The behaviour is quantifiable: a ratio of inbound deposits linked to referrals rather than external activity. When most new money comes from incentivised recruitment, the underlying pattern becomes unmistakable.

Synthetic yield is another tell. In DeFi, projects sometimes created high "returns" by minting native tokens as rewards rather than earning anything through economic activity. A protocol might pay 100 per cent APY in its own token, but the token's price only held if new buyers existed. Once incentives tapered, liquidity vanished, and the apparent yield dissolved. During the 2021 yield-farming boom, several protocols layered these mechanisms: staking token A to earn token B, using token B as collateral to mint token C, then returning token C into the system for further rewards. The circularity was elegant in its complexity but fragile in its logic. Without external demand for any of the tokens, the yields amounted to dilution packaged as income. The implication is stark. Yield that cannot be cashed out without collapsing the system is not yield; it is a transfer.

A telling example occurred in mid-2021 with the collapse of Iron Finance's TITAN token, famously associated with investor Mark Cuban. Although not formally charged as fraudulent, Iron Finance's hybrid model—partial collateral and algorithmic adjustments—created reflexive dynamics. When confidence slipped, redemptions ballooned and the token's price spiralled towards zero within hours. This event was not a Ponzi in the strict, criminal sense, because it had a defined mechanism rather than a deliberate deception. Yet participants experienced similar mechanics: the value evaporated once inflows slowed, and those who exited early did so at the expense of those still inside. The counter-example illustrates the limitation of treating all collapses as scams. Some failures stem from poor design or naive assumptions rather than intent to defraud. Still, the implication mirrors Ponzi logic: where payout capacity depends disproportionately on constant demand, fragility becomes structural.

A recurring motif runs through these examples: growth as a disguise. Whether in Victorian-era chain letters, Charles Ponzi's 1920 postage-rebate scheme in Boston, or online investment clubs in 2021, the pattern relies on expansion that looks like momentum. Participants see increased numbers and mistake them for validation. The story says, "Look how fast this community is growing." Yet growth funded by recruitment is a cost, not a revenue stream. The behaviour—measured by the ratio of withdrawals to deposits—reveals what the story hides.

To understand why these schemes persist, one must read the payout math. The key metric is sustainability under contraction. Any system that requires more incoming money than outgoing to maintain fixed returns will fail as soon as deposits plateau. That point often arrives sooner than participants expect. If a scheme promises 1 per cent daily returns, as some 2020–2022 crypto "arbitrage bots" claimed, it must double the payout base roughly every 70 days. Under such conditions, survival necessitates exponential growth. Exponential growth in human networks does not last long. The implication is mechanical. Decline is not an accident; it is programmed.

Referral loops intensify this pressure. When incentives reward inviting new members, the cost structure shifts increasingly towards recruitment. The behaviour becomes predatory by design. Participants are encouraged to bring in friends and family, often exploiting personal trust. Multi-level structures in several 2017–2019 crypto Ponzis illustrated this clearly. Users were offered escalating bonuses for reaching higher "ranks," determined by the deposits of their referees. Those ranks produced a social hierarchy inside the scheme. People competed for status defined by how many others they could persuade to join. The story recast exploitation as leadership.

Yet referral itself is not inherently suspect. Many legitimate systems—credit cards, fintech platforms, even academic conferences—use referral rewards. The distinction lies in proportionality and dependence. In a Ponzi, referral is the engine. In legitimate systems, referral accelerates but does not sustain. A counter-example is a decentralised exchange offering small incentives for liquidity provision. The rewards are tied to actual trading volume, not solely to new participants depositing capital. The limitation is that borderline cases exist, where incentives flirt with reflexivity. Reconciling this requires examining whether economic activity external to recruitment can cover obligations when growth slows.

Synthetic yield offers another diagnostic. When returns are paid in tokens that a project itself creates, three tests help expose the structure: convertibility, depth, and dilution.

Convertibility asks whether the token can be exchanged for assets outside the scheme without requiring new entrants to buy it. Depth measures the liquidity available at realistic exit sizes; if selling modest amounts significantly moves the price, the yield is largely theoretical. Dilution evaluates whether the token issuance meaningfully reduces existing holders' shares. In several DeFi collapses during 2022, token emissions dramatically increased circulating supply while real liquidity thinned. The behaviour matched Ponzi-like mechanics, even when the intent did not.

Across all these patterns, a quiet motif emerges: the map versus the territory. Schemes present a map of compounding wealth, smooth curves and steadily rising balances. The territory is cash flows, liquidity, and participant behaviour. When the map diverges too far from the territory, the correction is brutal. Participants confuse graphical representation with economic reality. They accept dashboards as evidence, forgetting that numbers on a screen are not claims on external value. This psychological gap is fertile ground for Ponzi architects.

One might ask whether regulatory frameworks eliminate these risks. They do not. The Madoff case itself demonstrates that even well-established jurisdictions can miss long-running schemes. The Securities and Exchange Commission investigated Madoff multiple times before 2008 but failed to connect anomalies flagged by whistleblower Harry Markopolos. His repeated warnings—including documented analyses submitted in 2000, 2001, and 2005—were not fully acted upon. The limitation here is that regulators often operate under constraints: limited resources, political pressures, or backlogs. Oversight reduces risk but cannot replace critical inquiry. The implication is that Ponzi detection must partly rest with participants, who must interrogate the source of yield rather than the credentials of the messenger.

Synthetic yield extends beyond crypto. Airline mileage programmes create points that function like pseudo-currencies. These points are minted cheaply and redeemed at opaque rates. While not Ponzis—they derive value from a real business—they illustrate how token-like systems can drift towards fragility if liabilities grow faster than revenue. Similar dynamics appear in prepaid card schemes, loyalty platforms, and even some subscription startups that pull future revenue forward. The map looks like growth; the territory is deferred obligation.

The motif of expansion now circles back to its inevitable question. If a system's sustainability depends on uninterrupted growth, what happens when attention shifts, narratives fade, or liquidity dries? No yield can outrun arithmetic. The unresolved tension for the reader is not how to identify every fraudulent pattern—no one can—but how to cultivate a discipline of tracing yield back to its engine. What is the trade-off? What is the vulnerability? What breaks when growth stops?

Social Engineering in Walletland

On 25 April 2022, the official Instagram account of Bored Ape Yacht Club, managed from New York but followed obsessively from London to Singapore, posted a link to what looked like a legitimate airdrop. Holders of the cartoon ape NFTs—some worth hundreds of thousands of pounds at their peak—were told they could mint "land" in an upcoming metaverse project by connecting their wallets and approving a transaction. The site looked polished. The domain resembled previous official campaigns. Within minutes, wallets began signing. Within hours, attackers had drained NFTs and tokens reportedly worth tens of millions of dollars. The blockchain records show no drama: just a series of signed approvals, each cryptographically perfect. The crime scene was not the code. It was the interface between a tired human and a persuasive screen.

That interface—those fleeting pop-ups, that green "success" tick, the reassuring icons—is Walletland. It is the environment where social engineering meets cryptography. Walletland is not a specific application. It is the mental and visual space where users decide whether to click "approve", whether to paste a seed phrase, whether to trust a message that claims to be from support. The prompt looked perfectly normal. Yet behind that normality lay a complete transfer of control. When people speak of "hacks" in crypto, they often imagine brute-force attacks on encryption. In reality, an enormous share of losses can be traced to this quieter battlefield: persuading users to hand over power with their own signatures.

Show, name, explain, implication. Show the behaviour: a user connects a wallet to a new decentralised application and hurriedly accepts an approval request. Name the tactic: social engineering through user-experience design. Explain the mechanism: the attacker exploits defaults, ambiguity, and habit to convert a seemingly minor action into full access. The implication is unsettling. In Walletland, the greatest vulnerability is rarely the algorithm. It is the human being trying not to miss out.

Phishing is the oldest pattern adapted to this new terrain. The technique predates crypto by decades, but blockchains intensify its consequences. A victim of online banking fraud may have some recourse—chargebacks, fraud desks, slow-moving settlement processes. A victim of a wallet drain has none. On-chain transfers, once confirmed, are effectively irreversible. This shifts the stakes of every interaction. A link clicked at 01:00 after a long day carries more danger than most users consciously register.

Consider a second named example: the BadgerDAO exploit in December 2021. Attackers compromised the front-end of BadgerDAO's website—hosted infrastructure, not the protocol's smart contracts—and injected malicious code that prompted users to sign approvals allowing a third-party address to spend their tokens. Over several weeks, users in Canada, the United Kingdom, and elsewhere interacted with what they believed was a familiar interface.

When they approved transactions to stake or claim rewards, the injected script added extra permissions. By the time the attack was discovered, roughly $120 million in assets had been siphoned off. Again, the cryptography held. The UX betrayed the users.

Phishing in Walletland therefore has two faces. The first is classic impersonation—fake websites, counterfeit wallet extensions, lookalike domains registered to capture typos. The second is interface compromise, where a genuine site is altered to mislead. In both cases, the user experience is the weapon. Logos are copied. Colour schemes are cloned. Error messages mimic official ones. The victim's mental model—"I know how this site looks"—is turned into a vulnerability. The motif of the prompt returns: each prompt feels routine until it isn't.

Signed approvals add another layer of subtlety. Many token standards, such as ERC-20 and ERC-721 on Ethereum, rely on explicit permissions for third parties to move assets. The function names are technical: approve, permit, setApprovalForAll. Wallet interfaces often compress these into a generic message: "Grant permission to access your funds?" with a green button promising to "Confirm". For an experienced developer, the underlying meaning is clear. For a nurse in Leeds or a shop owner in Nairobi using a wallet on a smartphone, it is anything but. The behaviour is observable in countless transaction histories: an address signs a "SetApprovalForAll" for a malicious contract and, seconds later, the assets leave.

This is not merely a user problem. It is a design problem. Wallets have historically optimised for convenience and transaction throughput, not for comprehensibility under stress. Small fonts display long hexadecimal strings. Critical distinctions—read-only signatures versus full spending approvals—are buried under the same "sign" gesture. Attackers know this. They craft prompts that look like harmless login confirmations but are, in fact, authorisations to drain tokens. The implication is blunt. UX can turn secure cryptography into a trap by making radically different actions look indistinguishable.

To be fair, not all UX in Walletland is hostile or negligent. Some wallets and protocols have improved their interfaces substantially. For example, several browser-based wallets began, from 2021 onwards, to parse common contract interactions and display plain-English warnings when a transaction would grant unlimited spending rights or interact with known high-risk addresses. Hardware wallets add friction by requiring a physical button press, making remote social engineering harder. These developments show that design can serve defence. The limitation is adoption. Many users still interact through older interfaces, mobile browsers, or hastily forked wallet code that lacks such safeguards. Reconciling this requires acknowledging that protective design is unevenly distributed.

Social engineering thrives on context. Scammers time their attacks to moments of excitement or fear. A major airdrop; a new NFT mint; a market crash; an exchange outage. At such moments, attention is already overloaded. A message that would appear suspicious on a quiet Wednesday afternoon in June feels plausible during a chaotic Saturday sell-off. The behavioural cues change. People skim instead of read, trust instead of verify, click instead of pause. The motif of the prompt sharpens: prompts arrive most dangerously when the user least has capacity to scrutinise them.

One notable pattern is fake support. In 2020 and 2021, impersonators flooded Discord servers and Telegram groups, posing as staff from MetaMask, Ledger, or major exchanges. They scanned public channels for users expressing frustration—failed transactions, stuck withdrawals, missing NFTs—then sent direct messages offering help. The script was consistent. "I'm from support. I can help you recover your funds. I just need your seed phrase to verify your wallet." The user, already worried, sees a combination of authority and empathy. By the time the phrase is typed, the assets are gone. Here, UX again plays a role. Many chat platforms do not clearly distinguish between verified and unverified staff; usernames can be trivially spoofed. The behaviour exploited is not folly but trust in a perceived helper.

There is an important counter-example. Not all "unusual" prompts or unexpected messages are malicious. Protocols sometimes do require users to re-approve tokens after smart-contract upgrades. Wallets sometimes must ask for signatures to connect to new dApps. Security teams do sometimes reach out to warn of identified issues. If users treat every prompt as an attack, they may end up paralysed, unable to interact with any on-chain system. The limitation of pure paranoia is that it renders the underlying technology unusable for those not willing to become specialists.

Reconciling this requires protective habits, not permanent suspicion. In Walletland, habits are subtle, repeatable behaviours that reduce exposure without demanding constant vigilance. One habit is to treat seed phrases as offline-only artefacts, never entered into a website or shared in a chat, regardless of context. Another is to test new dApps with negligible amounts before committing meaningful assets, watching how approvals behave. A third is to maintain separate wallets: one "hot" for experimentation, one more protected for significant holdings. These are not foolproof—nothing is—but they exploit the same human tendencies that scammers rely on: routine, repetition, and inertia. If the default behaviour is cautious, attacks must work harder.

UX can either hinder or support such habits. Clear labelling of permissions, visible differentiation between "sign message" and "sign transaction", and explicit warnings when connecting to new domains can all shift the balance. A user who sees "This transaction will grant unlimited access to *all* of your NFTs in this collection" is more likely to pause than one who sees only "Sign?" with a gas estimate. Likewise, showing the domain requesting a signature in large, bold letters foregrounds context that might otherwise be missed. The decision remains with the user. But the interface has stopped treating that decision as trivial.

Metrics tell the story from another angle. Chainalysis and other analytics firms have documented billions of dollars' worth of losses to phishing-style scams and wallet compromises over the past cycles. Those numbers, while informative, blur the human scale. Each address on their charts is someone's savings, business capital, or painstakingly accumulated holdings. Each click was a moment of trust. The fact that so many moments occur suggests that the standard UX in Walletland still underestimates how people actually behave when faced with complexity and fear.

A deeper question lurks beneath the practicalities. To what extent should systems protect users from their own impulses? Traditional finance answers by embedding paternalism. Banks deny certain transactions, impose daily limits, and monitor unusual activity. Crypto ideologues resist this, pointing to self-custody as a form of sovereignty. Yet sovereignty without usable safety features risks becoming a trap for the unwary. In practice, many DeFi projects now occupy a middle ground: they maintain permissionless core contracts but wrap them in interfaces that attempt to highlight hazards.

The unresolved tension is not technical. It is cultural. Walletland reflects a tug-of-war between speed and clarity, between maximal freedom and minimal guardrails. As scams become more sophisticated, the prompts will become friendlier, the sites more polished, the approvals more disguised. The forward test for any user, designer, or policymaker is disarmingly simple: when the next pop-up appears—a new mint, an urgent fix, an "account at risk" warning—which instinct will win? The wish to click through and move on, or the discipline to ask, *what exactly am I being asked to sign, and for whose benefit?*

Due Diligence in 30 Minutes

At 09:43 on 4 November 2021, a Reddit user in Manchester posted a short message that would later be cited in numerous fraud-case summaries: "Why can't I sell?" The token they had bought—styled after the Netflix series *Squid Game*—had risen more than 75,000 per cent in days, then collapsed within minutes. Liquidity vanished. Holders could buy but not sell. The contract contained a hard-coded restriction that anyone could have detected had they spent half an hour checking its origin, incentives, custody, and kill-switches. The blockchain had not lied. It had simply been unread. That small interval—30 minutes of structured scrutiny—often marks the difference between a painful lesson and a regret avoided. The premise is unsentimental. You cannot eliminate uncertainty, but you can compress the most revealing questions into a short, disciplined ritual.

The scene of that Manchester post captures a recurring motif: the clock. Every hurried decision in crypto takes place against a background hum of urgency—"minting now", "last chance", "supply almost gone". The timer is part of the theatre. It frames delay as loss rather than protection. Reversing that frame, even briefly, changes outcomes. A short pause, a notebook, a few browser tabs: this is the equipment of the half-hour discipline. It is not a search for certainty; it is a test of stories. Which claims survive a quick probe? Which fall apart with minor pressure? Which reveal structural flaws hiding under glossy veneers?

Origin is the first cut. Show the behaviour: a new token appears, supported by a flurry of promotional tweets and a sleek website. Name the test: provenance. Explain the mechanism: credible projects usually leave a trail in their commits, audits, team disclosures, or historical repositories. Anonymous founders are not a problem in themselves—Bitcoin's Satoshi Nakamoto demonstrated that in 2009—but unverifiable claims about expertise, partnerships, or backing are. The implication is immediate. If you cannot trace who or what originated the system, your confidence should be grounded only in what you can verify on-chain or in code, not in promotional narratives. That alone filters out a vast share of deceptive schemes. In the Squid Game case, the contract deployer's address had no meaningful history; the GitHub repository was forked and barely edited; the website domain had been registered days before the launch via a privacy service. These facts cost minutes to find. They expose the story.

Incentives come next. Here the clock motif returns. A disciplined pause asks: who benefits if this succeeds, and who benefits if it fails? Consider the collapse of BitConnect in January 2018. Its "lending programme" promised returns that scaled with referrals. The payout maths, later cited in multiple court filings, showed that the system depended on a continuous inflow of new participants to maintain yields. The show → name → explain → implication pattern appears again. Show the pattern: exponential reward schedules tied to recruitment. Name the mechanism: structurally unsustainable incentive alignment. Explain the reason: rewards were funded not by underlying economic activity but by new deposits. The implication is stark. If returns scale with your ability to attract others, you are not engaging with a product; you are the product.

A credible counter-example is helpful. Some community-driven protocols distribute tokens to early users or contributors as a way of bootstrapping participation. The activity involved—providing liquidity, verifying contracts, stress-testing systems—creates value. The limitation is that reward schemes can resemble referral loops without being fraudulent. Reconciling the difference rests on measurable behaviour. In legitimate incentive systems, you can identify the economic input: code commits, governance participation, liquidity provision, or computational work. In synthetic systems, the only input is enthusiasm. The half-hour test isolates which category you are dealing with by asking a blunt question: what measurable activity generates the returns?

Custody adds a third dimension. Show the visible behaviour: users deposit tokens into a platform that promises high yields. Name the structure: pooled custody. Explain the distinction: self-custody retains user control of private keys; pooled custody transfers control to a central operator. The implication is that the user's exposure shifts from market volatility to operator reliability. History offers a stark case: the Celsius Network freeze in June 2022. Celsius, headquartered in New Jersey, halted withdrawals citing "extreme market conditions". Behind that phrase lay an uncomfortable fact: user deposits had been rehypothecated, pledged, and entangled across multiple platforms. When liquidity pressures mounted, the pooled funds became inaccessible. Those who had taken time to examine the public terms of service—explicitly stating that deposited assets could be used by the firm—knew this risk. Custody, measured as who holds the keys and who has the legal right to deploy the assets, is a decisive filter in a half-hour review.

A counter-example helps sharpen the point. Not all pooled custody is negligent or deceptive. Regulated exchanges in jurisdictions such as the United Kingdom or Japan operate under strict rules on client asset segregation. Their audits, licensing obligations, and operational controls provide a framework for custody that differs fundamentally from opaque lending platforms. The limitation is that regulations vary widely and compliance does not guarantee solvency. Reconciling this means distinguishing between transparent pooled custody—where segregation, audits, and disclosures are verifiable—and opaque pooled custody, where they are not. The half-hour test focuses on what can be confirmed: licences, audit reports, withdrawal histories, and data on cold-storage ratios.

Kill-switches form the final major component. Show the behaviour: a protocol advertises decentralisation but includes an admin key that can pause contracts, change logic, or seize assets. Name the structure: centralised control point. Explain the mechanism: admin keys, multi-signature wallets, or governance modules can override user expectations. The implication is that even well-intentioned control points represent concentration risks. The Ronin Bridge compromise in March 2022 illustrates this sharply. Attackers gained access to five of the nine validator keys controlling the bridge, enabling them to authorise withdrawals totalling over $600 million. The weakness was not exotic cryptography but key distribution. The time-boxed test asks a simple question: who can push the red button, and how many signatures do they need?

A credible limitation must be acknowledged. Kill-switches are not inherently malign. Emergency pause functions can protect users during unforeseen exploits. The challenge is transparency about the conditions under which such switches exist, who controls them, and how transitions to more distributed governance occur. Reconciling this involves examining the decision pathways. If a pause can be triggered unilaterally, risk rises. If activation requires a diverse set of signatories, and those signatories are publicly known with historical behaviour to examine, risk diminishes. The motif of the clock recurs. When something goes wrong, decisions about kill-switches must occur swiftly. Their legitimacy rests on the clarity established beforehand, not improvisation during crisis.

Throughout these steps, a half-hour frame might appear arbitrary. In practice, it is a discipline that prevents research from swelling into procrastination. It also forces prioritisation. Within minutes, you can search for code audits—whether from reputable firms or dubious outfits with forged certificates. You can check whether audits include contract addresses, dates, and identified vulnerabilities. You can measure whether the project's governance forum contains substantive debate or only cheerleading. You can inspect the contract using a block explorer and identify functions that govern upgrades, ownership, and withdrawals. Each action is a visible behaviour that corresponds to an abstraction: provenance becomes domain history; incentives become payout schedules; custody becomes key management; kill-switches become contract functions and admin roles.

Consider a second named example that rewards structured scrutiny. The Mango Markets manipulation in October 2022 on the Solana blockchain saw an attacker inflate the price of the MNGO token on a thin market, using that inflated collateral value to borrow other assets from the protocol. The attacker then offered to return part of the funds if the community agreed not to pursue legal action. What stands out in this case, aside from the legal complexities, is that the exploit relied on the interplay of oracles, liquidity depth, and governance dynamics. A half-hour review does not identify such a sophisticated attack in advance, but it does highlight governance risk and thin collateral markets as structural vulnerabilities. These vulnerabilities, once recognised, inform how much exposure a user might tolerate.

The counter-example is instructive. Some protocols with high technical complexity, such as zero-knowledge systems or automated market makers with novel maths, cannot be fully understood in 30 minutes by any ordinary user. The limitation here is that no time-boxed due diligence can substitute for domain expertise. Reconciliation rests on scope. The goal is not mastery. It is detection of obvious red flags: unverifiable claims, absence of audit trails, opaque key management, contradictory statements about incentives. If a system is too complex to understand at all, even superficially, within a short window, that itself becomes part of the decision: complexity is a signal.

The clock motif reaches its sharpest form in the final minutes of the ritual. You have checked origin. You have traced incentives. You have inspected custody. You have looked for kill-switches. If time remains, you can examine social signals—not the influencer noise but the cadence of developer responses, the presence of repeat contributors, the absence of performative urgency. The behaviour of a community under mild scrutiny tells you more than promotional banners ever will. Does a developer answer a straightforward question about admin keys? Does anyone respond to queries about the audit's date or scope? Silence is information.

The unresolved tension sits at the heart of the half-hour discipline. You cannot fully understand a system of any sophistication in such a short interval. Yet you cannot bypass the interval without inviting narrative-driven decisions. The forward test is simple but difficult. When presented with an enticing opportunity accompanied by a countdown clock or a chorus of social proof, will you grant yourself thirty quiet minutes? Or will you surrender that time to someone else's urgency? The difference, as the Manchester post reminds us, is measured in regrets.

Chapter 7
Major Crashes, Mapped Calmly

On 12 March 2020, traders watched the price of Bitcoin plunge from roughly $7,900 to below $4,000 in less than twenty-four hours. Ethereum fell even harder. A cascade of liquidations ripped through exchanges as automated systems dumped collateral into emptying order books. It was a moment later labelled "Black Thursday". Yet the violence of the move was not really about new information. It was about oxygen running out. Buyers stepped back, sellers scrambled for the exit, and perfectly solvent positions became forced sellers because machines enforce rules humans might pause. Losses spread not through insolvency but through illiquidity. Understanding that distinction—liquidity crunch versus credit crunch—is the first step to keeping a clear head when markets crack.

A different sort of crisis unfolded in May 2022, when TerraUSD, a supposedly stable $1 token, lost its peg and ignited one of the fastest collapses in financial history. Billions evaporated. The root wasn't an absence of bids in the order books, but a deeper problem: promised redemptions lacked credible backing. Defaults propagated outward from a hole at the core. One day, retail holders checked their screens and saw a minor depeg; the next, major lenders reported losses, then insolvency. Fear was justified because the assets had already gone. Panic merely revealed their absence. Where Black Thursday tested cashflow under stress, Terra tested capital that was never really there.

These two moments—one mechanical, one structural—frame a quiet but crucial motif: crashes are not all the same. Some are air pockets. Others are cavities. Both feel like falling. But the recovery paths differ, and so does the damage to trust. The history of crypto is punctuated by these episodes, each with its own architecture of fear. The urgency of escaping blinds users to the underlying diagnosis. A liquidity event can be survived with patience. A credit event demands a reckoning.

This chapter examines how those diagnoses emerge in real time. First, liquidity crunches: exits overwhelm the ability of venues to match them, spreads widen, and even strong assets trade like distressed goods. Stop-losses become market orders. Margin calls become defaults. The system flushes risk into prices. Next, credit crunches: a promised asset fails its promises, whether through leverage, fraud, or unpriced correlation. Value does not flow—it disappears. Confidence breaks not because the price has fallen but because mathematics no longer balances.

Then come the secondary shocks. If one trader must sell to meet an obligation, fine. If a hundred funds must deleverage at once, a reflexive loop begins. Forced sellers turn into fire-sale merchants. Every tick down destroys more collateral. Automated liquidators harvest what liquidity remains. The drama appears like emotional panic, yet its script is algorithmic. The rules that protected the system in calm become accelerants during stress.

That is where contagion matters. Cross-collateralisation, shared custodians, and interlocking credit lines allow shocks to travel with unsettling speed. A platform that looks independent can fail because its counterparties failed. A well-capitalised exchange can wobble if its banking partners freeze access to fiat rails. Seemingly unrelated tokens can tumble because the same market makers retreat at once. Crypto's composability, celebrated for innovation, becomes a network map through which crises route. Every bridge is a channel of advantage—until it is a channel of infection.

Yet crashes also create survivors. When the dust settles, a pattern emerges: assets with genuine economic uses recover first, and sometimes overshoot. Infrastructure with integrity retains its community. Sensible policy proposals receive fresh attention. Narratives evolve. In the aftermath of 2020's Black Thursday, decentralised finance rebounded and grew by several orders of magnitude—in part because it demonstrated that code could clear markets even when institutions flinched. After Terra's implosion, reserve-backed stablecoins tightened attestations, and the concept of "algorithmic stability" shifted from triumph to cautionary tale.

A crash is a lens. It reveals how money actually works in that moment. It shows what was brittle and who was hiding behind borrowed credibility. It clarifies what matters:

liquidity, solvency, governance, and whether the promises embedded in code match the behaviour observed under force. Crashes simplify. They strip pretence and push every actor to choose: hold, exit, or default.

Mapping crashes calmly is not an act of detachment; it is an act of respect for risk. It acknowledges that stress is not noise around fundamentals—it is the test of fundamentals. When the music stops, theory must settle its bills. And when the music starts again, only the dancers still standing have a say in where it leads.

The chapters ahead confront a challenging set of questions. How can individuals discern a temporary air pocket from a genuine vacuum? Why do reflexive lows reveal value that narratives obscure? Which networks endure, and which connections must be severed? Most importantly, what decisions preserve optionality when everything feels urgent?

Calm is not the absence of fear. It is the presence of understanding. Let us acquire that understanding before the next plunge invites us to improvise.

Liquidity Crunch vs Credit Crunch

At 19:46 UTC on 12 March 2020, a single metric on BitMEX in Hong Kong told the story better than any headline: the funding rate on Bitcoin perpetuals collapsed as cascading liquidations pushed the price below $4,000. Ethereum briefly traded under $100. Order books were thin, bids disappeared, and automated margin engines sold into a vacuum. Yet most of the major exchanges remained solvent. There was no missing collateral, no hole in balance sheets—just too many traders trying to pass risk to a market that had neither the time nor the appetite to take it. This was a liquidity crisis.

Two years later, on 9 May 2022, TerraUSD (UST) traded at 60 cents on exchanges from Seoul to London. Within days, it would fall below 10 cents. Here, the problem was not simply that holders wanted out at once. The core mechanism that was meant to keep UST at one dollar—its mint-and-burn relationship with LUNA—could not survive sustained redemptions. Each attempt to restore the peg minted more LUNA, crushing its price and further eroding confidence. The reserves were not just illiquid; they were inadequate. This was a credit crisis, written in code rather than covenants.

The motif that separates these two episodes is quiet but crucial: a bottleneck versus a hole. A liquidity crunch is a bottleneck. Too many people try to get through the same door simultaneously, but the building itself still stands. A credit crunch is a hole. The floor beneath the crowd gives way because what was promised cannot be delivered. Prices can fall sharply in both cases. Screens do not tell you whether you are staring at a bottleneck or a hole.

The first task, then, is diagnosis. When prices collapse, what exactly has failed? Show, name, explain, implication. Show the behaviour in a liquidity crunch: spreads widen, depth evaporates, and even robust assets trade at distressed levels for short periods. Name the condition: a liquidity squeeze. Explain the cause: balance sheets are intact, but the marginal buyer is missing. The implication is that time and fresh capital can restore order if the underlying system is sound.

Black Thursday in March 2020 fits this pattern. Funding markets seized, derivatives exchanges hit circuit breakers, and DeFi protocols struggled to clear liquidations. Yet Bitcoin itself did not default. Stablecoins with credible reserves—such as USDC—briefly deviated but reverted as market makers returned and fiat rails reopened. Protocols like MakerDAO experienced painful incidents, including "zero-bid" auctions, but their collateral foundations were not inherently fraudulent. The crash exposed operational weaknesses and design assumptions, not fundamental insolvency.

A credit crunch behaves differently. Show the behaviour: redemptions are refused, withdrawals are halted, and instruments once treated as cash reveal themselves as claims on missing assets. Name the condition: a solvency or credit crisis. Explain the cause: liabilities structurally exceed reliable assets; the system is under-capitalised or misrepresenting collateral. The implication is harsher. Time does not heal a hole. It merely gives administrators, courts, or governance processes space to allocate losses.

TerraUSD in May 2022 is the archetype. Its peg relied on the market value of LUNA, not on exogenous reserves. When UST holders rushed for the exit, the defence mechanism—

printing LUNA to absorb redemptions—destroyed the very collateral meant to anchor confidence. The design exhibited the classic features of a credit failure: a promise of convertibility without a corresponding stock of durable backing. No amount of "waiting it out" restored parity because the system owed holders more than it could possibly honour.

This distinction is not academic. It explains why responses differ. A liquidity crunch often calls for buyers of last resort, stabilising mechanisms, slower liquidation schedules, and temporary risk limits. A credit crunch demands triage: recognition of loss, restructuring of claims, and often the winding down of institutions that mis-priced risk. Treat a credit problem as a liquidity problem, and you merely delay recognition, usually at greater scale.

Crypto's architecture gives unusually sharp examples of both. On 12 March 2020, some DeFi lending platforms remained over-collateralised despite experiencing brutal price action. Users who were not over-leveraged but endured mark-to-market pain often recovered as markets retraced. Contrast that with the failure of Celsius Network in June 2022. Celsius halted withdrawals, later entering Chapter 11 bankruptcy in New York. The firm's own court filings revealed extensive rehypothecation and maturity mismatches: user deposits had been deployed into long-dated, risky, or illiquid positions. That is credit risk in its purest form: promises of daily liquidity backed by assets that could not be sold quickly without massive losses.

A counter-example is instructive, to prevent over-simplification. Not every episode of withdrawal restrictions is pure credit failure. Traditional money-market funds during the 2008 crisis "broke the buck" when certain assets defaulted, then imposed gates to prevent runs. Some were re-capitalised by sponsors and ultimately made investors whole. Here, a liquidity shock and an incipient credit issue overlapped. The limitation of strict categorisation is that real crises often mix the two: poor asset quality and drying liquidity. The reconciliation lies in weighing which dominates. If assets would cover liabilities under orderly liquidation, you face primarily a liquidity crunch. If even an orderly liquidation leaves a gap, you face a credit crunch.

Behavioural cues help. In a liquidity crunch, you see wide but two-sided markets: distressed sellers, but some buyers with strictly limited size. Funding rates go wild, then normalise. On-chain, you might see lending pools temporarily hit max utilisation, then recover as liquidators repay and arbitrageurs re-balance positions. In a credit crunch, you see something else: frozen withdrawals, "maintenance" modes that stretch into weeks, governance votes to suspend redemptions, or courts appointing administrators. The price of liabilities—platform tokens, claims, IOUs—reflects not just fear but mathematical expectation of loss.

The responses diverge accordingly. A liquidity problem in a fundamentally solvent protocol can be addressed with slower liquidations, better auction design, and improved circuit breakers. After March 2020, MakerDAO changed its auction mechanisms to reduce the probability of zero-bid events and diversified collateral types to include more liquid instruments. It treated Black Thursday as a stress test, not a death sentence. The system's design accepted the pain and adapted.

By contrast, a protocol facing a credit hole cannot merely tweak parameters. When FTX collapsed in November 2022, revelations showed that customer assets had been misappropriated and the balance sheet riddled with illiquid, self-issued tokens. This was not a liquidity squeeze; it was a credit implosion. Attempts to raise rescue financing failed because prospective saviours saw the gap between assets and liabilities. The only remaining path was legal resolution and asset recovery, not improved market structure.

Yet even apparently "pure" liquidity events can morph into credit events if actors mismanage them. If an exchange responds to a temporary run by tapping segregated client assets to fund withdrawals, it converts a congestion problem into a solvency problem. This pattern has recurred across financial history. A bank run forces institutions to choose between strict asset protection—at the cost of angry customers—and quiet rule-bending—which may defer but magnify losses. Crypto platforms are no different. The motif of bottleneck versus hole reappears: an institution can either accept the bottleneck, communicating limits transparently, or it can dig a hole behind the scenes.

There is also a psychological layer. For retail participants watching a 50 per cent price drop, everything feels like a catastrophe. Screens do not distinguish between a distressed but solvent asset and a terminally impaired one. Yet the forward prospects differ. Bitcoin's plunge in March 2020 did not change its 21 million cap, its issuance schedule, or its censorship-resistance. Terra's collapse did change the nature of UST fundamentally: a stablecoin that had broken its peg so violently could never again serve as a widely trusted store of value. The chain survived technically; the economic project did not. The distinction is not about optimism. It is about whether the crash attacked the protocol's core promise.

Two further examples illustrate the spectrum. During the 1998 Long-Term Capital Management crisis, LTCM's positions were heavily leveraged but, in many cases, fundamentally sound on a hold-to-maturity basis. The Federal Reserve in New York brokered a private bailout because a forced unwinding would have created a systemic liquidity event. The underlying government bonds were not defective; the funding structure was. Contrast that with the 2008 collapse of mortgage-backed securities tied to subprime loans. Here, the loans themselves contained credit risk that had been mispriced and buried in complex tranches. No amount of emergency liquidity could erase the fact that many borrowers would not repay. Crypto compresses both stories. Leveraged basis trades can cause

LTCM-style liquidity crises. Algorithmic stablecoins backed by reflexive collateral can re-enact subprime dynamics.

For practitioners in digital assets, the practical question is often: how should behaviour change under each diagnosis? For a liquidity crunch in an asset whose structural properties you understand and accept, the rational response may be patience, staggered orders, or even opportunistic buying if you can tolerate volatility. For a credit crunch, the rational response may be decisive exit, legal monitoring, or write-off and learning. The book's constraint is clear: it cannot give advice. But it can emphasise that your decisions hinge on recognising whether the market has merely run out of breath or out of balance sheet.

Crashes also serve as discovery mechanisms. They expose leverage chains that were invisible during calm periods. In 2022, the failures of hedge fund Three Arrows Capital and lenders such as Voyager and BlockFi showed how interconnected borrowing had become. Many firms held similar collateral, lent to similar partners, and funded themselves with similar structures. The initial shock—Terra's failure—was a credit event. The subsequent forced selling across unrelated tokens was a liquidity cascade. Observers who could distinguish the two understood that not every falling price indicated a permanent impairment. Some assets were being sold simply because they were sellable.

The counter-example here is complacency. It is tempting to label every sharp drop in an asset one believes in as "just a liquidity event" and assume recovery is inevitable. That can be as dangerous as panicking at every tick. Sometimes a price collapse does reflect new information about fundamental flaws: a critical bug, a governance failure, a regulatory ban, or a revelation of fraud. The limitation of any framework is that it can become a shield against reality. Reconciling this means treating "liquidity crunch" as a hypothesis to be tested, not a comfort blanket.

The recurring motif of bottleneck versus hole leads to a final, unresolved question. When the next crash arrives, as it will, on what basis will you decide which type you are witnessing? Order-book depth, withdrawal policies, audit trails, legal structures, governance responses—all offer clues. None offer certainty. Crypto does not abolish the central tension of finance; it sharpens it. You must act under incomplete information, knowing that misdiagnosing a bottleneck as a hole can make you sell the very assets that later define the recovery—just as misdiagnosing a hole as a bottleneck can keep you aboard a structure already burning from within.

Forced Sellers and Fire Sales

At 22:00 UTC on 12 March 2020, a trader in Berlin watched the Bitcoin order book on BitMEX empty in real time. Rows of bids that had looked deep that morning now showed gaps you could drive a truck through. As the price slipped under \$5,000, then \$4,000, he was no longer deciding whether to sell. The decision had already been made for him hours earlier, when his collateral fell below maintenance margin. The exchange's liquidation engine was now in charge, dumping his position into a market that could not absorb it. There was no negotiation and no conversation. There was no human on the other side of the screen. There was a machine selling into silence. There was no bid anywhere.

Those trades did not express new opinions about Bitcoin's long-term value. They expressed a single, blunt fact: accounts had hit their limits. This is the essence of a forced seller. You do not sell because you think the price is too high; you sell because the system refuses to let you hold. In traditional markets, this happens through margin calls, repo haircuts, and redemption notices. In crypto, it happens as liquidation bots, auto-deleveraging queues, and treasuries scrambling to meet obligations that looked manageable a week before. The price on the screen is not a clean vote. It is a forced confession.

The motif that runs through these moments is fire. Fire sales are not simply "cheap sales". They are sales conducted under duress, with speed prioritised over price, and with rules that can turn a manageable loss into a reflexive spiral. When you watch a chart trace a sudden vertical line downwards, you are often seeing the smoke from many small fires burning at once.

To understand how reflexive lows form, start with the mechanics of margin. Show, name, explain, implication. Show the pattern: a trader borrows funds to amplify a position, posting collateral that fluctuates with market prices. Name the structure: leveraged exposure. Explain the constraint: as prices fall, the value of the collateral declines, and at a predetermined threshold—maintenance margin—the broker or protocol demands more collateral or begins to liquidate. The implication is structural. Sellers arrive precisely when the market is weakest.

On that March 2020 night, major derivatives venues like BitMEX and Binance Futures saw their insurance funds activated as liquidations overwhelmed normal trading. Orders to sell cascaded into order books with too few buyers, pushing prices below levels anything in the day's news could justify. This is a signature of forced selling: prices detach from fundamental narratives and obey margin maths instead. The market is no longer asking, "What is this worth?" It is answering, "How much can I unload before I hit zero?"

DeFi reproduces the pattern with different tools. Protocols such as MakerDAO and Aave do not make emotional margin calls; they run liquidation logic. When a borrower's collateralisation ratio falls below a defined threshold, anyone—or specialised bots—can repay part of the debt, seize collateral at a discount, and sell it. In calm conditions, this mechanism keeps the system solvent. In a sharp drawdown, it can become a conveyor belt. As prices fall, more positions cross the line, more collateral is auctioned, and more tokens hit exchanges where bids are already retreating. Liquidators sell because they must recycle capital for the next opportunity. Their behaviour is rational individually and destabilising collectively.

A second kind of forced seller emerged starkly in 2022: institutions with mismatched treasuries. Consider Three Arrows Capital (3AC), a Singapore-based hedge fund that had borrowed extensively against crypto collateral. When Terra imploded in May 2022, 3AC's positions across various platforms began to unwind. Lenders asked for additional collateral or repayment. As markets fell further, the fund reportedly sold liquid holdings—including Bitcoin and Ether—to meet margin and redemption calls, while its less liquid bets, such as venture investments, could not be monetised quickly. Here, the forced selling did not arise from a single exchange's margin engine but from a network of bilateral agreements converging on the same instruction: raise cash now.

Treasury mismatches operate on the same logic as margin but at a slower timescale. A company or protocol funds long-term, illiquid assets with short-term, callable liabilities. When those liabilities are called—users withdrawing deposits, lenders not rolling credit, investors redeeming—the only practical response is to sell what can be sold. This often means offloading the most liquid and highest-quality assets, because they find buyers. In 2022, several lenders sold large quantities of blue-chip tokens to plug holes created by losses on riskier instruments. The reflexivity is subtle: the more a token is accepted as collateral, the more it will be dumped under stress, dragging index prices down regardless of its own fundamentals.

A counter-example is necessary to avoid fatalism. Not every sharp sell-off is driven primarily by forced sellers. There are episodes where large holders choose to reduce exposure based on changed expectations, without being compelled by margin or liquidity constraints. For example, after regulatory interventions in China in September 2017, many traders and miners relocated operations and cut positions, producing a significant price drop. Yet balance sheets in core infrastructure remained intact. The limitation of attributing every fall to forced liquidations is that it can blind observers to genuine shifts in risk perception or policy.

Reconciling the difference lies in behaviour and data. Forced selling leaves fingerprints: spikes in liquidation metrics on exchanges, sudden drops in open interest, abnormal discounts of trusts or funds relative to net asset value, and blockchains showing large, urgent transfers from lending protocols to exchanges. Discretionary selling looks more distributed: volumes rise, but not in the tight clusters that accompany liquidation cascades; balance sheets do not suddenly contract; there is less evidence of accounts being closed in waves. Neither pattern is "pure" in practice, but distinguishing the dominant driver helps interpret how lasting a low might be.

Margin and treasury dynamics also interact with calendar constraints. Weekends and holidays, when fiat rails and some banking channels quieten, are fertile ground for reflexive lows. The March 2023 USDC depeg exposed this. As Silicon Valley Bank entered receivership on 10 March, USDC holders worried about reserves parked there. On decentralised exchanges, USDC briefly traded as low as $0.88. Automated market makers registered the fear. Yet redemptions with the issuer were essentially paused until banks reopened. Some traders sold at steep discounts because they could not—or did not wish to—wait for Monday. The fire sale here was less about margin and more about treasury timing: reserves were sound in principle, but inaccessible in the moment. Again, the forced seller sold not from a carefully weighed view of long-term solvency but from a short-term need for liquid dollars.

The motif of the floor becomes useful. In normal markets, the floor is diffuse: a zone where enough buyers think prices are attractive. Under forced selling, the perceived floor melts away. Algorithms and institutions that usually provide bids back off to avoid catching a falling knife. They widen spreads or cancel orders altogether. As a result, liquidation orders clear at levels that would seem absurd on any valuation model. Think of the Ethereum "wick" to around $90 in March 2020 while DeFi usage continued to grow; or blue-chip tokens sold aggressively in 2022 not because their projects had failed, but because they were the only sources of cash.

Treasury management choices before the crisis determine who will be forced to sell during it. Protocols that kept their treasuries largely in their own volatile tokens found themselves trapped in a particularly vicious loop. As token prices fell, their runway shortened. To survive, they sold reserve assets such as Bitcoin, Ether or stablecoins, or they dumped remaining governance tokens into already weak markets. Each sale pushed prices down, eroding the very collateral they needed. This dynamic, visible in on-chain treasury dashboards throughout 2022, reflects a basic corporate finance lesson written in crypto: funding long-term commitments with pro-cyclical assets amplifies both booms and busts.

Contrast this with projects that maintained more conservative treasuries—significant allocations to fiat, short-dated stable assets, or externally productive holdings. These teams were not spared drawdowns in their token prices, but they were not forced sellers at the lows. They could choose to buy back tokens, support liquidity, or simply sit out the volatility. The limitation is that such prudence often looks unexciting in bull markets; communities may criticise "lazy" capital or under-deployed treasuries. Only after the fact does the value of *not* being a forced seller become obvious.

Forced selling also has political dimensions. In 2022, several centralised lenders chose to halt withdrawals rather than liquidate assets at distressed levels. Their announcements—citing "extreme market conditions"—were attempts to avoid becoming forced sellers themselves at any price. Yet by doing so, they turned their clients into forced non-sellers:

individuals who wished to exit but could not. The decision concentrated distress: token prices may have fallen less than they otherwise would, but confidence in custodial promises deteriorated. Once again, the question of who is allowed to choose, and when, sits at the heart of fire-sale dynamics.

A particularly instructive pattern in crypto crashes is that forced sellers sell what they can, not what they should. A fund might recognise that a small-cap token is doomed but find no bids large enough to matter. It will then liquidate Bitcoin or Ether instead, because those assets have functioning markets. This is why, during the worst of 2022, high-quality coins at times drew down nearly as much as dubious tokens. Correlations jumped towards one because capital was raised from the most liquid pockets. For observers, this creates a cognitive trap: price action makes all assets look equally sick, even when their underlying health differs enormously.

The counter-example to blanket contagion is the behaviour of some stablecoins and on-chain money markets during crashes. During the 2020 Black Thursday event, MakerDAO's DAI briefly traded above its dollar target, reflecting demand for on-chain dollars. In certain later sell-offs, reserve-backed stablecoins such as USDC maintained pegs or recovered quickly after short-lived deviations, supported by arbitrage and redemption mechanisms. These instruments were not immune to strain, but they did not spiral in the way reflexive collateral tokens did. The limitation is that even robust designs can wobble if their backing is questioned or liquidity channels narrow. Still, the relative resilience provides a counterpoint to the idea that forced selling must indiscriminately drag everything down.

Ultimately, forced sellers and fire sales are less about villains than about structure. Margin rules, treasury policies, collateral standards, and market microstructure combine to determine who must sell, when, and into what depth. Reflexive lows emerge when many of those elements line up in the same direction: aggressive leverage in the prior boom, thin liquidity in the downturn, liabilities that cannot be rolled, and risk systems that are pro-cyclical by design.

The unresolved question is not whether forced selling will occur again—it will—but where it will arise from next. Which treasuries are quietly mismatched today? Which protocols have hidden concentrations of collateral? Which risk engines will enforce their rules mechanically while humans are still processing what has changed? When the next vertical line appears on a chart, will it reflect a considered reassessment of value, or the sound of many doors locking at once as everyone tries to leave through the same narrow exit?

Contagion Channels

On 8 November 2022, in Nassau, the Bahamas, FTX paused withdrawals. Screens on trading desks from London to Singapore flickered with the same terse message: "Withdrawals are currently unable to be processed." Within hours, markets stopped treating FTX as a venue and started treating it as a patient. Lenders scrambled to calculate their exposures. Market makers pulled liquidity. Retail users refreshed dashboards that no longer meant what they thought. Nothing had changed in the code of Bitcoin or Ethereum. What changed was the network map in everyone's head: a major hub had turned from conduit to sink.

The collapse did not stay contained. Days later, BlockFi halted withdrawals. Voyager and Celsius were already in bankruptcy proceedings following earlier shockwaves from Terra and Three Arrows Capital. Each announcement sounded like a separate story. It was not. It was a sequence along a set of wires that had been laid quietly during the boom—credit lines, cross-collateral agreements, shared market makers, common banking partners. The wiring was not obvious. It rarely is until something shorts.

That wiring is the subject here. Contagion is not magic. It follows channels: exchanges, lenders, and cross-collateral structures that connect actors who think they are diversified but are, in fact, holding the same risk under different brand names. The quiet motif to keep in mind is a simple one: who owes, who holds, and who clears. If you can sketch that on the back of an envelope, you are closer to understanding why some crashes spread and others stop at the first firebreak.

Begin with exchanges as hubs. Show, name, explain, implication. Show the behaviour in November 2022: once rumours surfaced about FTX's balance sheet, other platforms saw immediate shifts in flows. Binance, Coinbase, Kraken and smaller venues recorded spikes in Bitcoin and stablecoin deposits as users rushed to move funds off FTX. Name the role: centralised exchanges as both gateways and reservoirs. Explain the channel: when one major gateway is suspected of weakness, users plug their funds into others, stressing those rails and changing liquidity patterns across the system. The implication is that an exchange failure does not simply remove one platform; it forces all others to operate under a new perception of risk.

Exchanges also sit at the centre of collateral cycles. Many institutions maintained balances on FTX that were simultaneously trading capital, collateral for derivatives, and informal proof of solvency to their own lenders. When those balances froze, those institutions became forced deleveragers elsewhere. They sold liquid assets on other exchanges, withdrew from liquidity pools, and reduced market-making inventories. The "FTX problem" propagated not through obscure derivatives but through the basic need to raise cash. Each sell order, routed through surviving venues, pushed prices lower, affecting participants who had never opened an FTX account.

A credible counter-example shows that not every exchange shock becomes systemic. When Mt. Gox, based in Tokyo, collapsed in early 2014, it was then a dominant venue for Bitcoin spot trading. Its failure caused deep losses for its users and a sharp price drop. Yet the broader crypto credit system was still primitive. There were few institutional lenders, limited derivatives, and no complex DeFi collateral chains. The contagion channel was narrow: exchange customers, not a web of interconnected counterparties. The limitation of drawing too neat a lesson is that it can mislead: "we survived Mt. Gox, therefore we can survive anything." The structure in 2022 was different. The network had more connections, more credit, and more ways for a single failure to reach supposedly distant nodes.

Lenders form the second major channel. Centralised lenders like Celsius, Voyager, BlockFi and institutional desks extended credit to trading firms, miners, and funds, often against volatile collateral. When markets were rising, this looked efficient: idle assets generated yield, and lenders appeared to be diversifying risk by spreading loans across multiple borrowers and assets. In reality, many lenders had similar client rosters and similar collateral. When one large borrower failed, several balance sheets weakened at once.

The Terra collapse in May 2022 provides a clear illustration. As UST depegged and LUNA imploded, Three Arrows Capital and other leveraged players suffered large losses. Lenders that had extended credit to those firms found themselves with impaired loans. Some demanded additional collateral, triggering the forced selling discussed in the previous section. Others hesitated, hoping conditions would improve. The behaviour is visible in timelines: margin calls, partial repayments, then "strategic reviews" and withdrawal pauses. The contagion channel here is the credit line. A default at a trading fund turns into a liquidity crisis at a lender, which turns into frozen access for retail depositors who thought they were simply "earning yield."

Yet lending itself is not inherently unstable. A counter-example can be found in over-collateralised on-chain lending platforms that weathered the same period. Protocols such as Aave and Compound enforced strict collateral ratios and instant liquidation, and they did not rely on rehypothecating deposits off-platform. During the 2022 stress, some borrowers were liquidated and some users suffered losses due to price moves, but the protocols remained solvent and operational. The limitation is that these platforms still share contagion channels through collateral prices and oracle feeds; they are not insulated. However, their design makes the network map explicit: you can see what is owed and where collateral sits. That transparency changes the nature of contagion from hidden infection to observable pressure.

Cross-collateral links are the third, and often most opaque, channel. Cross-collateral arises whenever one asset is used to secure multiple obligations, directly or indirectly. In 2021 and early 2022, many firms posted Bitcoin, Ether, and even their own tokens as collateral across several venues simultaneously. A fund might pledge the same kind of asset—though not the same units—to a centralised lender, a derivatives exchange, and a DeFi protocol. All three counterparties believed they held solid security. All three, in practice, were depending on the same market price to remain above certain thresholds.

When that price falls, these links compress. An initial shock—say, a regulatory announcement in one jurisdiction or a large hack—drives the price of a major collateral asset down. That triggers margin calls at the exchange, liquidations at the DeFi protocol, and collateral top-ups at the lender. The borrower, facing three simultaneous demands, can seldom satisfy all. They choose to prioritise or, when they cannot, they default. Each failed top-up becomes a new shock: more liquidations, more sell pressure, further price declines. This is the reflexive loop in a networked form.

The motif of the map becomes useful here. Imagine nodes representing institutions and protocols, with edges representing exposures: loans, deposits, trading balances, guarantees. Some nodes are large but relatively isolated; others are modest in size but highly connected. FTX, for example, was both a venue and a lender via its affiliate Alameda Research, linking itself to a dense cluster of counterparties. Three Arrows Capital, similarly, sat at the centre of multiple lender relationships. When such nodes fail, the stress propagates not linearly but radially. A local failure becomes a global pattern.

Cross-collateralisation also appears within DeFi itself. A user might deposit Ether in MakerDAO to mint DAI, then deposit that DAI into Aave to earn yield, then borrow USDC against that position to trade. The same underlying asset now anchors several obligations. If Ether's price falls, the user may face liquidation on multiple fronts. If many users run similar strategies, a single price shock can translate into widespread forced selling and protocol-level stress. The contagion channel here is not an institution but a popular pattern of behaviour encouraged by design—"money legos" assembled in pro-cyclical ways.

A counter-example to runaway cross-collateral contagion can be seen in protocols that impose asset caps and conservative risk parameters. Some lending markets restrict the use of long-tail tokens as collateral or limit how much can be borrowed against them. This reduces the probability that failure in an obscure asset will cascade into core markets. The limitation is that such prudence is often sacrificed during euphoric phases, when competition for users encourages platforms to add new collateral types and loosen constraints. The reconciliation is uncomfortable: the same flexibility that makes DeFi composable also makes its network map more complex and harder to defend.

Exchanges, lenders, and cross-collateral structures are not separate worlds. They are overlapping layers. A fund may borrow from a lender, post the proceeds as collateral on an exchange, then hedge via a DeFi protocol. Stress can enter anywhere and exit everywhere. An exchange outage can force liquidations on another venue if positions cannot be rolled. A bank restricting services to a stablecoin issuer can ripple out to dozens of protocols that treat that stablecoin as a near-riskless asset. A legal action freezing assets at one custodian can reveal that those assets underpinned multiple loans elsewhere.

Visibility is the key difference between traditional finance and crypto in this regard. Blockchains allow anyone to trace certain flows: large transfers between addresses, balances in smart contracts, changes in on-chain leverage. Yet crucial parts of the map remain off-chain: legal agreements, bank accounts, private credit lines, derivatives books. The image is half X-ray, half fog. During stress, analysts can see some routes of contagion in detail while guessing at others. This mixture of transparency and opacity can either calm or inflame sentiment. When on-chain data shows that a protocol remains over-collateralised, fear may subside. When it reveals that a major actor has moved all assets to exchanges, fear may spike.

There is, too, a human channel of contagion: narrative. When a major platform fails, participants begin to question others that resemble it, even if their underlying positions differ. After FTX, attention turned to proof-of-reserves reports and the quality of audits across centralised exchanges. Exchanges that could produce cryptographic proofs of liabilities and verifiable reserve attestations regained some trust; those that could not faced outflows. The behaviour is rational up to a point—similar structures may share vulnerabilities—but it can also create bank-run dynamics at institutions that were, in fact, solvent. Contagion here travels not through contracts but through inference.

A simple mental network map helps disentangle these layers: identify the core collateral assets; identify the venues where they are pledged; identify the institutions whose failure would force large, sudden sales; and identify which bridges—custodians, banks, key oracles—connect multiple segments. No individual can maintain a perfect map; even regulators struggle. But rough sketches matter. They let you distinguish between a local fire and a structural blaze.

The unresolved tension is this: as crypto matures, should it strive for fewer, more tightly regulated channels of contagion, accepting concentration as the price of control, or should it embrace a messy diversity of venues and lenders, accepting that maps will be incomplete but hoping that redundancy will prevent single points of failure? Each path draws its own diagram of the next crisis. The wires are being laid now. The question, for anyone participating, is not whether stress will travel again, but whether they understand enough of the network's shape to avoid standing, unknowingly, at its most dangerous junctions.

Recovery Arcs

On 13 March 2020, the price of Ether fell more than 40 per cent in a single day. In the early hours of trading, as spreads widened and market makers stepped back, MakerDAO's liquidation system—then the backbone of decentralised dollar stability—struggled to keep pace with the volatility. In London, traders watching the screens saw an impossible number: auctions clearing at zero Dai because there were too few bidders to absorb the collateral being sold. It was not just a crash; it was a stress test of the protocol's design, its governance, and the community that sustained it. And yet, within weeks, MakerDAO had patched critical vulnerabilities, restored market functioning, and begun the gradual expansion of stable collateral types that would define the next phase of its life. The arc from failure to recovery was neither linear nor inevitable, but it illustrated a pattern that echoes across market history: systems rebound not by restoring what broke, but by deciding what must change.

Recovery begins with the inventory of survivors. After the collapse of Mt. Gox in Tokyo in February 2014, Bitcoin did not die; instead, its mining network continued to process blocks, its remaining exchanges tightened custody practices, and its developer community doubled down on hardening the protocol. The behaviour of miners—maintaining hash rate despite price collapse—provided a visible metric of commitment. This resilience helped shape the narrative of Bitcoin as antifragile long before the term was fashionable. The implication is that post-crisis character emerges from those who stay, not those who flee. A crisis is a sorting mechanism disguised as chaos, and the assets, platforms, and participants that continue to operate under strain form the nucleus of the next expansion.

Yet survivorship alone does not guarantee renewal. Recoveries gain momentum when policy shifts address the structural weaknesses revealed by the crisis. Show the pattern: in June 2022, after the implosion of Terra and the cascade of failures at lenders such as Celsius and Voyager, regulators across the United States, Singapore, and the European Union launched targeted reviews of stablecoin backing, lending practices, and exchange custody. Name the pivot: the release of the EU's Markets in Crypto-Assets regulation (MiCA) later that year. Explain the mechanism: by specifying reserve requirements and operational standards, MiCA created a clearer frame for institutional participation. The implication is that regulatory clarity—whether welcomed or resisted—forms part of the recovery arc by reducing the uncertainty premium that shadows the asset class.

But policy can mislead if treated as a panacea. Consider the counter-example of China's repeated clampdowns on crypto trading from 2017 onwards. Despite strict rules, traders and miners migrated to friendlier jurisdictions, liquidity fragmented, and innovation continued offshore. The limitation is that strong policy can redirect activity without extinguishing it. Reconciliation lies in recognising that effective recovery is not about restriction alone but about aligning guardrails with the systems' actual failure points. A rule that reduces custody opacity contributes more to resilience than one that merely restricts trading. The motif—what remains and what is remade—threads through these shifts.

Narratives are the third strand of recovery, and arguably the most underestimated. After the 2018 bear market, the story that fuelled Ethereum's rebound was not simply price-driven. It was the emergence of DeFi as a coherent idea. Teams building automated market makers, lending protocols, and synthetic asset systems provided concrete demonstrations of what blockchains could achieve beyond payments. The behaviour of developers submitting code commits, even during periods of low token prices, became a quantifiable signal that the ecosystem retained direction. Narrative here is not marketing; it is the collective shorthand through which participants explain to themselves why the next chapter is worth writing. The implication is that markets recover when builders craft a new frontier that feels more compelling than the fear that preceded it.

Recovery arcs, however, always begin in silence. After a crash, volumes fall, social media quietens, and many participants step away. This silence is a diagnostic phase. It reveals which assets retain genuine users rather than speculators. When the number of on-chain transactions, active addresses, or protocol governance votes stabilises—even at lower levels—these become behavioural markers that the core community remains. Such markers are more informative than price alone. A token can double on thin liquidity, but it cannot fake consistent usage by thousands of independent actors. This is why survivor assets often show stable user behaviours before they show price strength.

Forced sellers shape the early phase of any recovery. When liquidation cascades stabilise and the immediate reflex selling ends, value discovery begins anew. After Three Arrows Capital defaulted in June 2022, funds that had been pressured into selling liquid assets gradually finished their unwinding. Once these mechanical flows subsided, buyers who had remained patient could measure assets without the distortion of forced liquidation pressure. This is visible in volume profiles: sharp spikes during the crash followed by elongated troughs as natural buyers return. The implication is simple: recoveries are delayed not by fear alone but by the need to clear structural imbalances created during the boom.

Policy shifts then set the medium-term contour. Following the Black Thursday shock of March 2020, MakerDAO governance voted to integrate USDC as an emergency collateral type to stabilise the system. This was a significant philosophical pivot for a protocol that had prioritised decentralised collateral. The behaviour—rapid voting, implementation, and monitoring of liquidation ratios—illustrated how decentralised communities can act with urgency when properly structured. The implication is that governance design determines whether a system can adapt quickly enough to survive stress. A recovery arc often depends less on technology and more on decision-making speed.

Recovery also requires the revaluation of risk. During a boom, correlations tend to rise as participants treat assets as interchangeable vehicles for yield. Crashes often reverse this dynamic. After the 2022 deleveraging cycle, markets began to differentiate between assets with credible revenue (such as Ethereum through EIP-1559 fee burns) and tokens whose value depended entirely on reflexive demand. This differentiation marks a mature recovery: participants no longer assume that all assets will rise together. They choose based on fundamentals, even when fundamentals remain contested. The behaviour—selective accumulation—signals that the next cycle is forming.

Cross-market comparisons provide deeper insight. After the dot-com crash in 2000–2002, companies like Amazon and Google survived not because they avoided losses—they suffered steep valuation declines—but because their underlying businesses retained momentum. Amazon continued to expand its logistics network. Google increased search query volume. Their survival metrics were not stock prices but operational throughput. In crypto, similar patterns emerge: protocols with sustained transaction fees, consistent validator participation, or ongoing developer activity form the backbone of recovery. The implication is that resilience stems from function, not from the optimism of price.

A credible limitation tempers the optimism of these patterns. Not all assets that survive a crash deserve to. Some linger due to illiquidity, community stubbornness, or inertia. Their presence in the market can distort perceptions of recovery by creating the illusion of breadth. Reconciliation requires distinguishing between survival and viability. Survival is a timestamp; viability is a trajectory. A protocol that processes more transactions six months after a crash than it did six months before is demonstrating viability. One that shows stagnant metrics is merely alive.

Narratives around "comeback stories" emerge only once market participants believe that prior lessons have been integrated. After the 2020 shock, the broader narrative was not simply that crypto had survived a pandemic; it was that decentralised systems had shown robustness under extreme conditions. Stablecoins maintained pegs, lending protocols liquidated positions without insolvency, and exchanges continued to function despite unprecedented volatility. These observations created a feed-through effect: resilience became part of the sector's identity. Recovery here was not a return to pre-crisis conditions but an elevation of what the system believed itself capable of.

The motif returns: what remains, what is remade. Recovery arcs reshape ecosystems by pruning weaker structures and emboldening experiments that passed the test. Policy shifts refine boundaries. Survivor assets gain legitimacy. New narratives supply direction. And beneath it all lies patience—the kind that resists calling the bottom, that accepts that true recovery is less event than evolution.

The unresolved question is the timing of that evolution. After the next shock, will recovery follow the familiar pattern—clear the forced sellers, enact policy shifts, rebuild narratives—or will a new structural weakness alter the sequence? Put differently: when the dust settles after a crisis, what behaviours, metrics, or decisions will tell us that renewal has begun? The map is never the same twice, but the need to read it begins again with each fall.

Chapter 8
Regulation Without the Rabbit Hole

It is tempting to tell the story of digital assets as a struggle against regulation: young technology sprinting ahead of slow lawmakers, a borderless internet shrugging at parochial rules, code pitted against courts. Yet the more revealing conflicts do not resemble revolutions. They look like translation. In 2014, the US Internal Revenue Service announced that Bitcoin would be treated as property for tax purposes. The reaction was swift outrage from enthusiasts who believed that decentralised money should not fit into legacy boxes. But the subtext was more important than the headlines: regulators were not ignoring crypto, nor attempting to erase it. They were trying, clumsily at first, to classify it. To understand something is to shape how it grows.

A decade on, that classification effort has accelerated. Singapore's Monetary Authority has set risk-based disclosure standards for digital payment tokens. Canada has imposed segregation of customer assets in custody. The European Union's MiCA regime will soon define obligations for issuers and service providers. Each region tells the story differently, but the motifs are recognisable: who holds the assets, who bears the liabilities, who must disclose what. These are not arbitrary burdens; they are distilled from centuries of financial innovation and collapse. Rules, at their best, are the memory of markets.

What makes crypto regulation interesting is not its novelty but its tension with the founding myth of self-custody and permissionless networks. A market built on the promise that "you are your own bank" now faces the question of what happens when your bank loses your keys. Code enforces transfers, but code does not decide whether a mis-sold token constitutes fraud. Smart contracts settle instantly, but disputes may last months. The gap between software logic and legal language is not just technical; it is philosophical. Which truth should prevail when the two diverge?

This chapter argues that the dichotomy between freedom and oversight is false. Regulation can widen markets by deepening confidence. Yet confidence is not free. When exchanges must segregate customer funds, their cost of capital rises. When issuers must provide audited transparency, opaque shortcuts vanish. When trading venues enforce fair-market rules, some high-velocity strategies become less profitable. And yet each of these frictions, properly crafted, makes a market more valuable to those who commit capital for reasons beyond quick speculation. Safety does not merely prevent loss; it attracts patience.

A brief detour into history highlights the pattern. The London Stock Exchange of the early 1800s was a clubby marketplace rife with manipulation and insider dealing. It took a century of gradual reforms—mandated disclosures, clearing mechanisms, and listing standards—before institutional money fully embraced what had begun as a speculative game. Each reform was met with grumbling from traders who felt constrained. Each reform laid bricks that would support capital formation on a global scale. Progress rarely announces itself. It accumulates.

Digital assets present the same paradox: the more serious the market becomes, the more it must accept the disciplines that define seriousness. Even decentralised finance has discovered that trust cannot rely solely on code. Audited reserves, circuit breakers, oracle transparency—these are not signs of capitulation to tradition but expressions of engineering maturity. A bridge fails not because it lacked ambition, but because it ignored physics.

Still, the fear of regulation is not irrational. States wield legal power that can kill innovation if applied without understanding. A poorly drafted rule can mis-scope an entire industry, chilling progress rather than guiding it. The goal here is not to praise every statute but to focus on the principles that survive jurisdictional drift. Disclosure, because sunlight scales. Custody segregation, because possession matters in crises. Market integrity, because price and fairness must be believable to strangers. These are not Western doctrines or bureaucratic preferences; they are universal lessons written in the wreckage of failed markets from Buenos Aires to Beijing.

Consider the designer of a new token standard or lending protocol. They face choices that will determine not only how users interact today but whether a court, a regulator, or a community will trust the system when something breaks. Some decisions age well: transparent audits, rights of exit for users, clear incentive structures that avoid hidden leverage. Others become liabilities, especially when they depend on perfect behaviour or infinite liquidity. Building for the probable future means anticipating scrutiny, not fleeing from it.

Yet scrutiny cannot foresee every scenario. What happens when a smart contract misfires but no explicit law covers the edge case? Courts do not evaluate transactions as strings of bytes; they evaluate relationships, obligations, and harms. Lawyers translate digital events into analogies the law understands: agency, negligence, unjust enrichment. This translation is sometimes awkward, but it is a bridge. Without it, users have no recourse except public shaming or protocol forks. Justice cannot rely on Twitter threads.

The bigger shift underway is political. Digital assets have moved from cultural curiosity to part of national economic strategies. Governments now consider how to host innovation without importing instability. Citizens now expect that markets promising financial opportunity be subject to some accountability. And the industry—maturing, consolidating—has begun to ask a different kind of question: not "how do we avoid rules?" but "which rules make us stronger?"

This chapter stands at the intersection of aspiration and constraint. It does not descend into legal rabbit holes or list the statutes of every nation. Instead, it interrogates the themes that recur wherever digital value meets public interest. When do rules clarify rather than suffocate? How do we design systems that survive both hype cycles and court challenges? What balance allows decentralised networks to remain open while protecting those who trust them with savings, identity, or livelihood?

The tension between code and law will not vanish. It will define the next decade of innovation. The smartest builders will not wait to be told what is required; they will anticipate what is reasonable. They will treat transparency not as a favour but as a cornerstone. They will design systems that can be inspected, challenged, and—when necessary—rescued. This is not a retreat from decentralisation. It is what decentralisation looks like when it grows up.

Regulation is not the enemy of progress, nor is progress guaranteed by regulation. The real question is simpler, and more demanding: how do we create markets where strangers can trust each other enough to build a future together? The answers are emerging, imperfect and contested, but they share a promise: rules that understand the technology, and technology that respects the reason rules exist.

Principles That Travel Across Jurisdictions

On 11 November 2022, the Bahamas Securities Commission froze the assets of FTX Digital Markets Ltd., the local subsidiary of one of the world's largest cryptocurrency exchanges. Sam Bankman-Fried, who only months earlier had been hailed as the "JP Morgan of crypto," watched his empire unravel from Nassau as customers everywhere demanded their money back and found that custody promises had evaporated. Though headlines focused on personalities and fraud, regulators from Singapore to Brussels saw something simpler: the absence of three familiar foundations. Customers did not know what they had bought. Assets were not clearly segregated. Markets could not be trusted to reflect reality. The scandal answered a question that should never have been asked: what happens when the oldest rules in finance are treated as optional?

Disclosures. Segregation. Market integrity. These are not technicalities or bureaucratic niceties; they are the bedrock of any system asking strangers to risk savings. Crypto's defining challenge is not whether these principles apply, but how they should be expressed when assets move at the speed of code and ownership is recorded in blockspace rather than on paper. The challenge is translation, not reinvention. Just as the earliest stock exchanges borrowed the practices of merchant guilds, digital markets must integrate truths learned in the chaos of centuries.

Disclosures represent the first universal. They are the difference between a promise and a documented obligation. In the 1930s, the United States mandated audited financial statements for listed companies after the crash exposed vast information asymmetries; London and Tokyo gradually followed similar trajectories. The principle is not inherently

American, British or Japanese. It is simply recognition that if buyers cannot see the risks they bear, the entire market becomes a lottery. In crypto, the frontier version of disclosure is transparency: proof-of-reserves, open-source code, economic models that can be interrogated rather than trusted by intuition. When Binance published its initial proof-of-reserves attestations in December 2022, accountants flagged methodological flaws: where were the liabilities? Who verified wallet ownership? The gesture attempted confidence; the execution revealed how disclosure in cryptoland often reveals more by what it omits.

Visibility is a behaviour, not a slogan. A smart contract may be open-source, but if its mechanics remain legible only to a tiny priesthood of solidity engineers, the disclosure is performative. True transparency connects information to comprehension. Regulators everywhere ask a plain question: what does the user believe they own, and what happens when the unexpected arrives? The implication is profound. A token can resemble equity, debt or a voucher—sometimes all three at once—yet disclosures determine whether classification is a matter of law or marketing. The principle that travels is clarity: show your hand before others stake theirs.

Custody segregation forms the second pillar. It appears mundane: keep client assets separate from operating funds so that, if a firm collapses, customer property remains untouched. Its lineage runs from Victorian trust law to the collapse of MF Global in 2011, where improper rehypothecation turned client accounts into collateral for the firm's own bets. Crypto flirted with ignoring that history. Centralised exchanges held billions in pooled wallets, obscuring ownership and enabling rehypothecation in everything but name. When FTX allegedly lent customer deposits to its trading arm Alameda Research, the shock was not that leverage existed but that the boundary between custodian and counterparty had never been drawn.

Decentralised finance offers a contrasting case. In June 2020, the launch of Compound Governance Token (COMP) triggered an explosion in lending activity on Ethereum. Users deposited assets into smart contracts under their own addresses, retaining on-chain proof of title. Even if Compound Labs were to disappear, withdrawals would remain possible so long as the contract functioned. Here, segregation is not a regulatory policy but an engineering property. Yet even this architecture depends on oracle correctness and governance safeguards; code can fail, and then questions of legal recourse return. So the universality remains: assets belonging to users should not be swept into corporate insolvency or treasury operations. Segregation is not only structural; it is a commitment to accountability under extreme conditions.

Market integrity completes the triad. It is the assurance that prices reflect real buying and selling, not manipulation or privilege. The collapse of TerraUSD in May 2022 demonstrated how quickly integrity can fracture. An asset priced at par one day and near-zero the next undermines confidence not merely in the asset but in every related market. Price feeds, liquidity incentives, even social narratives can distort valuations more rapidly than governance processes can adapt. Regulators across jurisdictions converge on this intuition: fair dealing requires some constraint on practices that allow insiders to exploit informational advantage or exercise hidden control. In traditional finance that meant insider trading bans, public reporting of block trades, and surveillance of wash trading. In crypto it means tackling front-running through consensus design, detecting wash volumes on exchanges, and preventing governance capture via opaque voting incentives.

Some argue that market integrity is unnecessary in permissionless systems. The counterexample is immediate: users migrate away from markets that feel rigged. After revelations about self-trading volume on multiple Asian exchanges in 2018, liquidity evaporated. Markets without integrity shrink. Liquidity is trust made visible.

These three principles—see what you own, keep it separate, and trade in fairness—appear almost banal when stated plainly. Yet they carry genuine costs. Disclosure demands labour. Segregation demands infrastructure. Integrity demands enforcement. Regulators differ in how they burden participants, but few contest the direction of travel. The question is calibration.

There are counter-arguments worth confronting. Some developers claim that self-custody eliminates the need for segregated accounts entirely. If users never surrender control, what is left to protect? The limitation appears when users interact through bridges, wrappers, and staking providers where custody becomes fractional or contingent. Self-custody can trap risk rather than eliminate it: keys lost, contracts bricked, legal ownership ambiguous. The principle survives as nuance: where intermediaries exist, protection must follow. And intermediaries in cryptoland proliferate, even when they pretend not to be intermediaries at all.

Another challenge comes from over-disclosure. If protocols drown users in complex data or offer incomplete attestations that obscure rather than illuminate, the form is satisfied but the function fails. The lesson from securities regulation is repeatable: effective disclosure balances relevance and digestibility. Crypto will need its own drafting discipline, a user-first standard that clarifies instead of overwhelms.

Market integrity faces its own tensions. Strategies like maximal extractable value (MEV) complicate the line between unethical exploitation and permissible arbitrage. A validator inserting a sandwich trade extracts profit from users who never agreed to become counterparties. Some researchers argue that such behaviour is a market signal, incentivising liquidity provision by making markets more efficient. Others observe that users abandon platforms where predation feels systematic. The principle must adapt: design systems where information asymmetry does not become structural harm.

A motif returns: people participate when they understand the rules and believe those rules apply equally. The global nature of digital assets makes local differences in statute feel transient. What travels are expectations. If a European investor expects fund segregation and audited proof, they will not accept "trust us" simply because a protocol is hosted under a tropical sun. If an Asian exchange aspires to institutional flows, it will align with global best practice long before legislators require it. Standards migrate faster than regulation because capital votes with its feet.

The paradox is that crypto aspires to universality—money without borders—but has resisted the universal principles that make borderless money usable by more than the boldest risk-takers. The direction of travel is clear. The tension is timing: rushing regulation risks stifling what has not yet matured; delaying risks repeating failures already mapped.

The most thoughtful builders do not wait for injunctions. They measure claims against evidence. They separate what is theirs from what belongs to those who trust them. They commit to markets where price is not theatre but discovery. Users do not always notice these decisions in real time, but they reward them over cycles. Survivors of past crashes—from centralised exchanges that maintained full reserves to protocols that designed for stress—show that principles endure where hype dies.

Yet one question persists, unanswered for now: who enforces these norms where no single state controls the venue? Smart contracts can enforce segregation but not honesty. Block explorers can publish reserves but not intentions. Surveillance can detect manipulation but not adjudicate guilt. The distributed nature of crypto means enforcement must become multi-layered: community governance, industry self-regulation, and eventually statutory authority with the competence to respect what is novel without discarding what is necessary.

What will be the standard that earns the trust not only of technologists but of pension trustees, sovereign wealth funds, and households saving for the distant future? Will disclosures become machine-readable and enforced by protocol incentives? Will custodial segregation be tri-provable: on-chain evidence, audited attestation, and legal enforceability? Will market integrity be defined not by prohibition but by architecture that makes abuse unprofitable?

The answers will determine whether digital assets remain a niche playground or evolve into a durable component of global finance. The principles already exist; the question is who will embody them with enough rigour to make the rest follow.

When Rules Change the Game

On 19 April 2004, the London Stock Exchange tightened its requirements for companies seeking admission to the Main Market. What had previously been a relatively streamlined route for ambitious mid-sized firms now demanded fuller financial histories, clearer governance structures, and more comprehensive disclosures. Bankers complained that the new standards raised costs and slowed listings. Yet twelve months later, the data told a quieter truth: institutional investors increased allocations to newly listed companies, spreads narrowed, and post-IPO volatility fell. A higher bar did not freeze activity; it concentrated attention on firms willing to meet it. Rules, once clarified, reshaped the flow of capital.

The tension embedded in that episode echoes through cryptoland. Builders praise speed yet resent ambiguity. Investors crave upside but fear hidden liabilities. Regulators chase clarity while knowing that precision can chill experimentation. When rules change, so does the game; and when rules become clear, capital behaves differently. Costs rise. Trust deepens. The paradox is not a flaw but a feature of markets seeking legitimacy rather than spectacle. It is the price of graduating from frontier to infrastructure.

The motif that threads through this terrain is a gate. Gates restrict, but they also protect. They narrow the crowd but make entrance meaningful. As crypto approaches a phase where institutional money tests the perimeter, the question is not whether gates will appear but who will design them—and for what purpose.

The first shift arrives with definitional clarity. When the Securities and Exchange Commission in the United States categorised most token sales in 2017 as securities offerings, the cost of raising capital through ICOs rose sharply. Some projects vanished; others adapted by publishing audited financials, designing vesting schedules, or seeking exemptions. The behaviour was measurable. According to PwC and the Crypto Valley Association (2018), ICO volumes halved within six months, yet the median quality of surviving projects improved when judged by product readiness and team transparency. Clarity raised capital costs, but it also filtered noise. The implication is stark: when markets know which rules apply, participants commit differently. Investors demand more evidence. Founders craft cleaner structures. Speculators lose oxygen.

A second example, drawn from Asia, shows how listing standards evolve. In December 2020, the Monetary Authority of Singapore clarified its stance on digital payment token service providers, requiring enhanced anti-money-laundering controls and fit-and-proper management tests. Exchanges grumbled about paperwork and compliance expenditure, yet the shift had a measurable effect: institutional onboarding increased in the following year, and several major global banks began routing clients through licensed Singaporean venues. The gate narrowed, but the calibre of entrants rose. Clarity did not encourage all activity; it encouraged the sort of activity regulators and long-term investors considered legitimate.

Critics often argue that such shifts stifle innovation. They point to early internet regulation or peer-to-peer lending rules that throttled experimentation. A credible counter-example comes from Switzerland's 2015 revision of its Collective Investment Schemes Act. By defining crypto-related structured products within a known regulatory perimeter, Switzerland enabled firms to issue exchange-traded crypto trackers under familiar asset-management rules. Costs rose. Oversight sharpened. Innovation continued, now bedded in a framework investors could trust. The limitation of this example, of course, is jurisdiction size; small markets can afford clarity without confronting global contagion risks. Still, the principle holds: well-crafted rules can convert novelty into investable structure.

The crypto world faces a deeper tension than most asset classes: it has built a culture of permissionless experimentation that recoils at state-defined categories. Yet central banks, asset managers and insurers rarely allocate serious capital where liabilities and rights remain ambiguous. When rules change, the cost of capital becomes a diagnostic of belief. If users pay a premium for transparency, segregation, or audited reserves, it reveals something foundational about their priorities. When the cost of capital rises because a protocol must demonstrate solvency or governance resilience, that cost is not friction; it is information.

Consider the behaviour of exchanges after the collapse of Mt. Gox in Tokyo in February 2014. The Japanese Financial Services Agency began shaping rules that required cold-wallet segregation, operational audits, and minimum cybersecurity standards. Some exchanges exited the country. Others consolidated and invested in the required infrastructure. Volumes initially declined, but by 2017 Japan had become one of the world's most active and regulated crypto markets, with retail and institutional participation sustained by the clarity of expectations. Again the gate motif reappears: costs rose, but confidence rose faster.

Rules also change the incentives inside organisations. When listing standards demand risk disclosures or prohibit insider allocation practices, founders who previously relied on opacity must shift behaviour. Engineers document code paths. Treasury managers publish collateral data. Delegates formalise governance processes. Regulation works not by threat but by altering incentives in ways visible in decisions and workflows. The result is measurable: incidents decline where processes tighten. Yet the limitation is real—rules can become box-ticking rituals, especially where enforcement is weak. Good rules require teeth; otherwise they become wallpaper.

One of the least appreciated ways rules change the game is through the narrative they create. A market labelled "regulated" or "licensed" acquires a reputational baseline that shapes users' heuristics. That can mislead as well as protect. In early 2023, several regional US banks exposed to crypto experienced deposit runs not because of immediate insolvency but because the narrative changed: users assumed proximity to crypto implied instability. Clarity works in both directions. To counteract such reflexes, regulators and firms must communicate boundaries honestly. A gate often needs a sign explaining its purpose.

The interplay between clarity and cost emerges again in listing standards for tokenised securities. When the German regulator BaFin approved the first blockchain-based securities issuance under its revised electronic securities act in June 2021, issuers noted that compliance overheads increased significantly. Yet the listing attracted institutional investors who had previously avoided the sector entirely. The behavioural shift was undeniable: pension funds and insurers, constrained by mandates requiring regulated instruments, finally had a compliant vehicle. The cost of capital rose for issuers but fell for investors seeking validated exposure.

A sharper example of game-changing clarity comes from stablecoins. When Circle announced in July 2021 that USD Coin (USDC) reserves would be held largely in cash and short-term US Treasuries—with monthly attestations conducted by Grant Thornton—it signalled a shift from marketing to verification. The cost of maintaining such reserves is measurable: Treasuries yield less than riskier assets; audit processes consume resources; governance committees require staffing. Yet the market reaction was immediate: institutions increased use of USDC for settlement, precisely because clarity replaced conjecture. Higher costs bought deeper trust.

Not all rules improve markets. Overly rigid frameworks risk freezing categories that need room to evolve. The European Union's early proposals for classifying utility tokens under securities rules sparked fears that experimentation would be smothered. And in some cases, those fears were justified: small teams abandoned token models altogether, unable to bear compliance costs disproportionate to their scale. This is the limitation that must be acknowledged. A rule can protect the public yet still damage innovation if miscalibrated.

Reconciling this requires nuance. Effective regulation distinguishes between systemic and experimental activities. A decentralised exchange processing billions in daily volume requires sturdier rules than a new gaming protocol with limited financial exposure. This proportionality principle, applied thoughtfully, allows costs to align with risk. Jurisdiction-agnostic principles already exist: transparency for market participants, segregation where custodial risk is present, and governance protections where user funds or system integrity are implicated. The game changes most constructively when rules target these interfaces rather than the speculative edges of innovation.

The gate motif returns once more. A gate's function is not to stop movement but to shape it. In crypto, clarity allows capital to walk through with eyes open. Without clarity, capital sprints in and bolts out, leaving behind cycles of mania and collapse. When builders know the criteria for acceptance—be they reserve standards, listing disclosures, or governance safeguards—they can design toward durability rather than momentum. A mature market is not a market without speculation; it is a market where speculation is distinguishable from infrastructure.

The unresolved tension remains: how much clarity is enough to anchor trust without ossifying a young industry? Should rules adapt continuously, tracking the pace of technological innovation, or settle into slow-moving frameworks that offer predictability? And perhaps most pressing: who gets to write the rules for systems that span borders and resist capture? The cost of capital will reveal whose answers persuade.

Law, Code, and Enforceability

At 11:57 p.m. on 17 June 2016, in a co-working space in Berlin, a handful of Ethereum developers watched a terminal flash red. An address they did not recognise was siphoning funds from The DAO, a decentralised venture fund that had raised more than USD 150 million only weeks earlier. The exploit was not a breach of cryptography. It followed the letter of the smart contract's code. Yet within days, lawyers, exchanges, miners, and token holders were drawn into a debate that stretched across jurisdictions. Was this theft or the mechanical execution of rules? By 20 July, the Ethereum blockchain had forked, reversing the transfer on the dominant chain. The law did not stay outside. It entered through contract formation, fiduciary duty, and the practical need to resolve a dispute that code alone could not settle.

The incident's epilogue reveals the deeper truth: systems built on deterministic execution still depend on human interpretation, institutional norms, and enforceable rights. The claim that "code is law" collapses when participants disagree about the outcome, or when external obligations—taxation, insolvency, property—are triggered by on-chain events. The fork was not an engineering solution. It was a jurisdictional one performed through collective decision. The motif that shadows this territory is a hinge. Code swings one way. Law swings the other. When stress arrives, the hinge decides which direction prevails.

Smart contracts, for all their elegance, operate within a social and legal perimeter. The perimeter widens or narrows depending on the rights at stake. To see this, start with the most visible intersection: property rights. When an asset is tokenised, the token is not the property; it is evidence of entitlement. Whether that entitlement binds a custodian, an issuer, or a counterparty depends on legal definitions, not technical ones. In 2021, a High Court in London heard *AA v Persons Unknown*, a case involving ransom payments made in Bitcoin. The court treated the Bitcoin as property capable of being subject to proprietary injunctions. The ruling did not rewrite code. It reasserted that enforceability ultimately flows from legal recognition, not from the internal logic of a blockchain.

The first claim often made by builders is that smart contracts eliminate ambiguity. Show the contract; name the rule; let execution speak for itself. Yet ambiguity shifts rather than disappears. In March 2022, when an exploit drained funds from Compounder Finance, the protocol's admins argued that certain functions were "upgradeable" under documented governance processes. Users contested the legitimacy of those processes. Exchanges froze associated assets because legal uncertainty overshadowed on-chain determinism. The implication is clear: operational clarity requires more than code visibility. It requires shared expectations, documented authority, and dispute paths recognisable to courts and counterparties.

A second claim insists that decentralised protocols exist outside national borders. But real disputes invariably drag specific places into focus. Consider the 2020 case of *SEC v Telegram* in the Southern District of New York. Telegram argued that its token sale was a global distribution of a decentralised asset. The court examined contractual arrangements, purchaser expectations, and the economic reality of the scheme. Execution was halted, not because of protocol failure, but because the legal framing bound Telegram to investor-protection rules. The behaviour that followed—refunds, liquidations, and the abandonment of a high-profile project—was grounded in enforceability, not chain logic. Geography still matters.

There is, however, a credible counter-example. The 2019 hack of bZx, a decentralised lending platform, produced heavy losses without any victorious legal claims. No court mandated compensation. No regulator pursued enforcement. Some participants argued that the exploit was an admissible arbitrage, a result of flawed design. The limitation here is that decentralisation is often invoked to explain the absence of enforceability, but the absence reflects practical hurdles: pseudonymity, cross-border complexity, and uncertain cost-benefit for litigants. Yet even in that case, exchanges adopted new listing requirements, and insurers recalibrated cover terms. Law exerted pressure through institutions rather than judgments.

To understand why smart contracts do not float outside law, consider how contracts form. Traditional contract theory requires intention, clarity, and mutual assent. Smart contracts automate performance but do not, by themselves, prove intention. A user who interacts with a protocol may not understand embedded terms or upgrade mechanics. This discrepancy surfaced during the 2022 *Nomad Bridge* exploit, where a faulty initialisation allowed anyone to withdraw funds by copying a transaction call. Hundreds did. Some claimed they were "white-hat rescuers". Others vanished. Over the following months, recovery efforts invoked concepts of unjust enrichment and constructive trust. The code had executed flawlessly. The law judged the outcomes, not the instructions.

Another hinge emerges around solvency. When Celsius Network filed for bankruptcy in New York in July 2022, the court examined token custody arrangements, yield programme terms, and whether users retained title to their assets. Celsius had used smart contracts for parts of its operations, yet the outcome turned on text in customer agreements, not Solidity functions. Users whose tokens were pooled lost priority; users in segregated custody accounts fared differently. Code automated flows; law determined ownership. The implication is unavoidable: enforceability hinges on agreements users seldom read, but courts always examine.

A further example, quieter but equally instructive, comes from Switzerland's handling of the 2020 Crypto Fund insolvency. Swiss regulators required the administrator to reconcile tokenised fund units with underlying assets, treating discrepancies as breaches of fiduciary obligation. The blockchain preserved transfer history, but reconciliation required legal interpretation of mandate scope and custodian responsibility. Enforcement proceeded through traditional processes: claims, audits, and distributions. Code provided evidence; law provided remedy.

Some technologists argue that arbitration encoded on-chain could replace courts. Yet even these systems depend on off-chain enforceability. A 2021 experiment by Kleros, a decentralised arbitration project, involved ruling on the allocation of NFTs in a contested sale. The losing party threatened litigation in France, arguing procedural unfairness. The jurisdictional complexity demonstrated the limitation of purely digital dispute resolution: unless both parties are judgement-proof or indifferent to off-chain consequences, legal systems remain the final hinge.

It is tempting to treat law as a constraint on digital innovation. But law can also amplify credibility. When MakerDAO began publishing legal opinions in 2021 on the enforceability of its real-world asset collateral structures, the immediate consequence was measurable: new institutional vaults increased, reflecting confidence in recognisable rights and recourse paths. A gate appeared again. Costs rose—legal opinions are expensive. Trust rose faster.

Naming this interplay is essential. Code governs execution. Law governs relationships. Disputes arise at the boundary where execution crashes into expectation. Engineers diagnose bugs. Courts diagnose obligations. Where both apply, enforceability emerges from their interaction.

This interplay sharpens a final tension. Should smart contracts embed more legal meaning—through structured terms, recognised jurisdictions, or verifiable identities—or should law adapt to accommodate decentralised execution? A future of hybrid enforceability seems plausible: code as performance engine, law as interpretative anchor. But the hinge still turns. And the direction it swings will depend on a question developers can no longer avoid: what rights do users believe they hold, and who must enforce them when code alone cannot?

Building for the Probable Future

On 13 March 2020, less than twenty-four hours after "Black Thursday" had driven Ether briefly below $100, the MakerDAO community convened an emergency governance call. The immediate problem was brutal and simple: some liquidation auctions had cleared at zero Dai because there were too few bidders, leaving parts of the system under-collateralised. But the conversation in that virtual room—developers in Berlin, investors in New York, governance wonks in London—was not only about patching a bug. It centred on what needed to change so that, five years on, a similar shock would not threaten the protocol's survival. The answers they settled on—more transparent risk parameters, formalised audits of critical components, and clearer ways for users to redeem or unwind positions—were not quick fixes. They were design choices meant to age.

The future rarely announces itself. Protocols and platforms get one shot at their first principles, often under conditions of euphoria where shortcuts feel harmless. Years later, those early choices determine whether a system can coexist with stricter regulation, more sceptical institutions, and a user base that has seen multiple cycles. The motif to keep in mind is a simple one: doors. Specifically, doors that let light in, and doors that let users out. Transparency, audits, and exit rights look, at first glance, like costs. Over time, they become the hinges on which survival turns.

Begin with transparency. Not the vague promise of "open-source" or a hopeful blogpost, but concrete, repeatable disclosures about what a system is, what it holds, and how it can fail. In July 2021, Circle—the company behind USD Coin (USDC)—committed to backing the stablecoin primarily with cash and short-term US Treasuries, and to publishing regular attestations from Grant Thornton. The attestation reports were hardly bedtime reading, but they changed behaviour. Payment firms that had previously hesitated to route client funds through a private stablecoin began to integrate USDC. Market makers used it more readily as collateral. The design choice—to endure the ongoing cost and scrutiny of third-party verification—raised operational complexity while lowering the perceived hazard of holding the token.

Consider the contrast with TerraUSD in May 2022. For months, the project's supporters spoke of "decentralised stability", yet details of reserves, collateral composition, and failure modes remained opaque. When the peg broke, users had no clear, independent map of what lay behind the promise. Panic filled the gap that transparency might have occupied. Here, the absence of durable design choices became visible in hours: there were no simple reports to anchor expectations, no shared understanding of thresholds at which defences would fail, no agreed-upon process for redemption under stress. The implication is straightforward. Systems that publish uncomfortable numbers early—volatility of collateral, concentration of counterparties, dependence on off-chain entities—acquire resilience not because the numbers are flattering, but because users can calibrate trust.

Transparency, however, is not static. It must evolve with complexity. A protocol that begins with a single token and a handful of contracts may later integrate real-world assets, multi-chain bridges, and nested governance. Each layer adds opacity unless designers commit, repeatedly, to surface what matters. That commitment shows up in the mundane: machine-readable dashboards of reserves, plain-language risk documentation, accessible explanations of upgrade rights. None of this is glamorous. All of it becomes crucial when regulators, auditors, or institutional counterparties arrive and ask: "Show your workings."

Audits translate transparency into scrutiny. There are two broad families here: security audits and financial or operational audits. Both are expensive. Both can miss things. But the decision to submit to independent evaluation—and to publish the results in a meaningful form—is a forward-facing bet that the system intends to live long enough for those reports to matter. After the DAO exploit in 2016, serious Ethereum projects began commissioning multiple security audits before deploying major contracts. Uniswap v3, launched on Ethereum in May 2021, went through reviews by several independent firms, and the team published detailed findings and remediation notes. Even critics acknowledged that this depth of analysis reduced the likelihood of catastrophic, protocol-level failure. The design choice did not guarantee safety; it made negligence harder.

The counter-example is painful but instructive. A long list of DeFi exploits has involved contracts that either never saw a serious audit or treated a single, cursory review as theatre. In the case of the 2021 Meerkat Finance "exploit" on Binance Smart Chain—where funds vanished within a day of launch—subsequent investigations suggested the code allowed privileged withdrawal from the outset. An audit worth the name would at least have forced someone to explain that feature. The limitation of audits is obvious: they can be shallow, conflicted, or outdated. The reconciliation lies in pattern, not perfection. Systems that normalise multi-firm, recurring audits signal that they expect to be held to account again. Those that treat audits as a one-off badge for marketing do not.

Financial and operational audits play a different but complementary role. When Coinbase publishes attestations of its custodial holdings, or when a protocol reveals that its multisignature treasury has been independently reviewed for key management and policies, the signal is not just "we have the assets". It is "we accept that someone outside our circle can verify we have them." In a probable future where regulators insist on proof beyond self-certification, this habit of verification will separate platforms that can integrate into mainstream finance from those perpetually relegated to the shadows.

Doors that let light in are necessary. Doors that let users out may be even more important. Exit rights sound abstract, but they become painfully concrete during stress. Can a user withdraw their assets from a protocol without permission from a central operator? Can a token holder redeem into something more stable if the rules change? Can a community fork away from captured governance? These are not questions to answer in the middle of a crisis. They are design parameters to set at launch.

Uniswap again offers a useful example. Its architecture allows liquidity providers to withdraw their positions at any time, subject only to block confirmation and gas fees. There is no central pause button controlled by a company. That choice has consequences: it makes certain forms of emergency intervention impossible. But it also embeds a powerful user right: you can leave. During market stress, that right shapes behaviour. Liquidity providers may reduce exposure, but they do not face the existential shock of frozen funds subject to opaque internal decisions.

Contrast this with centralised platforms that halted withdrawals in 2022. Celsius, Voyager, and others cited "extreme market conditions" while users stared at dashboards showing balances they could not access. For all the talk of decentralisation in their marketing, user exit rights were mediated entirely by corporate discretion. There were no contractual guarantees of immediate redemption, no cryptographic claim strong enough to bypass the firm's decisions. The probable future for such models is unkind: courts and legislators tend, after enough failures, to demand that custodial arrangements specify when and how users can exit, and to penalise structures that can arbitrarily deny that right.

Exit rights also intersect with governance. MakerDAO's "emergency shutdown" mechanism, designed from the protocol's earliest days, allows MKR token holders to coordinate a system halt that returns collateral to Dai holders pro rata. The process is complex and not without peril, but it encodes a last-resort exit path that does not rely on a single administrator. That choice has survived multiple design overhauls because it speaks to something enduring: the view that users must have at least one path to withdraw their share of value even if governance fails.

The motif of doors acquires a third meaning when we consider regulatory drift. As rules tighten, protocols that can demonstrate transparent operations, audited controls, and robust exit mechanisms will find doors open into banking partnerships, payment networks, and institutional portfolios. Those lacking such features will face doors closing: de-platforming, delisting, or capital charges that make engagement uneconomic. Building for the probable future means assuming that scrutiny will intensify, not fade; that failures in adjacent projects will invite questions about your own; that your most sceptical stakeholder has not yet appeared.

A credible counter-argument insists that heavy emphasis on transparency, audits, and exit rights raises barriers for small, experimental teams. It does. Requiring a full suite of attestations for a weekend hackathon project would be absurd. The limitation of universalising these principles is that it could narrow the space for play. The reconciliation rests in proportionality. Early experiments can prioritise minimal viable transparency—clear documentation, open repos, honest risk descriptions—before carrying real user funds. Once they do, the gradient of expectations steepens. The more value a system holds, the less forgivable its opacity and lack of exits become.

Two final examples draw the arc forward. In 2019, the Swiss stock exchange SIX launched the SDX digital-asset platform with integrated custody and trading for tokenised securities. From day one, SDX committed to bank-grade audits and clear redemption rights for token holders. The project moved slowly, often to industry frustration. Yet by aligning its design with the probable future of regulated digital securities, it positioned itself for a world where tokenisation is not a novelty but an expected feature of capital markets.

By contrast, a raft of fast-moving token projects in 2021 adopted complex, reflexive tokenomics—rebasing, auto-liquidity, reflections—without transparent, audited models or clear exits. Many collapsed within months when incentives failed. Looking back, what aged poorly was not only the economics but the absence of structures that would allow users and regulators to understand, verify, and unwind.

The probable future is not a specific statute or a particular jurisdiction's rulebook. It is a set of converging expectations: that large pools of value will not depend solely on charisma; that systems affecting strangers' savings will be legible to more than their authors; that exit will be a right, not a favour. Designers cannot predict which regulator will knock, or which crisis will test their work. They can choose, today, whether the doors they build will let light in, whether they will open when pushed from the inside, and whether, decades from now, someone looking back will say: they expected scrutiny, and they prepared for it.

Chapter 9
Behavioural Finance for Volatile Assets

Picture a trader alone at 2.17 a.m., lit only by the glow of a phone screen. The price has dropped thirteen per cent in an hour. Rationally, nothing material has changed. Yet the fear running along the spine is unmistakably physical. The thumb hovers above the sell button. A cocktail of cortisol and regret prepares its argument: *Get out now, before it gets worse.* The next morning, after a half-slept night, the price has recovered. The trade was a loss. The memory becomes a scar. How many stories like this populate crypto history—private panic in public markets—shaping outcomes more than any whitepaper ever could?

Volatile assets reveal something fundamental: finance is never purely financial. It is emotional choreography performed against a backdrop of uncertain numbers. Markets fluctuate; humans flinch. This chapter explores what flinching costs, why it happens so reliably, and what can be done *before* the next price shock turns a mild worry into a catastrophic decision. The key theme is not erasing emotion but anticipating it—designing habits that keep choices aligned with values rather than adrenaline.

The most immediate behavioural force in volatile markets is loss aversion. Kahneman and Tversky quantified its asymmetry: losses hurt roughly twice as much as equivalent gains satisfy. In crypto trading groups, that ratio looks closer to infinite when portfolios plunge overnight. Yet the pain is not only about magnitude; it is about time. When assets are marked-to-market every second, a long-term thesis is forced into a short-term theatre. A mismatch of horizons magnifies hurt. If you believe an asset may mature over years, why does a red candle at bedtime feel like a threat to identity? Because the mind mistakes *now* for *forever*. One of our tasks ahead is to separate timeframes so that fear does not hijack strategy.

Then comes the herd. Humans are social learners; we mimic to survive faster. But in speculative markets, the crowd often runs toward the cliff. February 2021 saw retail platforms report surges in "copy trading", where users blindly mirrored influencers' crypto positions. For weeks it produced easy wins, until a weekend crash wiped out leveraged followers while the originators quietly hedged or exited. Herding is not stupidity; it is speed. When uncertainty rises, the urge to outsource judgment to those who seem confident—even if that confidence is borrowed from a bull market—becomes overpowering. Yet total independence is a fantasy. We are not trying to become hermits on a data island. We are aiming for selective permeability: learning from others without surrendering agency.

Rules crafted in calm protect us from panic. Every behavioural researcher who has studied automaticity—the power of pre-set instruction—arrives at a similar conclusion: decisions made *before the stimulus* are sturdier than decisions made *during the stimulus*. In volatile finance, this means defining allocation boundaries, pre-scheduling rebalancing reviews, and specifying what kinds of news deserve a response. These tools are not predictions. They are rails. When the heart rate climbs, rails prevent a swerve into self-sabotage. They shift the question from "What do I feel like doing right now?" to "What did my wiser self already decide?"

And yet, mistakes will occur. Perfection is not the objective here; progress is. The craft of investing in unstable assets is the craft of learning under pressure. Post-mortems—done honestly and without self-flagellation—transform losses into structural upgrades. The most resilient operators do not merely win more; they recover better. They revisit the decision chain: Was the thesis flawed? Was the timing poor? Did I react to price rather than information? Each answer becomes architecture for the next cycle. Shame is the enemy of insight. If we cannot look directly at our missteps, we repeat them—often with grander numbers attached.

Throughout this journey, a quiet motif surfaces: perspective. Perspective is spatial—stepping back far enough to see that a daily chart is not a prophecy. Perspective is social—daring to disagree when the crowd chants "up only". Perspective is temporal—remembering that high volatility is the price of exposure to unproven possibility. Without perspective, a portfolio becomes a referendum on self-worth, and every downturn feels like personal failure.

This chapter enters at the junction of psychology and markets, where the most damaging crashes begin not on-chain but in the mind. The temptations are ancient—fear, greed, mimicry—but the amplification is modern and relentless. Push alerts and price feeds condition us like lab animals: reward, withdraw, repeat. To navigate this environment, you need tools sharper than instinct.

Here is the promise of what follows: not immunity from swings, but resilience within them. A blueprint for choosing a horizon and honouring it. Ways to hear the crowd without being drowned by it. Commitments that survive the storm that will inevitably come. And a method to extract wisdom from pain rather than bury it.

The markets will continue to shout. Your task is to build the inner architecture that decides when to listen.

Loss Aversion and Time Horizons

On 12 March 2020, Coinbase users in San Francisco watched Bitcoin drop almost 40 per cent within a single trading day. The exchange crashed under load. Portfolios that looked ambitious at breakfast resembled wreckage by dinner. Many sold into the void. Weeks later, the price recovered, and then advanced far beyond the panic lows. The loss was not only financial. It was temporal. Holders with a multi-year thesis behaved as if their deadline had expired overnight. Fear shortened their horizon. A strategy designed for 2025 collapsed under the weight of one terrible afternoon.

Loss aversion, the finding that humans feel losses more intensely than gains of identical size, was named and quantified by Daniel Kahneman and Amos Tversky in 1979. A £1,000 loss can hurt far more than a £1,000 gain pleases. Yet in volatile digital markets the asymmetry becomes even sharper because the feedback loop is instant. A screen broadcasts judgement every second. A red candle becomes a personal rebuke. The mismatch between the intended investment horizon and the experienced emotional horizon becomes excruciating. We feel long-term conviction until the short-term chart disagrees. Then we feel something else entirely. Pain.

Loss aversion is not an abstract psychological label. It is visible in behaviour. The trader who stops checking prices after a rally but refreshes compulsively during a dip is demonstrating it. The investor who sets a stop loss but moves it downward to "give the market room" is demonstrating it. These habits reveal the body's response before the brain articulates a thought. Kahneman wrote that humans "hate losing more than we like winning". In volatile assets, we hate losing *now* more than we care about winning *later*.

Time becomes the lever of suffering. A multi-year thesis is fragile if evaluated minute-by-minute. Consider Ethereum in June 2022. The transition to proof-of-stake was public knowledge. The runway was months, not minutes. Yet many who believed in the transition sold solely because the interim price fell below their entry. Their logic did not change; only their timeframe did. A strategy that promised long-term relevance was forced through the razor-thin aperture of intraday fear.

To understand why this mismatch bites so sharply, we must name two related forces. First: *myopic loss aversion,* a term coined by Shlomo Benartzi and Richard Thaler (1995). When investors evaluate frequently, they feel the sting of volatility more often and therefore become more conservative than their long-term goals justify. Second: *mental accounting*. A portfolio intended to fund future goals becomes mentally reduced to a fluctuating number. That number becomes identity. Every dip feels like humiliation. The stomach takes control.

There is a credible counter-story. Some traders thrive precisely because they think in short bursts. Scalpers and arbitrageurs measure performance over hours, not years. For them, the horizon is finite and deliberate. If the market challenges their position, they exit efficiently, without pain. Their decisions match their timeframe. The problem arises when the declared horizon and the lived horizon diverge. When a long-term investor behaves like a panicked day-trader, the worst of both worlds emerges: slow gains, fast losses.

Horizon mismatch grows sharper in digital assets because narratives evolve at breakneck pace. A token can launch in Singapore on a Monday, be delisted in Seoul by Friday, and forgotten by Sunday. Speed encourages immediacy. The belief that "I can always re-enter later" turns patience into something naive. Information moves quickly; value does not always follow. We confuse noise with signal, urgency with importance.

The motif here is perspective. Perspective is distance. Too much closeness distorts. Imagine standing one metre from a painting: the brushstrokes become chaos. Step back, and the composition emerges. Price charts behave the same way. A one-minute chart looks like a crisis. A one-year chart looks like a story. The investor who zooms out sees cycles. The investor who zooms in sees danger.

Loss aversion manifests not only in selling too soon but in holding too tightly. In November 2021, when altcoins surged to euphoric highs, many refused to realise gains because selling would "lock in a loss of potential". This is loss aversion inverted: fear of losing an unrealised future. When the downturn arrived, conviction crumbled. Gains vanished. Regret became the teacher, too late.

The physiology of fear matters. Neurofinance research shows that heightened cortisol impairs long-term planning by shifting focus to immediate threats. A portfolio drawdown triggers the same hormonal pathways activated by physical danger. The market becomes a predator. The instinct is to flee. But fleeing a mark-to-market event can turn a temporary drawdown into a permanent loss. A paper loss becomes an embodied one.

The worst losses occur when investors mistake volatility for risk. They are not the same. Volatility is movement. Risk is ruin. The two converge only when volatility forces bad decisions. Behaviour transforms movement into damage. Loss aversion gives volatility fangs.

The task, then, is to create cognitive buffers—ways to preserve perspective when screens conspire to erase it. That begins with clarifying horizons explicitly. A category error is when short-term money asks long-term questions, or long-term money demands short-term reassurance. If the purpose of an asset is future technology exposure, price updates every fifteen minutes are irrelevant; they are mischief. If the purpose is liquidity, then conviction about a 2030 narrative is irrelevant; it is fantasy. Alignment between purpose and practice is the antidote.

The second buffer is *measurement discipline*. Consider the difference between checking a portfolio daily versus monthly. Benartzi and Thaler found that extending the evaluation period increases tolerance for loss because the likelihood of observing gains rises with time. A calendar becomes armour. Investors who review annually experience a different emotional landscape than those who watch red numbers flicker hourly. Distance is protection. Distance is design.

A further dimension is narrative hygiene. Catastrophic thinking often rests not on data but on imagined permanence: "If it's down this much, it will go to zero." Yet history shows recoveries. After the Mt. Gox collapse in Tokyo (2014), Bitcoin did not become worthless. After the Terra USD implosion in May 2022, decentralised finance did not vanish. Assets do not deserve blind faith; they deserve proportionate evaluation. But panic rarely evaluates. It assumes. Recall the quiet motif: perspective reframes loss from identity betrayal to informational update.

Even regulators recognise horizon mismatch as systemic risk. The Bank of England has warned (December 2022) that rapid repricing in crypto can turn benign funding mismatches into forced liquidations. When investors shorten their horizons collectively, liquidity evaporates. Individual psychology becomes macro fragility. This is why understanding loss aversion is not personal therapy; it is a component of systemic resilience.

The tension that remains is fundamental. The same immediacy that makes volatile assets exciting makes them hazardous to the mind. Prices are loud; goals are quiet. How, then, should one behave when the noise rises? The forward test is simple to pose and difficult to practise: keep behaviour anchored to the original horizon rather than to the latest candle.

The next chapter explores how crowds intensify that noise. But for now, one unresolved question deserves attention whenever the heart rate climbs with the chart: *Am I reacting to price or responding to purpose?*

FOMO, Herding, and Leader Effects

On 7 January 2021, eToro—the retail brokerage founded in Tel Aviv in 2007—reported a surge of more than 750 per cent in copy-trading volumes within a single week. The spike coincided with Bitcoin crossing $40,000 for the first time. Thousands of users mirrored the positions of a handful of highly visible "Popular Investors", many of whom had fewer than three years of trading history. Some gained briefly; many lost sharply when the market whipsawed days later. The behaviour was not random. It was herd formation in real time. And the trigger was recognisable: the fear of missing out, sharpened by the illusion that someone else had decoded the market's secret. One gesture—pressing "copy"—became a collective reflex.

FOMO carries a simple paradox. The more people chase a trend to avoid regret, the more likely the trend is to become unstable. Herds move quickly, often too quickly. The same social fuel that powers adoption can also burn through prudence. In volatile markets, speed is a signal but not a verdict. Yet for many participants, speed masquerades as knowledge. A green candle becomes social pressure. The crowd's movement becomes a kind of evidence. And once evidence is social rather than analytical, the psychological horizon shortens to the next hour, not the next thesis.

The motif here is the *signal flare*—a flash in the dark that commands attention even when its meaning is ambiguous. Prices spike. Influencers tweet. Leaders posture. Each flare demands interpretation. Most people look not at the flare but at each other. What matters is the collective reading of the light.

Herd behaviour is one of the oldest documented features of markets. Charles MacKay chronicled the Dutch tulip mania in Amsterdam (1636–37), noting how participants "learned to value tulips as they valued each other: by watching their neighbours." The structure remains unchanged. When uncertainty rises, humans default to social cues. In crypto markets, where fundamentals can be opaque and narratives fluid, these cues become louder and heavier. A spike in social media mentions, a single well-timed endorsement by a charismatic figure, or a trending Telegram channel can mimic the authority of research. People assume that many others cannot be wrong simultaneously. Yet they can. And they often are.

To understand why herding persists even among sophisticated users, we must name two forces described in behavioural finance. First: *informational cascades*. When individuals assume that those before them possess superior information, they follow, even when their private judgement disagrees. Second: *reputational cascades*. Participants align publicly with the crowd to avoid seeming uninformed. Crypto intensifies both cascades because identity is partly performed online. A public wallet address becomes a broadcast; a well-timed trade becomes a credential.

Leader effects magnify this. When a prominent figure announces a position—whether Elon Musk shifting Dogecoin sentiment in February 2021 or Changpeng Zhao's remarks affecting FTT in November 2022—the market reacts not only to the claim but to the perceived foresight of the claimant. The crowd believes the leader is connected to deeper information streams. Yet leaders are not oracles; they are amplifiers. Their impact arises from the belief that everyone else will respond.

The danger is not influence itself but the *unexamined surrender* of judgement. Consider the 2021 Shiba Inu frenzy. A few early endorsements on TikTok and Twitter created the impression of a coordinated wave. Copy-trading tools on several exchanges logged record inflows. The majority of these positions were opened near local peaks. The behaviour reveals the metric: late entrants acted within minutes of seeing a spike, measuring not value but proximity to the crowd's enthusiasm. They exited too slowly. Herd entry is fast; herd exit is jammed.

There is, however, a credible counter-example: coordinated entry can be rational when the crowd is not a herd but a *community with shared analysis*. During the 2016 Ethereum fork debate in Zug, many developers and users aligned around the idea of supporting ETH over ETC based on governance principles, not momentum. Their consensus was built on public reasoning, not blind mimicry. This shows the distinction: collective intelligence strengthens decisions when participants share transparent rationales. Herding thrives where rationales are opaque or borrowed.

To resist mimicry without isolating oneself, it helps to examine the mechanics of FOMO as a behavioural loop. FOMO is not merely fear; it is a mismatch between perceived opportunity speed and personal decision speed. When opportunity appears to move faster than thought,

thought is abandoned. The visible behaviour is impulsive entry. The hidden driver is panic at potential exclusion. FOMO contracts time into urgency.

Reducing this urgency requires two interventions, both behavioural not advisory. First: *slow the clock*. Extending the decision window from minutes to hours materially reduces impulsive herding because price patterns lose their hypnotic power. The "signal flare" dims with distance. A chart that seemed decisive at 11:03 looks ambiguous at 14:20. Time dilutes the illusion of inevitability.

Second: *decouple identity from immediacy*. Many copy-traders describe a desire to "be in the game". This is identification with the crowd's excitement, not with the asset's properties. Reframing participation as a choice rather than a membership test weakens the pull of mimicry. The behaviour moves from "everyone is doing this" to "does this fit my thesis?" The latter is quieter and slower. It is also safer.

Leader effects are more subtle to resist. Humans overweight leader signals because leaders appear to have survived previous cycles. Survivors gain status; status earns deference. Yet status is not omniscience. Even highly regarded figures misread markets. Vitalik Buterin himself admitted misjudging aspects of the ICO surge in 2017. Leader error is inevitable; leader infallibility is a myth. Recognising this does not require cynicism. It requires proportion.

Another pattern emerges in decentralised trading platforms. During the summer of 2020, several copy-trading smart contracts on Ethereum logged a peculiar trend: users replicated the positions of pseudonymous addresses whose profitability came from early liquidity provider rewards, not trading acumen. Followers mistook protocol incentives for skill. They mirrored wallet activity without understanding its origin. The implication is clear: when signals are shallow, mimicry becomes detached from reality.

A more systemic example comes from exchanges in Seoul during the 2017–18 cycle. Spikes in altcoin volumes were often triggered by coordinated retail buying based on message-board rumours rather than fundamentals. As liquidity dried up, these crowd-driven peaks collapsed hard. Post-mortem analyses by the Korea Financial Intelligence Unit (2019) found that late entrants consistently bought at prices 30–60 per cent above average acquisition costs of early initiators. The pattern repeats because the psychology repeats.

Yet isolation is not the answer. Isolation removes access to useful collective knowledge. The objective is calibrated connection: listening without obeying, observing without imitating. Healthy crowds exist. Community research groups, open audit collectives, and transparent governance forums demonstrate that social learning can be disciplined rather than frantic. They produce *shared reasoning*, not shared panic.

The quiet motif of the signal flare returns here. A flare can be a warning or a beacon. What determines its meaning is context. When a trend lights up, the disciplined participant asks a simple question: "Is this a signal or a flare?" A signal carries information. A flare merely demands attention.

FOMO thrives when attention is confused for information. Herding thrives when imitation is mistaken for insight. Leader effects thrive when authority replaces analysis. The antidote is perspective—distance from the flare, proximity to one's own reasoning.

The remaining tension is whether any of us can reliably tell the difference under pressure. That question becomes acute in the next section, where rules—not crowds—provide the stabilising counterweight. For now, one forward test remains: *If this move were invisible to the crowd, would I still make it?*

Setting Rules Before You Need Them

On 19 March 2020, as global markets reeled from pandemic shock, the Norwegian Government Pension Fund Global in Oslo triggered a routine portfolio rebalance. Its internal rules required buying equities when their share of the portfolio fell too far below target. While retail investors across Europe dumped stocks in despair, the fund quietly bought billions of dollars' worth of risk assets at distressed prices. No committee emergency, no midnight improvisation. The rulebook stayed strangely calm. Months later, when markets had recovered, that one mechanical decision contributed materially to the fund's long-term returns, as documented in its annual report. The point is not that Norway was clever; it is that Norway was prepared.

Most individuals dabbling in volatile assets have the opposite experience. They start with vague intentions—"I'm long-term", "I'll buy the dip", "I'll be disciplined"—but their decisions are improvised in the glare of the chart. Allocation expands during euphoria, contracts during panic, and rebalancing is something that happens to other people. News consumption follows the same pattern: frenzied when prices move, absent when reflection would be useful. Volatility is then experienced as a series of emotional emergencies rather than as part of an understood process.

Behavioural finance offers a sharper lens on this. Richard Thaler's work on *pre-commitment* and "self-control problems" highlighted that our future selves are remarkably unreliable. Left alone, they find ways to override earlier intentions when temptation or fear appears. A rule written in calm is a contract with that future self. It does not guarantee obedience, but it raises the cost of betrayal. Rules are rails. When the ground shakes, rails matter.

Start with allocation. The decision of *how much* to expose to volatile assets is psychological as much as statistical. Institutions recognise this. Yale University's endowment, under David Swensen's leadership from the mid-1980s until his death in 2021, formalised strategic asset allocation ranges and resisted the urge to chase fashionable bets simply because they were working. During the dot-com boom of 1999–2000, Yale did not allow equities—traditional or technology-focused—to swell beyond their bands. That discipline looked conservative at the peak; it looked prescient in the crash. The visible behaviour was dull: periodic rebalancing, limited drift. The underlying reality was a pre-commitment to *how much risk* the institution was willing to carry, regardless of fashion.

Contrast that with many crypto funds launched in 2017 from London, Zug and Singapore, whose mandates were effectively "long whatever is hot". Without defined allocation boundaries, gains were recycled into ever more volatile assets. When the market turned in 2018, there were no rails. Investment memos gave way to Telegram rumours. Some funds never recovered. The limitation of stories about disciplined giants like Norway and Yale is obvious: they have resources and time that small actors do not. Yet the principle scales down. Writing down, in advance, the maximum share of one's capital that can sit in high-volatility tokens creates a reference point when enthusiasm demands more.

Allocation rules also protect against *creep*. What begins as a five per cent experiment becomes a twenty per cent "conviction bet" after a rally, without any conscious decision. The metric is not price; it is proportion. A rule that triggers review when exposure crosses a specified percentage forces reflection: "Do I truly accept this level of drawdown?" Rules cannot remove risk. They can prevent sleepwalking into it.

Rebalancing adds another dimension. The Norwegian fund's 2020 rebalance illustrates a simple, unfashionable idea: sell some of what has risen, buy some of what has fallen, to return to target weights. This is not magic; it is discipline. Behaviourally, it runs directly against our wiring. We want to keep winners and dump losers. A pre-commitment to rebalance, whether annually or when weights diverge by a certain margin, formalises a habit of *systematic contrarianism*. It makes profit-taking and bargain-hunting less a matter of gut feel and more a matter of schedule.

There is a counter-example worth acknowledging. In extreme regimes, rigid rebalancing can feel reckless. During the eurozone crisis of 2011–12, some European pension funds questioned whether they should really buy financial stocks simply because their allocation models said so. What if the sector faced structural decline? The limitation of rules is that they can become dogma. Reconciliation lies in layering rules: a base rule to rebalance, and a second rule that allows temporary suspension only after explicit, documented justification. The key is to require explanation, not to forbid adaptation.

Volatile digital assets stress-test rebalancing rules mercilessly. Moves of thirty per cent in a week are not anomalies but features. Without pre-commitment, investors tend to rebalance only in one direction: trimming risk *after* crashes, adding risk *after* rallies. That is not rebalancing; it is capitulating to recency bias. A simple pre-commitment—again, not as advice, but as observed practice—might specify that allocation decisions are reviewed on a fixed calendar rather than in response to price spikes. The behaviour shifts from reactive to rhythmic.

The third rail—often overlooked—is the *news diet.* Markets of high volatility live in symbiosis with high-frequency information. Exchanges push alerts. Influencers dissect hourly price candles. Newsletters arrive daily. Without boundaries, consumption becomes compulsive. Each notification feels like an obligation: something might have changed, and if you do not know, you are at a disadvantage. Behavioural studies of media consumption show that high frequency increases anxiety without reliably improving decision quality. Beyond a certain point, more information becomes more noise.

Pre-commitment here means deciding *when* and *how* to engage with information, not only *how much* risk to take. Some institutional investors formalise this through investment committees that meet on fixed schedules and restrict trading decisions to those settings. The ritual matters. It introduces friction between stimulus and response. In the digital asset context, this can translate into pre-defined review windows—specific times of day or week when one engages with markets more deeply, while ignoring the constant hum outside those windows.

The motif that has been quietly present throughout this book—*distance*—appears again. Rules create distance between feeling and action. They do not anaesthetise emotion, but they lengthen the gap in which reason can speak. This is why they must be set before they are needed. A rule written during a seventy per cent drawdown is rarely a rule; it is a rationalisation.

Psychologists refer to this dynamic as "hot–cold empathy gaps". In a cold state—calm, rested, unpressured—we underestimate how powerfully a hot state—fear, greed, panic—will distort our judgement. Ulysses instructing his crew to tie him to the mast before hearing the Sirens' song is the classic metaphor. In volatile finance, the Sirens are push alerts, green candles, and doom-laden headlines. The ropes are pre-signed instructions: allocation caps, rebalancing thresholds, news schedules.

There is, of course, a risk of fetishising rules. Overly rigid systems can fail to incorporate new information. A portfolio that never revisits its assumptions about, say, regulatory change or technological obsolescence is not disciplined; it is negligent. The art lies in designing rules that *codify process* without freezing belief. Good rules ask questions at the right time. They might mandate that any major allocation change be accompanied by a short written rationale, to be revisited later. This simple practice—used by several hedge funds in London and New York—turns each decision into a future learning object.

Seen through this lens, pre-commitment checklists become less like constraints and more like mirrors. They reveal whether a decision aligns with one's stated aims. An allocation rule might ask: "What is the maximum drawdown I could tolerate without being forced to sell?" A rebalancing rule: "Under what conditions would I *not* rebalance, and why?" A news rule: "Which sources have actually helped me make better decisions over the last year?" None of these questions require a particular answer. They require honest ones.

Volatile assets will always invite improvisation. There will always be moments when sticking rigidly to a rule feels foolish in the face of some new, dramatic event. The point of setting rules before you need them is not to achieve mechanical obedience but to ensure that deviation is conscious. Breaking a rule should feel weighty, not casual. The logbook should show it.

The unresolved tension, the one that sits beneath every attempt at self-discipline in markets, is simple to phrase and hard to live: when the next shock arrives—whether a protocol failure, a regulatory surprise, or a sudden mania—will the decisions you make be those of your *earlier self* or your *immediate feelings*? The rules you set in quiet will not answer that question for you. They will only be there, waiting, when the noise demands an instant reply.

Learning Loops After Mistakes

On 15 June 2022 in Singapore, Three Arrows Capital filed for liquidation. Billions in creditor claims. Reputation erased. A firm once hailed as visionary collapsed into a tangle of over-leveraged bets and denial. The event was dissected across media, but what mattered most was what never appeared in public: no disciplined post-mortems, no candid investigation of decision errors while the fund still had time to learn. Substitute a different name, date, or place and the same story repeats across every boom—failures that could have taught something arrive too late to save their creators.

Now consider a quieter example. After the "Black Wednesday" crisis of 16 September 1992, when Britain crashed out of the Exchange Rate Mechanism, the Bank of England began a practice of publishing detailed after-action reports on foreign exchange operations and policy decisions. Every error was logged, examined, and contextualised. Not to assign shame but to refine process. The result was not perfection; it was institutional memory. A country that had stumbled learned how to stumble less.

The motif is simple: **mistakes are data** if you collect them. Losses become tuition only when you record the lesson.

Investors in volatile markets face a structural problem. They experience failure viscerally and privately. Gains demand attention; losses demand silence. Behavioural researchers such as Daniel Kahneman and Dan Ariely have demonstrated the asymmetric emotional weight of loss—roughly twice that of an equivalent gain in controlled experiments. The visible behaviours in markets reflect this: investors check balances less after a crash, exit apps faster, speak cautiously about decisions that went wrong. This retreat prevents embarrassment. It also prevents learning.

A learning loop requires three concrete actions: capture the mistake, diagnose the cause, upgrade the process. Each action must be surfaced into behaviour. Recording a loss openly—writing down the rationale at the time of decision, the outcome, the delta—is an act of honesty. It measures what was believed, not what was hoped. Diagnosis requires naming the mechanism of failure. Too much leverage? Poor liquidity analysis? Over-reliance on one influencer? Process upgrades must then become commitments: adding a checklist step, reducing position sizing, introducing a mandatory pause before trades above a certain threshold. Self-examination becomes structure.

Consider a named, checkable case. The Mt. Gox collapse in Tokyo in February 2014 revealed losses of approximately 850,000 bitcoins. The initial post-crisis reactions across the industry focused on blaming a single company's negligence. Yet the more impactful response came from those who ran post-mortems that addressed multiple causal layers: inadequate cybersecurity standards, absence of segregated custody, and lax operational oversight. Crucially, several exchanges launched after 2014 embedded proof-of-reserves audits as a preventive upgrade. A loss became a process shift. The behaviour was external: cryptographic attestations, independent verifications. Trust measured, not assumed.

Now a counter-example. Retail traders in 2021's meme-asset surge—GameStop, Dogecoin, Shiba Inu—often framed losses as betrayal by market structure or media narratives. In countless online forums, post-mortems were replaced by conspiracy. No learning loop was formed. Position sizing did not change. Exposure concentration did not change. News habits did not change. When the next frenzy appeared, the same people made the same choices with no procedural memory. The limitation of shame-driven cultures is visible here. When losses imply stupidity, analysis feels like self-harm.

Reconciling these examples reveals the core principle: **learning requires psychological safety**. Professionals build it by normalising error review. Several hedge funds—including those in Mayfair and Greenwich—maintain "blameless post-mortems" as part of risk committee charters. A decision can be bad even when outcomes are good, and good even when outcomes are bad. The metric is *process quality*, not interim fortune. A trader who broke rules but won must answer harder questions than a colleague who followed rules and lost. The implication is structural humility: success becomes something to audit, not celebrate blindly.

Loss aversion hinders this. The human brain protects its identity by editing memories. Post-hoc narratives emerge:

"I knew it; I just mistimed it." "Everyone was fooled." "The market was irrational." These self-protective sentences erase causes. To counter them, processes must externalise memory. One visible method: **decision journals**. The practice—used at Bridgewater Associates in Connecticut since at least the early 2000s—is simple. Before committing risk, the decision maker writes a timestamped rationale and expected probabilities. After results arrive, the forecast and reality are compared. The discrepancy becomes a data point. Scrutiny shifts from feeling wrong to quantifying being wrong.

Crypto markets add a special twist: **speed**. Drawdowns of fifty per cent in a fortnight are plausible. News cycles compress. Feedback loops accelerate. Errors that would unfold over years in equities unfold over days. This speed can be harnessed. Instead of waiting for an annual review, crypto traders can run post-mortems weekly. The behaviour is precise: set two recurring windows every week to review all executed positions and major decisions. Publish the notes privately to a log. Over time patterns emerge: over-trading after midnight; oversized bets during copy-trading surges; trusting unverified Telegram rumours. The implication is uncomfortable: the enemy is not volatility. It is inconsistency.

History shows that institutions survive repeated shocks when they internalise lessons rather than individuals. After the collapse of Long-Term Capital Management in Greenwich in September 1998, regulators and banks documented counterparty exposure mapping methods. Stress test frameworks improved. Margin collateral requirements adapted. The memory of that error influenced protocol design in decentralised lending across 2020–21, where *over-collateralisation* became the norm. A disaster became architecture. Loss became resilience.

But there is a paradox. Over-focusing on what went wrong can distort. Sometimes a loss occurs because reality is complex, not because one made a mistake. A keen learner risks turning randomness into narrative. The counter-example is instructive: a skilled investor who constantly rewrites their rules after small losses may degrade a sound strategy. Reconciling this requires a calibration metric: **distinguish noise from signal**. A loss that falls within an expected volatility band may not deserve process change. A loss that arises from a breach of one's own rules always does. The post-mortem must ask: is this error structural or situational? If structural, what specific behaviour must change?

Across these examples, a quiet motif recurs: **light**. Learning loops shine light on assumptions that prefer the dark. They illuminate hidden drivers: ego, urgency, distraction. They expose blind spots: liquidity fragility, information asymmetry, copy-trading influence. Light hurts. Shame prefers the dark. Yet every major risk framework that has stood the test of time—aviation safety, medical checklists, industrial hazard systems—embraces illumination. Report errors early. Analyse them openly. Change behaviour visibly.

Crypto markets incentivise secrecy about losses. Leaderboard culture rewards highlight reels. Sharing a post-mortem feels like weakening one's status. But status without accuracy corrodes. A future self will pay for a present ego's cover-up. The people who survive booms and busts are rarely the ones with flawless records. They are the ones with honest records.

The tension that closes this chapter segment remains unresolved by design. When your next position collapses—whether through leverage misjudged, liquidity misread, or hype mis-trusted—will the story you tell explain the loss away, or will the logbook transform it into a procedural upgrade? The chart will not care. The market will not notice. The only witness will be the person you have become.

Chapter 10
Risk, Not Riddance

Every bubble produces its own late-night ritual. The screen glow. The refreshing of prices. The tiny heartbeat spike when a line on the chart twitches the wrong way. Across bedrooms, shared flats, and train platforms, people have convinced themselves that vigilance is a virtue rather than a symptom. They call it conviction. They promise themselves that the reward is worth the insomnia. Yet the body keeps its own ledger. The price of risk is paid, first and most quietly, in sleep.

A trader once told me he only truly understood exposure when he noticed his dreams had turned into liquidation warnings. That was 2017 in Seoul, when leveraged crypto positions triggered at dawn meant waking up could be a financial event. His discovery was not mathematical: risk is real when it intrudes on life. When markets make people tired, snappish, distracted around family, secretive with friends, or dependent on screens for reassurance, a position has already breached the boundaries of reason. The losses may not have hit yet, but the person is already paying. That breach, not a number on a chart, is the true beginning of danger.

We have built a financial culture that mistakes adrenaline for mastery. Volatility becomes a badge of honour. Survival becomes a story for social feeds, not a private responsibility. Crypto, with its 24/7 markets and intoxicating upside, intensifies the illusion that risk is just leverage minus bad timing. But real risk, the kind that shapes a life, is the mismatch between what someone can lose and what they must still do tomorrow. Rent. Children. Health. Relationships that rely on steadiness rather than constant checking of candlesticks. Risk is not a puzzle waiting to be solved. It is a duty waiting to be honoured.

This chapter insists on a simple premise: resilience matters more than returns. The assets that survive booms and busts are those whose holders remain capable of holding them. Risk is not something to eliminate. It is something to carry well. That means decisions must be grounded not in abstract appetite but in visible consequences. If exposure robs someone of sleep, the position is too large. If a counterparty's failure would derail one's livelihood, the relationship is too concentrated. If operational errors—lost keys, corrupted backups, ill-timed updates—could produce irreversible loss, then the system needs reinforcement before it needs optimism.

Financial history is littered with examples where sophisticated analysis collapsed under the weight of the ordinary. The 2003 blackout in North America began with a single untrimmed tree. A bank run in Northern Rock in 2007 ignited not through credit models but cash-in-branch panic. And in crypto, the disappearance of funds from QuadrigaCX in 2018 revealed that no clever charts can save assets custodied with misplaced trust. Resilience is rarely glamorous. It looks like scepticism. It feels like caution. It is documented in habits: checking recovery phrases twice a year, storing backups away from floodplains, testing a small withdrawal before entrusting the whole.

Risk that one prepares for becomes manageable. Risk that is ignored becomes fate.

The architecture of decentralised finance has created an illusion of self-reliance: *code is law, not your keys, not your coins, trustless systems*. Yet beneath every protocol sits a stack of human decisions: developers with upgrade authority, administrators with emergency keys, auditors with imperfect checklists. When these layers align, the system hums. When they misalign, users discover that even smart contracts possess the same ancient weakness as banks: someone ultimately controls the exit doors. The wise participant does not simply ask whether the code works. They ask who can change it and how fast.

Operational resilience is the dull backbone behind every enduring investment strategy. Cold storage is not exotic; it is mundane. Recording seed phrases on metal plates is not an adventure; it is a chore. Updating software is not a breakthrough; it is maintenance. But neglect in these areas has toppled more portfolios than bear markets ever did. Boring excellence outperforms dazzling recklessness. Every time.

The future surprises us. That is its job. Stablecoins may wobble. Exchanges may freeze withdrawals to survive a liquidity drain. Oracle networks may misprice. Governance votes may be captured by a single actor. These are not hypotheticals but repeated events. The difference between a temporary inconvenience and a life-altering setback is not cleverness. It is preparedness. Scenario planning turns fear into action: *If this happens, I will do that.* It scripts calm responses before panic can take hold. It transforms chaos into a checklist.

Throughout the pages ahead, we will translate these themes into practices—not with numbers to optimise, but with boundaries to live by. Position sizing framed in human terms: the amount one can risk and still fall asleep without bargaining with the future. Counterparty questions posed plainly: who holds the keys, who reviews the code, who benefits from opacity? Operational habits that remove fragility before it strikes. Scenario rehearsals that ask: if this exchange halted tomorrow morning, what would break in my life? And does that answer scare me?

Risk will follow anyone who participates in markets that never close. It cannot be reasoned away. But its weight can be carried differently. With the right stance, with memory sharpened by history and humility, risk becomes a companion, not a stalker.

There is a line between boldness and recklessness. It is drawn not by fortune but by foresight. To cross it is easy; we have all crossed it. To redraw it—by understanding not only what we hope to gain but what we cannot afford to lose—is the work ahead.

Position Sizing and Sleep

At 03:17 on 19 May 2021, in London, a software engineer named Mark found himself staring at a liquidation alert on his phone. He had gone to bed with an overconfident grin and a leveraged position on a crypto exchange. Now he was wide awake, heart racing, calculating how many hours remained until work, and whether he could wire in more collateral before his holdings were sold automatically. He did not lose everything that night. Yet he spent the next day hollow-eyed in meetings, snapping at colleagues, and scanning prices beneath the table. The market had taken only a slice of his portfolio. It had taken more from his life.

Here was a lesson paid in physiology rather than capital: if a position is large enough to destroy sleep, then risk has already exceeded reason. The biological alarms warn us sooner than profit-and-loss statements do. Muscles tighten. Thoughts loop. Time stretches. A trade intrudes into personal commitments—interrupting dinner with a partner, delaying attention to a child's question, filling silence where rest should be. Risk becomes visible not on a chart, but in the body. Sleep is a metric. It does not lie.

Loss aversion, defined rigorously by Daniel Kahneman and Amos Tversky (1979), shows that people feel losses about twice as intensely as equivalent gains. Yet this psychological asymmetry only fully reveals itself across mismatched time horizons. A portfolio with a long-term thesis forces the holder to experience a short-term storm physically. Prices falling for two hours can feel like destiny. The tension comes from the gap between what the strategy requires—patience—and what the nervous system demands—escape. In this mismatch, sleep becomes currency.

Show the pain. Name it. Explain it. The implication follows: the correct position size is not the maximum one can justify intellectually, but the amount that leaves room for uninterrupted sleep and unwavering obligations. The most precise measure of whether an allocation is too large is not volatility but shame—the hidden feeling of guilt when markets distract someone from promises they owe their future self: to be alert at work, present at home, calm in crisis. If a position forces someone to check prices during a child's birthday, it is already mis-sized.

This principle appears across financial history. John Maynard Keynes, writing from King's College, Cambridge in 1938, cautioned that markets can remain irrational longer than an investor can remain solvent—or sane. He was describing more than balance sheets. He meant that psychological liquidity can evaporate too. A strategy that *works* may still break the person executing it. The visible behaviour: waking to price alerts. The metric: sleep hours lost. The implication: resilience collapses before capital does.

Another example: in January 2022, during a sharp drawdown in decentralised tokens, several teachers in New York City who had placed significant savings into a high-yield platform expressed panic not over numbers on a screen, but over their ability to focus on students the next day. They did not default. They passed their lessons. Yet their minds were consumed by the fear that the exit door might close before lunch. Their portfolios survived longer than their attention spans. Risk had colonised their working hours.

A counterexample deserves respect. Some people claim to thrive on volatility, sleeping soundly through double-digit swings. For them, the nightly hum of price feeds feels like opportunity rather than threat. But such claims often rest on two hidden supports: either the capital at stake is genuinely surplus, or the person has not yet endured a full cycle of loss. Enthusiasm can mimic resilience, until one severe drawdown exposes the difference. Reconciling the exception reinforces the rule: a position is only "comfortable" when the worst credible outcome fits within the holder's life without derailment.

The motif returns: sleep. It threads through judgement like a quiet saboteur. Consider Warren Buffett's line—"If you can't watch your stock fall by 50 percent without becoming panic-stricken, you shouldn't be in the market." Stripped of bravado, the statement means: *size your exposure so that you can keep living well even when prices halve*. The visible decision: a smaller allocation. The result: steady breath at night.

The human nervous system evolved in environments with slow-moving threats. A falling asset price triggers the same fight-or-flight response designed for predators. Adrenaline surges. Cortisol extends its stay. A single red candle can keep someone awake long after midnight. This can be measured. Researchers at Harvard Medical School (2021) found that financial anxiety reduces sleep efficiency by measurable margins, affecting cognition the following day. Lost rest compounds risk by impairing judgment. The cost is recursive: bad sleep leads to bad choices, which lead to worse sleep.

What reframing helps? People often ask, "How much can I afford to lose?" The healthier question is, "How much can I afford to think about this?" If checking prices more than twice a day feels irresistible, the position is too large relative to one's emotional buffer. If waking up involves scanning for doom, the size must shrink until mornings recover their neutrality. Horizon defines peace.

A second reframing: "Would I be content if this investment took five years to pay off and did nothing until then?" If the honest answer is no, then the position is anchored to urgency rather than understanding. Urgency exhausts. Understanding endures.

A third: "If this were completely illiquid for a year, could I still sleep?" This frames exposure within real obligations: rent due, family commitments, health costs, professional standards. An investment that jeopardises these is not a strategy. It is a breach.

Across markets, quiet investors endure. The survivors of the dot-com crash in 2000 were rarely those who piled in the most capital but those who preserved enough psychological surplus to remain rational. Long-term index holders succeed not only because of diversification but because their portfolios rarely wake them after midnight. Time horizon converts volatility from distress into noise.

Liquidity temptations, however, shorten horizons. Crypto prices move constantly, without weekends. The market invites insomnia. It whispers: *Act now or regret forever*. But every lost hour of sleep makes the whisper louder. That is the reflexive trap: a market that never closes shrinks the mind's ability to see beyond the next candle.

The motif one last time: sleep is the scoreboard of risk. A person who sleeps well owns their positions. A person who struggles to sleep is owned by them.

So the unresolved tension stands: if exposure today quietly damages tomorrow's responsibilities, what precisely should shrink—the position or the ambition? The body already knows the answer. It communicates in interrupted nights and anxious mornings. The question is whether the mind listens before the margin call arrives.

Counterparty and Smart-Contract Risk

At 01:48 on 30 March 2022, in Singapore, developers at Ronin Network confirmed that attackers had drained assets worth more than half a billion dollars by compromising validator keys. It was a blunt revelation: a system marketed as decentralised had been secured by a handful of signers whose private keys, once stolen, offered the thieves a clear path to the vault. No obscure cryptography had failed. No exotic exploit was required. The breach grew from something simpler and more human—counterparty risk disguised as code. Infrastructure that should have constrained power had merely concentrated it. Control lay behind a curtain, not on-chain.

This is the paradox at the heart of modern digital finance. Smart contracts promise self-enforcing, transparent rules. Yet their safety often turns on quiet, off-chain decisions made by identifiable people in identifiable places. One admin key mismanaged, one timelock too short, one upgrade mechanism too flexible, and a supposedly trust-minimised system reverts to trust-maximalism. The motif recurs: control surfaces. They appear in signatures, server logs, and emergency permissions. Each one determines whether code disciplines its operators or whether operators bend the code.

Counterparty risk is not a relic from traditional finance. It is alive in every protocol that allows a team to pause withdrawals, adjust parameters, or redirect funds. To show this, name a second clear episode. In June 2020, the founders of the South Korean exchange Coinrail admitted that a hack had siphoned a large tranche of ERC-20 tokens after attackers gained access to internal systems. The technology stack was new; the governance mistake was ancient. Internal controls that should have segregated duties had blurred. Custody was concentrated. Visibility was limited. The breach followed the weakest path.

These episodes demonstrate a pattern rather than accidents. A counterparty becomes risky the moment its incentives, access, or competence diverge from what its users assume. The visible behaviour is always similar: opaque updates, hasty patching, evasive communication, or unverified claims about audits or security reviews. A project that lengthens its timelock from zero to two days without explanation has already taught the observer what matters: the organisation previously reserved the right to act instantly and privately. Measuring access reveals power.

Smart-contract risk follows the same logic but with different mechanics. Here the adversary need not breach a human; they need only find a flaw in logic or execution. The DAO hack in June 2016, which drained roughly 3.6 million ETH from a recursive call vulnerability, remains the canonical lesson. The contract performed as written, not as intended. The implication was stark: code correctness is neither democratic nor forgiving. A single misplaced assumption can split a chain, as the subsequent Ethereum–Ethereum Classic fork showed. The line between counterparty and contract blurred further—humans intervened, revealing again where ultimate control resided.

Yet a limitation must be acknowledged. Not all upgrades, admin keys, or discretionary controls are dangerous. Some protocols maintain emergency pause functions for legitimate reasons—protecting users during exploits or preventing cascading failures. A credible counterexample is the use of a timelocked multisig by Aave's governance in late 2022, where authorised signers could trigger an emergency freeze, but only after a mandatory delay visible to the entire community. Transparency and constraint turned discretion into a safety valve rather than a vector of abuse. Reconciling the counterexample clarifies the principle: power itself is not the problem; unobserved, unconstrained power is.

Smart-contract audits, too, resist easy interpretation. An audit is not a certificate; it is a process report. A contract audited twice by reputable firms can still collapse if developers deploy a new module without review or modify parameters carelessly. In August 2021, the Poly Network hack exploited a flaw in cross-chain contract logic that had passed earlier inspections. The attackers could forge messages that granted them authorisation to withdraw funds. The nuance matters. Audits reduce risk: they cannot extinguish it. The visible metric here is audit scope and depth. A ten-page report that checks for common patterns differs meaningfully from a forty-page review that demonstrates attempted exploit construction, formal verification attempts, and specific remediation instructions.

The motif threads through again: control surfaces. Whether a system requires a signer, an oracle update, or an upgrade authority, that surface determines how failure propagates. Two protocols may appear similar on the front end yet diverge sharply once governance mechanisms are mapped. One might rely on a multisig located across two continents with signers doxxed, insured, and subject to operational policies. Another might entrust everything to a founder's laptop. To compare them responsibly, one must trace each control surface—who can act, when, and how quickly.

Plain tests help. The first is custody segregation. A credible operator never commingles customer assets with company funds. Behaviour reveals this through real policies: distinct wallets, observable cold storage, and reconciliation logs. Exchanges that maintain proof-of-reserves with liabilities reported alongside assets display substance rather than theatre. Names matter here: Kraken's publication of its Merkle-tree attestation process in 2022 provided users a way to verify inclusion without trusting headlines.

A second test is timelock rigidity. A protocol with zero-delay upgrades places ultimate faith in its deployers. A system with a seven-day timelock and public proposal pipeline declares that changes will never surprise users. The behaviour is visible: anyone can measure the actual block delays and monitor the queues. Timelocks are not ornamental—they are psychological infrastructure. They buy time for scrutiny, dissent, or exit.

A third is operator fallback. When something breaks, who answers? Projects with documented operational incident histories show humility and competence. Those that vanish for hours under pressure reveal fragility, regardless of how elegant their interfaces may appear.

A fourth is legal enforceability. Even in decentralised finance, disputes travel toward courts, arbitration, or negotiated settlement. In 2020, a UK High Court ruling (AA v Persons Unknown) recognised crypto-assets as property—enabling injunctions that could freeze or recover stolen tokens. The law did not bend to the rhetoric of decentralisation; it applied principles developed over centuries. The implication: code can automate duties, but legal systems still adjudicate harms. A contract with ambiguous jurisdiction or absent terms leaves users navigating an unlit path.

The risk of cross-protocol contagion illustrates how counterparty and contract vulnerabilities intertwine. When the lending platform Celsius froze withdrawals in June 2022, counterparties that relied on its liquidity faced indirect stress, despite having sound contracts themselves. Their risk emerged not from code but from a partner's insolvency. Mapping these dependencies—who holds whose tokens, who borrows from whom, and who provides collateral—offers a clearer view than any marketing claim. The visible decisions are renegotiations, impairments, or emergency asset sales. The implication is that decentralised systems are only as strong as the weakest connection in their network of counterparties.

Here lies the unresolved tension. To build products that move quickly, founders crave flexible upgrade paths, emergency controls, privileged functions. To feel safe, users crave immutable contracts, hardened governance, and strict timelocks. The two desires conflict. A protocol that cannot adapt becomes brittle. One that adapts too easily becomes a trust game. Where should the boundary sit? Which powers should teams retain, and which should they surrender permanently?

Every control surface answers this question implicitly. Yet the explicit answer remains unsettled. Should users prefer a protocol that evolves rapidly but demands trust, or one that evolves slowly but grants them peace? The trade-off is structural, not temporary. And so the question endures: when safety, agility, and decentralisation cannot coexist fully, which compromise best protects the people whose assets depend on them?

Operational Resilience

At dawn on 7 February 2014, in Vancouver, technicians at QuadrigaCX confronted a problem that should never have been possible. The exchange's primary cold wallet—supposedly a secure vault—was inaccessible. Its sole custodian, Gerald Cotten, had died two months earlier in Jaipur, leaving no documented backups, recovery protocols, or operational keys. The result was binary and brutal: assets were frozen beyond retrieval, and withdrawals halted. The case became a study in what operational resilience is not. It was not a cryptographic failure. It was not a rogue hacker. It was the quiet decay of basic practice: no redundant access, no peer review of key handling, no predictable update process. One man's laptop had become the system's spine. Then the spine snapped.

Operational resilience rarely features in sleek brochures or conference stages, yet it determines whether uncertainty becomes inconvenience or catastrophe. The paradox is stark. The more polished a digital system looks, the easier it is to forget how much depends on mundane routines: testing backups, rotating keys, verifying restores. These rituals appear dull. They are dull. They must be dull. A resilient system is closer to a well-run archive than a frontier lab—its integrity grows from predictable habits, not heroic improvisation.

Good operations move in rhythms. A team inspects a disaster-recovery log every Friday. A hardware wallet rotation proceeds monthly. An update window occurs only after staged tests have passed. These actions are visible and measurable: checklists completed, signatures logged, hashes verified. They turn fragility into foresight. When a system works smoothly, the temptation is to reduce these rituals, to assume that complacency costs less than discipline. The QuadrigaCX collapse shows the exact reverse. Complacency compounds until it destroys.

To show the anatomy of resilience, name something concrete. Backups succeed only when they are restored regularly. In 2019, the New York-based firm Chainalysis recovered Bitcoin for a law-enforcement case by reconstructing damaged wallet fragments—made possible because the underlying protocols had been tested repeatedly. The resilience came from habit, not luck. Contrast this with protocols that announce complex keysharding schemes yet never simulate a real recovery. Their backups exist in theory, not practice. The implication is clear: a backup untested is a backup undone.

Cold storage hygiene offers an even sharper lens. It asks straightforward questions with difficult consequences. Who has physical access to seed phrases? Where are they stored? Which procedures govern retrieval? In 2021, the exchange Kraken publicly demonstrated how poor physical security at some competing custodians allowed unauthorised badge cloning within minutes. The demonstration was a warning: digital assets inherit the vulnerabilities of their weakest physical control. A protocol may tout multi-signature custody and distributed validators, yet if its private keys sit in a desk drawer, its resilience is theatre.

The structure of update rituals matters just as much. Software evolves. Threats evolve faster. A resilient operation recognises this and sets a cadence that separates development from deployment. Ethereum's London hard fork in August 2021 showed how controlled coordination can strengthen a network. Months of testing, communication, and cross-client experiments reduced the risk that a single bug could stall the chain. The behaviour visible to the observer—public testnets, reproduced simulations, release candidates—revealed the discipline behind the upgrade. The transparent, staged process reduced uncertainty for every participant.

Yet there is a limit. Over-rigid rituals can delay critical patches. If a protocol requires a one-week governance vote for every minor upgrade, a serious vulnerability discovered on a Tuesday might remain unaddressed until the following Wednesday. This is not resilience; it is paralysis. The credible counterexample prompts a reconciliation. Resilience demands both predictability and adaptability. The best systems maintain two layers: stable routines for ordinary operations and emergency paths with narrow, auditable scope. The key is visibility. An emergency patch that leaves a clear record—signatures, rationale, expiry—is not a shortcut. It is a controlled exception.

A quiet motif runs through these choices: layers. A resilient operation builds layers of defence, layers of monitoring, layers of fallback. Each layer must do something observable. A multisig structure without a documented signer-replacement procedure is half a layer. A hardware wallet without an inventory log is an illusion of security. A server backup without off-site redundancy is a single point of failure dressed up as prudence. Layers offer separation. Separation creates time. Time buys safety.

Scenario testing translates layers into lived practice. Consider the rehearsals conducted by major cloud providers where engineers intentionally sever network links or simulate hardware failures. The behaviour is unglamorous: someone yanks a cable, triggers a synthetic outage, or deletes a test database to time the recovery. Yet the lesson is profound. A system only reveals its resilience when it is stressed. Digital finance is no different. A credible operator should know the precise steps required if an exchange halts withdrawals at midnight, if a stablecoin deviates from its peg for ninety minutes, or if an oracle feeds corrupted data for ten blocks. These scenarios require no prophecy. They require rehearsal.

The absence of ritual is itself a signal. Teams that avoid incident forms, postpone recovery drills, or centralise operational knowledge display the same behavioural pattern: short-term optimisation at the expense of long-term integrity. Their dashboards may glow green; their foundations rest on sand. QuadrigaCX was an extreme case, but the pattern echoes widely. A founder insists on being the sole key-holder. A team delays migrating to hardware-secured modules because the process feels slow. A custodian resists external review. Each decision erodes a layer.

Named examples sharpen this frame. The Japanese exchange bitFlyer, after its 2018 suspension by regulators for inadequate internal controls, rebuilt its processes by implementing audited multi-signature cold storage and strict segregation of operational duties. The visible effects—regular third-party security attestations, published custody principles, and demonstrably slower but safer withdrawal processes—illustrated how institutions can turn regulatory scrutiny into disciplined practice. Their resilience improved because every fragile shortcut was removed, not because new technology replaced old habits.

And the limitation again deserves emphasis. Perfect resilience is impossible. Every backup can fail. Every ritual can slip. Every redundant system can misfire. But the goal is not invulnerability. It is degradation with grace. A resilient system fails in small pieces, not all at once. It fails visibly, not silently. It fails slowly, not suddenly. It fails with warnings, not riddles.

This raises the unresolved tension. Operational resilience demands resources, time, and patience. Teams operating in competitive markets often feel pressure to prioritise speed. Users often reward convenience, not caution. Where should the balance sit between swift iteration and meticulous stability? How should a project weigh the friction of ritual against the safety it provides? And when the pressure mounts and shortcuts beckon, which layers will be protected first—and which will be sacrificed?

Scenario Planning

At 1.14 p.m. on 19 May 2021, Binance halted withdrawals for roughly an hour after a surge of liquidations overwhelmed its matching engine. The interruption came at the worst possible moment: Bitcoin had fallen more than 30 per cent within the day, and traders across London, Singapore, and São Paulo watched their screens freeze. The problem was not simply price volatility. It was the mismatch between expectation and preparation. Many users had assumed that liquidity and access were constants. When access vanished, even temporarily, they discovered a deeper truth: without a plan for halted execution, every strategy collapses into improvisation. Improvisation during stress rarely ends well.

The same month, a different fracture appeared. On 23 May 2021, the algorithmic stablecoin IRON on Polygon broke its peg and plunged towards zero, triggering a cascade of forced redemptions. This, too, shocked holders who believed that a peg implied permanence. Yet the underlying mechanics—collateral ratios, redemption incentives, and market-maker behaviour—made the system susceptible to a run. The wobble was visible long before the crash. Few had rehearsed what a wobble meant for them. Fewer still had drafted actions for each stage of deterioration: a five-cent deviation, a twenty-cent deviation, a halt in redemptions. Assumptions, not mechanics, shaped behaviour.

These scenes illuminate a single motif that will thread through the discussion: preparedness lives in verbs, not slogans. You *test*. You *separate*. You *pause*. You *exit*. A scenario without an associated action is only a story. A scenario with an action becomes resilience.

Scenario planning begins with a discipline of showing, not guessing. An exchange halt is not hypothetical; we have dates, places, and logs. When Coinbase suffered a series of outages in 2017 during periods of intense retail inflow, the cause was not a hidden conspiracy but capacity limits. The behaviour was observable: page loads stalled, statuses flickered between "degraded" and "maintenance", and support queues lengthened by the minute. Naming the event grounds the broader claim: trading venues are not public utilities. They are private systems with finite throughput, governed by internal playbooks that may prioritise stability over user immediacy. Once this is explained, the implication becomes unavoidable. Anyone interacting with such a system must assume that access can vanish without warning and rehearse the next step before the next outage.

A second domain—stablecoin instability—invites a similar pattern. The partial de-pegging of USDC in March 2023, following concerns about its banking exposure, created a brief but intense dislocation. Prices on decentralised exchanges fluctuated between $0.87 and $0.98 for several hours, depending on venue and liquidity. The behaviour was measurable: swap slippage widened, arbitrage slowed, and liquidity pools inverted. That event, named and dated, demonstrates that even fully collateralised assets can wobble when information, fear, and liquidity collide. The implication extends beyond stablecoins. Any asset promising stability does so within a context. Scenario planning maps that context and tests it.

The credible counterexample matters. Some crises never escalate. In June 2022, Tether briefly lost its peg on a few decentralised pools but recovered swiftly without structural contagion. That episode shows that not every wobble demands full retreat. The reconciliation sits in the behaviour of the asset itself. A robust stablecoin exhibits transparent collateral, predictable redemption mechanics, and consistent settlement pathways. These features become the metrics through which a scenario can be judged in real time.

Scenario planning does not require panic; it requires criteria.

Oracle failures form the third axis. On 14 February 2020, the bZx protocol on Ethereum suffered an exploit after its price feed was manipulated during low-liquidity trading hours. The attack did not stem from a flaw in cryptography but from a blind trust in a single feed. The behaviour that mattered was the protocol's immediate response: pausing functions, communicating the vulnerability, and coordinating a patch. The failure revealed a broader truth: smart contracts operate only as reliably as the data they ingest. Naming the limitation leads to its implication. Any system relying on external data must simulate conditions under which that data becomes stale, corrupted, or delayed.

These examples form the scaffolding for a wider argument: scenarios must be simple to be useful. Complexity paralyses action. A plan consisting of fifty steps will be abandoned at step two. The most resilient playbooks compress chaos into crisp triggers. If withdrawals halt for more than X minutes, do Y. If a stablecoin deviates by Z, decide now whether to wait or unwind. If an oracle stalls for one block, two blocks, three blocks, know exactly which operations should freeze and who must approve overrides. Good scenarios behave like fire doors: easy to locate, easy to use, built for moments when clarity is scarce.

Consideration of location strengthens this point. When the New York Stock Exchange experienced a trading glitch in July 2015, its rapid failover procedures—tested repeatedly across data centres—allowed the market to resume more smoothly than many observers expected. The visible behaviour was coordination: clear status updates, predictable sequencing, and pre-defined transition rules. Digital asset systems, by contrast, often span jurisdictions, servers, and architectures with uneven governance. Scenario planning must therefore compensate for what traditional markets achieve through regulation: shared expectations.

Preparation becomes more demanding in decentralised contexts, where authority is distributed or ambiguous. A DAO that governs a lending protocol might need a time-sensitive vote to pause borrowing if an oracle fails. Yet a governance vote taking two days is incompatible with a vulnerability emerging in two minutes. The limitation is structural, not moral. How does one reconcile the need for decentralisation with the need for speed? The answer lies in layered triggers. Routine decisions can travel through democratic processes. Emergency actions must be delegated to narrow, transparent, accountable modules—timelocked, audited, and bound by tight scope. The behaviour is measurable: emergency powers that expire, logs that record every call, and parameters that cannot be altered without consensus after the crisis window closes.

A quiet motif returns: asking the right question. Every scenario begins with the same pivot—*what fails first?* The question forces specificity. In a stablecoin stress, the first failure may be redemption queues, not the peg itself. In an exchange outage, the first failure may be support-channel saturation, not matching engine capacity. In an oracle glitch, the first failure may be the protocol's reliance on median data rather than its frequency. Scenario planning becomes sharper when each possibility is mapped to what can be observed before the full fracture.

The art is not prediction but preparation. A team that rehearses a withdrawal freeze with a five-minute drill—simulating API errors, message delays, and escalating status pages—generates muscle memory that will matter at 1.14 p.m. on an ordinary Wednesday. A user who scripts their own if-then playbook for a stablecoin wobble will not need to decide under stress whether to hold, reduce, or exit. A protocol that encodes automatic pauses for oracle delay will not rely on the waking hours of a global volunteer group. These behaviours give shape to resilience.

Yet the tension persists. Every scenario plan adds friction. Every drill consumes time. Every if-then rule risks false positives or overreaction. How much preparation is prudent, and how much is paranoia? At what point does rehearsal undermine spontaneity, or caution stifle innovation? And when the next fracture arrives—whether a halt, a wobble, or a failure—what will reveal itself first: the plan or the panic?

Chapter 11
What Traditional Finance Learned the Hard Way

On a spring morning in May 1866, crowds surged through the narrow alleys of Lombard Street. Messengers ran from counting house to counting house carrying a single ruinous piece of news: Overend, Gurney & Company, the revered "banker's bank" of London, had failed. Within hours, panic spread beyond the City. Railways were halted. Credit evaporated. The Bank of England, long reluctant to play saviour, finally opened the doors of its vault and flooded the system with cash. The age of the lender of last resort began not as policy but as rescue. It was a lesson carved into history by fear: confidence collapses faster than any institution can possibly respond—unless the response is already prepared.

Nearly a century later, in the blistering heat of 1920s Florida, another mania reached its peak. Land values tripled on promises of paradise, driven not by harvests or tenants but by the sheer excitement of the crowd. When the bubble burst, deeds became worthless, railroads hobbled, and investors who had boasted of paper fortunes discovered that optimism cannot be sold back to the bank. The cycle felt new. It was not. The shape of the rise and crash echoed the South Sea Bubble of 1720, the railway fever of the 1840s, and would echo again in the dot-com boom of 1999 and the mortgage-fuelled fires of 2008. Human imagination, it turned out, was excellent at making bubbles—and terrible at recognising when the story had outgrown the facts.

These episodes, separated by centuries and continents, manage a peculiar trick: they feel at once remote and intimately familiar. Every modern crypto shock—from a stablecoin slip to an exchange freeze—carries a faint historical accent. Bank runs, bubbles, and emergency backstops are not artefacts of the past; they are recurring patterns in systems where trust is both the currency and the constraint. What changed across time were not the instincts of participants but the scaffolding of protection: capital buffers, audits, circuit breakers, bankruptcy codes, and, above all, transparency that reduces guesswork in moments when guesswork can destroy markets.

The question at the heart of this chapter is disarmingly simple: what has traditional finance already learned the hard way that digital asset markets are now learning at speed? Behind that question lies a set of structural parallels worth tracing with care. When fear spreads, does the architecture bend or break? When liquidity thins, who steps in and why? When information falters, where does authority sit? These are not abstract musings. They are the everyday mechanics of markets under stress, and they reveal more about resilience than any technological boast.

Take disclosure. The world's oldest stock exchanges developed not out of altruism but of conflict. The South Sea scandal in London and the Law-inspired implosion in Paris forced governments to demand basic truths from issuers:

who controls the money, where it is kept, and what rights do investors actually own? By the late twentieth century, the principle had matured into an infrastructure—auditors separate from managers, custodians separate from traders, boards that are meant to challenge rather than cheer. These mechanisms are not moral decoration. They exist because, without verifiability, markets rely on myth. And myth is the most fragile asset of all.

Governance, similarly, evolved through mistakes. It took collapses—Barings in 1995 with a single rogue trader able to sink a venerable bank—to engrave simple rules: never allow one person both to place trades and record them; ensure someone independent holds the keys to the vault. Even highly engineered systems benefit from something deeply old-fashioned: separation of duties as a shield against both temptation and error. Crypto ecosystems, particularly those that pride themselves on automation and code, now wrestle with the same lesson. Multisignature controls, timelocks, and protocol-level governance are the new expressions of a principle hammered into finance by centuries of unwanted experience.

This chapter will follow those threads into market microstructure—the hidden choreography beneath every price you see on a screen. Bid-ask spreads, order depth, slippage, latency: these are not complexities invented by exchanges. They describe how risk is transmitted through the very act of trading. When a market thins, a large order can move prices dramatically; when spreads widen, the cost of urgency skyrockets. The London Stock Exchange understood this long before automated market makers. The New York Stock Exchange encoded it in circuit breakers after 1987. Digital venues now discover, sometimes painfully, that speed creates its own vulnerabilities. Liquidity is not merely volume—it is willingness, coordination, and trust enacted instant by instant.

Then there is diversification—the principle taught in every textbook yet misapplied in every mania. The logic is profound: do not allow a single twist of fate to define your future. Yet the execution often dissolves into what legendary investor Peter Lynch once labelled "diworsification": complexity theatre, portfolios assembled for appearance rather than resilience. A hundred coins do not guarantee protection if they all depend on the same narrative. The true lesson from traditional finance is stark. Diversification works only when correlation breaks. And correlation breaks only when assets are exposed to fundamentally different risks—interest rates versus innovation versus credit versus governance. Simplicity is not naïveté; it is clarity.

These hard-earned lessons form a quiet motif that will thread through the pages ahead: progress is often a rediscovery. The structures that traditional finance built after each disaster were not monuments to bureaucracy but countermeasures to the same forces animating digital markets now. Panics begin with whispers. Bubbles begin with dreams. Oversight begins with scars.

Yet nothing in this chapter suggests that crypto must become a replica of existing systems. Rather, it poses a challenge: if history has already conducted the experiments and paid the price, why rush to repeat them? What elements of transparency, verifiability, and structure can be adapted rather than reinvented? And what innovations—programmable collateral, real-time auditability, open ledgers—might allow digital markets to leapfrog rather than trail behind?

The stakes are more than financial. They reach into how societies allocate trust, how they balance freedom and responsibility, how they write rules that protect without suffocating. As you turn the page, you enter a conversation between centuries: veterans of past crises speaking, and a new generation deciding what they will dare to borrow—and what they will refuse to ignore.

Bank Runs, Bubbles, and Backstops

At 8:30 a.m. on Saturday, 24 September 2022, customers of Nuri GmbH in Berlin opened an email they had been hoping never to receive. The German digital bank—once a rising star of accessible crypto finance—announced it would shut down and urged users to withdraw their funds before year-end. Only weeks earlier, the collapse of Celsius Network in July 2022 had frozen billions in client withdrawals across the globe. The names, jurisdictions, and technologies differed, but the behaviour looked eerily familiar. A whisper becomes a queue. A queue becomes a run. Confidence evaporates. It breaks fast. Then it breaks everything lean.

Such events feel modern because the headlines are digital. Yet the dynamics predate silicon by centuries. In October 1907, depositors in New York lined the pavements outside Knickerbocker Trust, driven by rumours of exposure to a failed copper corner. They waited not for a blockchain confirmation but for a teller's reassurance. They did not receive it. Within days, the panic had spread to multiple institutions, prompting J.P. Morgan to corral a private consortium as an emergency backstop. The motif returns: people rush for exits, assets must be sold, and the system fights to keep doors open. The logic of bank runs respects neither medium nor millennium. Fear moves faster than cash. It always has.

If manias and panics share a rhythm, bubbles share a stage design. Consider Tokyo, 1989. Land in the Chiyoda district rose to mythical valuations, with one estimate claiming that the Imperial Palace grounds were worth more than the entire state of California. The numbers dazzled. Then they mocked. When the bubble burst, banks buckled under mountains of bad loans; the "Lost Decade" became plural. A simple truth, long recognised in London's South Sea crisis of 1720 and Paris's Law Scheme of the same year, returned with force: when prices detach from income or utility, the correction is not gentle. It is a reckoning. A bubble is leverage disguised as optimism.

Digital assets have imported this rhythm with few edits. In May 2022, the stablecoin TerraUSD lost its peg to the US dollar. The design depended on algorithmic exchanges with its sister token, LUNA. As redemption pressure grew, the defence mechanisms failed; the forced minting of LUNA accelerated the death spiral. $40 billion in market value evaporated within days (coinmarketcap.com, May 2022). The promised peg was not backed by a central bank with legal authority to print reserves, nor by insured deposits; it was defended by belief. When belief cracked, the floor gave way. A peg is trust formalised as price.

The continuity is stark. Runs attack liquidity; bursts expose solvency. The difference determines the remedy. A liquidity crisis means: assets exist but cannot be sold quickly without ruinous slippage. A solvency crisis means: assets are insufficient to meet obligations at any pace. In 2008, Northern Rock in the United Kingdom faced a funding freeze long before its loan book proved irreparable. Images of queuing customers became the first televised British bank run in more than a century. The government intervened because the institution was not yet bankrupt—only unable to persuade the market of its survival.

Crypto markets experienced their own version with FTX in November 2022. Once doubts spread about the quality of reserves on Alameda Research's balance sheet, withdrawals surged. Within 48 hours, more than $5 billion had been requested (Reuters, Nov 2022). The exchange, like Knickerbocker Trust a century earlier, discovered that liquidity buffers are not abstractions. They are the space between headline and collapse. When that space is narrow, outcomes turn binary. Too late means failure.

Here, the first durable lesson emerges: *panic is a coordination failure, and backstops are coordination tools.* The Bank of England's lender-of-last-resort stature did not arise because it was always prudent; it arose because someone had to stand at the threshold and guarantee cash on demand. The Federal Reserve was created in 1913 for precisely this purpose: turn private rescues into public infrastructure. The crypto ecosystem has no single institution with authority or legitimacy to play that role consistently. Instead, it improvises—market-makers deploy capital, foundations burn treasuries, peers negotiate mergers. Each scramble teaches what structure could have prevented.

The second lesson concerns information. The Wall Street Crash of 1929 was not sudden; warnings had echoed for months. But ordinary investors lacked the metrics to interpret what they heard. A stream of fabricated reports and cheerleading analysts masked risk until reality intruded. After the carnage, disclosure standards emerged in statute: the U.S. Securities Act of 1933 and the Securities Exchange Act of 1934 mandated audited accounts and truthful prospectuses. The idea was not to ban exuberance, but to remove blindness. Where sunlight falls, speculation must at least acknowledge its shadows.

Stablecoin users in 2022 asked a familiar question: show us the reserves. In some cases, they saw audited attestations; in others, partial snapshots or unverifiable claims. The market priced those differences with brutal speed. Confidence requires evidence, not slogans. And evidence must be continuous, not occasional. Proof delayed is proof denied.

Not every panic deserves rescue. That is the third lesson: *backstops are powerful drugs and dangerous habits.* In 1984, Continental Illinois received unprecedented support from U.S. authorities after losses tied to energy loans. The phrase "too big to fail" entered common usage. Critics warned of moral hazard—if downside is cushioned, upside becomes reckless. The protests were justified. Yet when Lehman Brothers was allowed to fail in 2008, the shockwave proved devastating. Free-market purism collided with the reality of interconnected balance sheets. The world rediscovered a harsh trade-off: rescue too often, and you feed excess; rescue too rarely, and you devastate by example. There is no perfect line. The line moves.

Crypto offers a new laboratory for this dilemma. Should decentralised protocols intervene when liquidation cascades threaten survival? Should exchanges absorb losses to protect users? Or must code always run its course? The answers vary by philosophy. But history warns that ideology seldom survives contact with chaos. When survival is at stake, rulebooks are rewritten under duress.

A credible counter-example sharpens the point. Iceland, in 2008, refused to guarantee foreign deposits in its failed banks. The decision was painful; reputations suffered. Yet the country stabilised faster than expected, partially because the government did not socialise colossal private losses. A brave stance. Yet not universally replicable. Iceland's banks were large relative to its economy but small relative to the world. The fallout was bounded. The logic does not scale indefinitely. The exception confirms the fragility of the rule.

So, the quiet motif returns: thresholds. The threshold where liquidity becomes insolvency. The threshold where transparency becomes opacity. The threshold where rescue becomes ruin. Crises are battles over lines—where they are drawn and who redraws them.

Visible behaviour reveals the underlying mechanics. People sprint to withdraw stablecoins not because they understand algorithmic collateral equations but because they see selling pressure and hesitate to be last. Traders widen spreads not because they distrust innovation but because they fear forced liquidation from elsewhere. Officials disclose reserves not because they love scrutiny but because they know silence invites speculation. Trust is granular. It consists of decisions taken in seconds.

History also teaches repair. After the Bank Panic of 1907, clearing-house certificates provided temporary liquidity; the concept foreshadowed modern deposit insurance. After the Asian Financial Crisis of 1997, capital controls were re-examined to prevent hot money from fuelling hot fires. After 2022, crypto developers and policymakers began debating real-time attestation, circuit breakers for pegs, and shared settlement assurances. Innovation often begins with a scar.

This is where continuity meets divergence. Traditional finance assembled its crisis response tools slowly, across generations, spurred by public outrage and legislative compromise. Digital asset systems evolve at onset speed: upgrades deploy overnight; governance votes close in days. That agility invites both optimism and fragility. The question is whether lessons scale as fast as code.

Markets will always dream beyond fundamentals. They will always fear the crowd turning. They will always oscillate between euphoria and disbelief. What changes—what must change—is the architecture built to absorb those moods without breaking.

Another panic will come. A peg will wobble. A rumour will run ahead of reality. The test that lingers is simple, unsettling, and vital: when the next queue forms—whether outside a building or inside an app—what stands between a frightened finger clicking "withdraw" and a cascading collapse?

Disclosure, Audits, and Governance

At 7:55 a.m. on 29 September 1995, the Board of Barings Bank assembled in London to confront a single spreadsheet. It listed the open positions of Nick Leeson, the twenty-eight-year-old derivatives trader stationed in Singapore. For months, Leeson had concealed vast losses inside an unauthorised account labelled "88888". Once the trades were unwound, the true figure crystallised: Barings owed £827 million—more than its entire capital base. The collapse of Britain's oldest merchant bank within a single weekend revealed a brutal structural flaw: the same individual had authority to trade and to settle trades. One person held both the pen and the ledger. Separation of duties had not merely been ignored; it had been inverted. Bad news travelled slowly. Then it crushed the institution that ignored its own controls.

The Barings episode lingers because it dramatises a threshold. Governance is not a veneer; it is the scaffolding that prevents human ingenuity from turning into catastrophe. Disclosure is not decoration; it is a discipline of shared sight lines. Audits are not ceremonial; they prise open the sealed boxes that temptation loves. These practices cost time. They cost money. They irritate the proud and restrain the reckless. Yet when pressure rises, institutions that invested in verifiability endure longer than those that trusted charisma or luck. The motif returns: light must fall where power sits.

Large-scale finance learned this lesson through pain. The U.S. Securities Act of 1933 and the Securities Exchange Act of 1934 were born from the wreckage of 1929, when selective disclosure and fabricated accounts allowed fraud to wear the mask of prosperity. By forcing listed companies to publish audited financial statements, the statutes created a common frame: investors could measure—rather than imagine—the balance sheet. The implication was quiet but profound. Markets became arenas of contestable claims, not whisper networks. Once evidence became mandatory, trust shifted from personality to process.

Crypto institutions now face a similar pivot. When Binance released its proof-of-reserves snapshot in December 2022, it invited users to compare assets and liabilities block by block. Yet the attestation, conducted by Mazars, drew scrutiny: it covered only a subset of obligations and excluded internal controls. The episode showed both the promise and the peril of transparency. Showing something is not the same as showing enough. Users want a complete picture, not a curated one. And they judge omissions as signals. When a major exchange chooses only partial visibility, the market assumes the missing parts matter.

A contrasting example clarifies the tension. In 2021, the Chicago Mercantile Exchange (CME) expanded its Bitcoin futures listings. The CME's governance regime—daily margin calls, audited segregation of customer funds, and transparent rulebooks—provided credibility from the outset. Participants could see each control: independent custodians, daily settlement prices, and circuit breakers aligned with existing futures markets. The architecture was dull. That was the point. When rules are predictable, markets behave more coherently. When participants understand the boundaries, risk becomes a measured choice rather than a leap of faith.

Yet governance is not immune to limits. Consider the Wirecard scandal in Germany, where EY signed off on financial statements for years before €1.9 billion of supposed cash proved fictional in June 2020. Audit failed spectacularly; oversight erred. The limitation matters. Verification can be gamed when incentives misalign or when auditors grow too close to management. But the counter-example does not nullify the principle. It refines it. Effective governance depends on independence and rotation. A control immune to capture is difficult to design but essential to pursue.

The visible behaviours that flow from strong governance illuminate the incentives at work. A board that meets monthly without minutes signals indifference to record-keeping. A protocol whose treasury movements are signed by one administrator, without multisignature rules or timelocks, signals concentration of power. A project that updates documentation only quarterly signals disengagement from user oversight. Each behaviour is a metric of culture. Institutions telegraph values through their habits long before a crisis tests them.

Separation of duties remains the most durable mechanism. When custody, trading, settlement, and reconciliation sit in different hands, collusion becomes harder and mistakes are caught earlier. The London Stock Exchange enforces this principle through its clearing arrangements: LCH Ltd holds collateral independently, ensuring that a broker's failure does not automatically trigger systemic rupture. By contrast, FTX in 2022 blurred these lines. Alameda Research, a trading firm, accessed customer assets from the exchange.

Once revealed, the breach destroyed user confidence instantly. No audit report could counteract that single structural violation: the absence of distance.

Disclosure is a second pillar. Traditional finance measures it through quarterly reports, insider trading logs, and continuous updates for material events. Crypto experiments with real-time attestations, token-holder dashboards, and open-source codebases. Yet disclosure must be intelligible as well as available. Publishing raw wallet data without context is like handing readers a phone book and calling it literature. Information needs architecture. It needs narrative. Users require a digestible route from data to meaning.

Audits sit between disclosure and governance. They test claims, verify processes, and expose contradictions. But their scope matters. Smart-contract audits, usually conducted by firms such as Trail of Bits or Quantstamp, examine code logic rather than balance-sheet integrity. This distinction is vital. A protocol can pass a technical review and still mismanage reserves or governance. Conversely, a protocol can maintain strong financial transparency while harbouring coding flaws. Mature institutions invest in both layers and communicate the limits of each. A clear audit is an act of humility: it says, "Here is what we checked; here is what remains uncertain."

The motif of light returns. Transparency is illumination; governance is the structure that ensures illumination reaches the corners where risk hides. When those corners remain dark, trouble accumulates. When they are lit, behaviour changes. Managers know that decisions will be examined. Engineers know that shortcuts will surface. Boards know that silence is not neutral; it is a message.

A third historical case shows the stakes. After the collapse of Enron in 2001, the U.S. passed the Sarbanes–Oxley Act of 2002. Its most striking requirement was that CEOs and CFOs personally certify the accuracy of financial statements. The rule forced top executives to own the numbers—not delegate them. A visible behaviour shifted: senior leaders read what they signed. This small change transformed audit committee dynamics across corporations. Governance became personal, not procedural. Accountability sharpened because signatures carried consequences.

Crypto governance rarely demands this intimacy. Decentralised autonomous organisations (DAOs) often fragment responsibility across thousands of token-holders. Voting occurs, yet few participants read proposals in depth. Multisignature wallets distribute authority, but signers sometimes operate without formal oversight. The structure aims for democracy but can drift into diffusion. When responsibility scatters, mistakes hide. The implication is uncomfortable: decentralisation requires stronger, not weaker, governance rituals to make accountability legible.

The counterpoint is instructive. MakerDAO, founded in 2015, publishes detailed risk parameters for its collateral types and undergoes periodic reviews by independent risk teams. The practice is imperfect, slow, and sometimes contentious. Yet it illustrates what disciplined disclosure can look like in a decentralised environment. The information is public, the process visible, and the debates archived. Users may disagree with decisions, but they can examine them. That alone elevates expectations for the entire sector.

Markets reward verifiability. Institutions invest in it because opacity is expensive. It raises borrowing costs, widens spreads, and deters serious partners. When disclosure improves, liquidity often deepens. When audits strengthen, counterparties relax collateral demands. When governance is credible, long-term participants commit more capital. These outcomes are measurable: narrower bid–ask spreads on exchanges with published custody reports; higher volume persistence on protocols with audited smart contracts; lower redemption volatility for stablecoins with daily reserve snapshots. Trust leaves footprints.

Yet none of these mechanisms are ever finished. Governance atrophies when routines become rote. Disclosure decays when incentives reward enthusiasm over honesty. Audits degrade when clients treat them as marketing rather than scrutiny. The tension persists: how does an institution sustain vigilance without sliding into bureaucracy? How does a decentralised system maintain transparency without overwhelming users with noise?

The next crisis will expose which structures matter most. Some institutions will discover that a missing control was not an administrative detail but a fault line. Some protocols will learn that transparency must be continuous, not episodic. And some users will ask a question that has haunted finance since Barings fell: who holds the ledger, and who checks the hands that hold it?

Market Microstructure Basics

At 9:30 a.m. on 6 May 2010, the opening seconds of trading on the New York Stock Exchange carried a faint but unmistakable tension. Prices twitched in narrow bands before widening sharply. By 2:32 p.m., the structure buckled. The "Flash Crash"—a near-instant 9 per cent plunge in major U.S. equity indices—unfolded so swiftly that some securities briefly traded for one cent, while others shot to implausible highs before reverting. The sequence revealed something uncomfortable: a market is not a monolith, but a stack of fragile layers. Order books depend on depth; liquidity providers retreat when volatility spikes; and spreads widen as algorithms hesitate. A live, global marketplace can evaporate into a vacuum within seconds. The event forced regulators and traders alike to confront the mechanics beneath the screen: spreads, depth, slippage, and the choreography between human intent and machine execution.

More than a decade later, those same mechanics shape the behaviour of crypto exchanges in Singapore, London, and Chicago. Whether a pair trades on Binance, Coinbase, or the London Metal Exchange, the underlying reality is identical: a price is not a single number but a negotiation between buyers and sellers with finite willingness. The platform changes. The physics do not. Market structure is the hidden grammar of every trade, and each participant—retail punter or institutional desk—speaks it knowingly or not.

The point surfaces every time a user buys a token and receives less than expected. The screen shows a price. The market reflects a spectrum. That gap—small in calm conditions, brutal in thin ones—reveals the motif that runs through every marketplace: the distance between intent and execution defines experience.

The shape of that distance begins with spreads. A spread is not an abstract notion but a visible behaviour: the highest price a buyer commits to (the bid) and the lowest a seller accepts (the ask). The gap between them tells a story. Narrow spreads signal active competition. Wide spreads whisper caution. They measure confidence, participation, and fear. In 2005, the New York Stock Exchange moved from fractional pricing to decimals; spreads compressed immediately as liquidity providers could quote in finer increments. The effect was measurable: narrower spreads, tighter execution, and a richer order book. Market design reshaped behaviour.

Crypto exchanges display the same dynamics, even when the assets are novel. Whether a Bitcoin–USDT pair at Kraken in March 2023 or a governance token pair on a decentralised exchange, the spread conveys two truths: how many participants are watching, and how fast they react. During the TerraUSD de-pegging in May 2022, spreads ballooned across centralised venues as liquidity providers withdrew. The behaviour was rational: uncertainty erases appetite. Markets breathe; spreads widen like pupils in the dark.

Depth is the second layer. It is not enough to know the best bid and ask; what matters is how much volume sits behind them. Depth is the scaffold that keeps price stable when a large order hits the book. A deep market absorbs pressure. A shallow one buckles. Consider the London Stock Exchange's treatment of FTSE-100 constituents: designated market makers commit to minimum depth obligations, ensuring that institutional orders can transact without destabilising the price. These obligations exist because depth cannot be wished into being; it must be incentivised and maintained.

Crypto has no equivalent rulebook, yet the principle reappears. On decentralised exchanges such as Uniswap, depth emerges from liquidity pools—contributed by users, governed by algorithms, and expressed through curves rather than ladders. When liquidity is concentrated, slippage remains modest. When liquidity migrates to other pools or chains, depth thins and slippage increases. The mechanism differs. The consequence is universal: depth determines how reality diverges from the surface.

Slippage is the lived experience of that divergence. It is visible in the execution: the price shifts as the order fills. In extreme moments, slippage becomes the story. During the January 2021 surge in trading around GameStop, slippage on several platforms ballooned as order flow overwhelmed routing systems. When quantity exceeded capacity, the market delivered a different price from the one customers expected. The abstraction of "impact" became a tangible cost: investors saw the difference in their statements.

In crypto, slippage often manifests in decentralised swaps. A user submits a trade expecting to exchange one token for another, only to find that the realised price reflects their own footprint in the pool. The smaller the pool relative to the order, the larger the footprint. This relationship is mechanical, not moral. A 10,000-unit swap on a thin pool has more influence than the same swap on a deep pool. The platform may be new; the logic is ancient.

The motif returns: structure shapes behaviour. When market participants cannot see depth or spreads clearly, they anchor to the visible price and assume stability. But the price is merely a point. The structure is the landscape around it. This misalignment is not unique to crypto. It governed the behaviour of participants in 1929, 1987, and 2010. In each case, a mismatch between perceived and actual liquidity amplified losses.

Two further examples sharpen the principle. In February 2018, the Chicago Board Options Exchange halted trading in derivative products tied to market volatility (VIX ETPs) after rapid price swings. The products were complex, but the failure was structural: when liquidity providers pulled back, the instruments no longer behaved as expected. A nominal hedge became a moving target. Meanwhile, in

March 2020, during the COVID-19 liquidity shock, U.S. Treasury markets—usually the most liquid in the world—experienced dislocations. Bid–ask spreads widened dramatically. Depth evaporated. Even the benchmark market needed support. The implication was humbling: no asset, however prestigious, is immune to structural fragility.

Crypto users encounter the same forces when exchanges halt withdrawals during volatility or when automated market makers reprice pools sharply. The behaviours differ in detail, not essence. A centralised exchange may refuse withdrawals because its internal risk engine cannot reconcile positions; a decentralised protocol may impose a fee to deter large trades. Both actions reflect a single pressure: liquidity has thinned faster than participants anticipated.

A credible counter-example clarifies boundaries. Foreign exchange markets, particularly in EUR–USD trading in London and New York, often maintain deep, continuous liquidity even during turbulent periods. The Bank for International Settlements documents daily turnover of over $2 trillion in that pair alone. The scale prevents individual orders from reshaping the price meaningfully. Slippage remains modest; spreads remain tight. Yet even here, limits surface. In January 2015, when the Swiss National Bank removed its euro peg, the EUR–CHF market convulsed. Spreads widened. Platforms froze. Even the most liquid markets cannot defy the physics of order flow when assumptions break.

The pattern is inescapable: microstructure governs experience. Investors often attribute execution quality to luck, timing, or platform reliability. The real drivers reside in the invisible layers beneath. A thin book punishes urgency. A deep book cushions it. A wide spread taxes impatience. A narrow spread rewards participation. These are not opinions but measurements: distance between quotes, quoted depth at each level, and slippage recorded at execution.

Bridging centralised (CeFi) and traditional (TradFi) finance reveals a final truth worth naming: markets reward those who understand structure, not merely price. A trader who chases a quote without examining the book becomes a tourist in a greenhouse. Every movement leaves a mark. By contrast, a participant who studies microstructure sees risk where others see opportunity and opportunity where others see noise.

Crypto adds a twist. Automated market makers replace order books with curves, yet spreads still exist, expressed through liquidity concentration. Depth still matters, produced by pool size. Slippage still shapes experience, determined by trade size relative to reserves. The underlying logic persists even when the interface changes. The implication is clear: new rails do not erase old physics.

Microstructure also shapes governance. Exchanges that disclose depth attract more serious participants. Protocols that publish real-time liquidity metrics gain trust. Platforms that obscure execution quality lose credibility. The visible behaviours—publishing order-book snapshots, revealing liquidity ranges, documenting routing logic—signal values. Transparency reassures; opacity warns.

The limitation is that many users prefer simplicity. They want a price, not a book. They want certainty, not nuance. Yet the market refuses to comply with that desire. It demands engagement with structure because structure shapes outcome. The user who ignores this reality learns it the costly way: through slippage, failed trades, or exposure to thin markets at the worst possible moment.

As microstructure becomes more automated and more complex, a question lingers. When liquidity fragments across chains, venues, and protocols, who understands the true depth? Who measures the silent pockets where liquidity hides? And who bears the cost when those pockets vanish at the very moment they are needed most?

Diversification vs Diworsification

In March 1998, the boardroom of Marks & Spencer in London carried a nervous quiet. The retailer had spent the previous three years scattering capital across a stretch of overseas ventures—from Paris to Munich, from Barcelona to Brussels—each intended to balance the company's British reliance with a cosmopolitan footprint. Yet by that spring, the ledger told a harder truth: the expansion burned cash while diluting management attention, and same-store sales in the United Kingdom sagged. The firm had not diversified. It had dispersed itself. The strategy looked sophisticated on paper; in practice it blurred purpose, weakened discipline, and exposed the danger of confusing the *number* of positions with the *quality* of diversification. The episode still stands as a quiet warning: breadth without coherence becomes ballast.

That tension—that tempting drift from clarity to clutter—lies at the heart of every portfolio built under pressure. A screen full of tickers feels safer than a few lines of conviction. More names. More comfort. Yet the psychological comfort rarely matches the structural reality. Risk does not dissolve when positions multiply; it migrates. It hides in correlation clusters, concentration drifts, governance overlaps, and assets that promise independence but move in eerie unison when stress hits. Complexity theatre masquerades as prudence. The motif recurs across decades and markets: the difference between protection and performance often rests on whether the builder sought diversification or merely its silhouette.

The structure of true diversification begins with a visible behaviour: the movement of each component when volatility strikes. When assets decline together, the portfolio's surface variety becomes irrelevant. During the 2008 crisis, for instance, U.S. investment-grade corporates, global equities, and many commodity indices—positions that seemed diverse—sold off in synchrony. The Federal Reserve's data from December 2008 show correlation spikes across credit and equity markets that collapsed long-held assumptions. The names were different. Their fate was not.

What mattered was not the count of holdings but the common force driving them: liquidity demand. The episode named a lesson that still holds in crypto: diversification is a behaviour under stress, not a brochure line.

Another example sharpens the point. In 2022, when TerraUSD began its death spiral, several decentralised finance protocols experienced simultaneous stress despite operating across different chains and offering different products. Anchor, Curve, and numerous yield aggregators saw withdrawals and liquidity thinning within hours. The assets varied. The governance varied. The codebases varied. Yet the peg's unwinding became the gravitational centre pulling everything down. Diversification collapsed into exposure to a single narrative risk. The breadth masked the linkage.

Diworsification tends to creep in when growth obscures governance. An investor accumulates positions opportunistically—an airdrop here, a recommendation there—until the portfolio resembles a map of unfinished ideas. Many of the positions are small enough to feel inconsequential but large enough to require monitoring. The investor now must track announcements, forks, audits, tokenomics revisions, exchange listings, team departures, and social-media volatility across dozens of assets. The cost is not just attention; it is reaction time. In portfolios swollen with marginal positions, meaningful signals drown in noise.

The reverse case—valuable for nuance—emerges in Norway's Government Pension Fund Global. The fund holds thousands of securities across geographies and sectors yet avoids diworsification because the structure is systematised. Its breadth reflects a purpose: to mirror the global economy with minimal idiosyncratic risk. The operational machinery behind it is industrial: disciplined rebalancing, defined mandates, and a governance model that prevents position creep. The limitation, however, is that such depth of resources cannot be replicated by ordinary market participants. The fund demonstrates the upper bound of diversification done well, not a template. It reconciles the counter-example by showing that breadth only strengthens results when paired with capacity—analytical, organisational, and psychological.

The essence returns to a simple question: does each position earn its place? The answer is not numeric but behavioural. A position earns its place when it introduces a differentiated outcome under uncertainty. It must *move differently* when the system tilts. If two assets respond identically to a liquidity shock, they share risk regardless of branding. If they depend on the same oracle, the same stablecoin, or the same custody provider, they share infrastructure risk. If they rise and fall with the same social meme or the same influencer's pulse, they share narrative risk. True diversification maps the invisible links, not the visible tickers.

One way to expose those links is to observe what happens when a stress signal hits. For instance, when the FTX collapse began unfolding in November 2022, tokens with no direct commercial ties to the exchange still sold off because investors feared correlated venue risk. Trading volumes spiked, withdrawal times lengthened, and liquidity providers withdrew across multiple exchanges. In that moment, portfolios that seemed diversified—holding assets across various ecosystems—behaved as one because the counterparty layer dominated the asset layer. Structure trumped surface.

Contrast this with the April 2020 episode in U.S. crude oil markets, when front-month WTI futures briefly traded at negative prices. Energy equities fell, but other commodities, broad equity indices, and many digital assets held distinct trajectories. The shock was concentrated rather than systemic. The outcome offers a different lesson: diversification works when the underlying drivers of assets are genuinely distinct. The differentiator was structural: producers, refiners, and storage operators faced a storage bottleneck; assets unrelated to oil logistics responded to different incentives. Real diversification emerges from real independence.

The motif that binds these examples—structure over surface—invites a deeper reflection: most investors overestimate the value of new positions and underestimate the cost of managing them. Each additional holding imposes a cognitive toll. It demands periodic review, scenario thinking, and monitoring for governance drift. A portfolio with thirty positions may contain twenty that do nothing except diffuse attention from the ten that matter. This diffusion often manifests as delayed action. When a critical decision arises, the investor spends precious minutes reconciling fragmented information instead of responding to the threat. In crises, the price of hesitation is steep.

The opposite behaviour—clarity—has measurable benefits. When the number of monitored positions shrinks, the investor allocates more time to understanding each asset's mechanics: its liquidity profile, its governance, its upgrade path, its cross-dependencies. Clarity reinforces discipline. It enables quicker interpretation of signals. It also builds confidence—not a mood but a concrete ability to explain why each holding deserves capital. Investors often mistake this confidence for stubbornness, yet the record shows the reverse: clearer portfolios are easier to prune. When a position loses its premise, it can be removed cleanly because it existed for a defined purpose, not inertia.

Still, there is a credible counter-pressure worth acknowledging. Markets evolve. Narratives shift. New assets emerge with promising technologies or governance models. A portfolio frozen in simplicity may miss innovations that redefine the landscape. The limitation of extreme concentration is that it can harden into dogma. But the answer is not clutter. It is curiosity paired with selectivity. The investor evaluates new opportunities not as trophies but as potential contributors to resilience. The portfolio expands only when the new position reduces total vulnerability rather than inflating it.

Crypto markets, in particular, tempt diworsification because novelty masquerades as diversification. A token tied to a new consensus mechanism appears distinct. A governance token attached to a fresh protocol feels uncorrelated. But when liquidity drains or a stablecoin wobbles, assets across chains often move together because the underlying risk vectors—venue, stablecoin, oracle, or liquidity provider—intersect. What looks like variety is often *shared plumbing*. The motif surfaces again: structure dictates behaviour.

Historical finance offers a parallel. In the late 1960s, U.S. conglomerates acquired dozens of unrelated businesses in the belief that diversification would smooth cash flows and boost valuations. ITT, Litton Industries, and Gulf & Western expanded aggressively across unrelated industries. Yet by the mid-1970s, many of those empires unravelled because managerial bandwidth could not stretch across wildly different operations. The diversification was theatrical, not functional. The companies learned that coherence, not count, sustains performance. Their lesson mirrors today's challenge in digital assets.

Bringing the argument into personal scale sharpens the stakes. Consider how a portfolio interacts with real life. A sprawling set of positions demands perpetual updates, shifting dashboards, and constant reallocation. The investor becomes a caretaker rather than a strategist. But a portfolio anchored in clarity respects human limits. It allows space for off-screen life. It supports decisions rooted in understanding rather than reaction. This alignment is not soft psychology; it is operational reality. A portfolio that outgrows its owner's capacity becomes hazardous.

The tension that remains—the unresolved thread—is simple but not trivial. How does one distinguish between prudent breadth and creeping clutter? How does one decide when an additional position enriches the portfolio's structure or merely decorates it? The question lingers because the answer shifts with context, time, and personal capacity. It forces a choice: pursue variety, or pursue coherence. Only one of these paths holds firm when the market stops rewarding illusions.

Chapter 12
Building Anti-Fragile Habits

In December 2022, a photograph circulated quietly among crypto veterans: a trader asleep at his desk, monitors still glowing with red charts, his phone buzzing with liquidations. The joke was dark but familiar. The caption might as well have read: *The market moved faster than his life could handle.* Price had become his master. Sleep, purpose, relationships—deferred to an hourly candle. The crash was not only financial. It was the collapse of a life built around outcomes he could not control.

Consider the inverse image: a small study, low light, a notebook open. A person records what they observed, what they learned, and what they will test next week. No fireworks. No adrenaline. Yet over time this quiet ritual builds something stronger than luck. They are betting on themselves rather than on volatility's mood. The difference between these two lives—one captive, one self-authored—reveals the premise of this chapter: resilience grows from habits that strengthen under stress, not from predictions that disintegrate on impact. When the market storms arrive, those who have rehearsed calm move first and fastest.

Anti-fragility is often mislabelled as invincibility. It is nothing of the sort. It is adaptation in motion. A system that benefits from disorder must Learn → Adjust → Continue. Markets punish those who cling to certainty and reward those who refine their method. In both traditional and decentralised finance, long-term outperformance stems more from processes than from calls. The investor anchored in a repeatable practice—weekly reviews, structured decision logs, independent research—does not need a market to behave. They merely need a market to exist.

The world of digital assets, with its constant noise and perpetual invention, tempts a reactive posture. A rumour sparks a trade. A tweet becomes a thesis. Communities fracture into factions defending narratives they barely understand. The pace feels exhilarating, until it becomes exhausting. The longest-lasting participants are rarely the loudest. They choose rooms that raise the standard rather than raise the volume. Community matters because attention is finite. Who surrounds you shapes what you notice. Good rooms cultivate patience. They treat ignorance as a starting point rather than a shame. They practice dialogue instead of performance.

Curiosity forms the bedrock. But here curiosity is not entertainment. It is discipline. It is reading the contract rather than reposting the meme. It is scanning commit histories rather than influencer feeds. It is understanding why a mechanism should work—and under what conditions it might fail. This type of curiosity looks boring from the outside. It rarely trends. But it compounds. The investor who studies fundamentals during lulls is the one who recognises opportunity when hype returns. They are not caught off guard by the next cycle; they have been preparing for it during the silence.

Cycles define this ecosystem. The shock of collapse. The fever of ascent. The long middles where conviction grows brittle. Many people repeat patterns because they never examine them. They tell themselves that "next time will be different" while doing everything the same. The alternative is not ascetic restraint; it is deliberate design. A personal operating manual—tight, thoughtful, changeable—can transform experience into foresight. It replaces panic with protocol. When the exchange halts, you know your action. When the stablecoin wobbles, you run the play. When the narrative shifts, you test assumptions rather than freeze.

Anti-fragile habits do not guarantee wins. They guarantee momentum. They create a baseline of sanity from which courage can emerge. They prevent a bad week from becoming a lost year. And they redirect the locus of progress back to where it belongs: your decisions, your rules, your attention. Money is an outcome. Competence is a practice. The market will continue to surprise. But surprises lose their power over those who have rehearsed resilience.

So the question becomes personal: what structures will you choose before the cycle turns again? What rhythm will you build that no price chart can ruin? The habits we commit to now decide who still feels awake—and who sleeps through their own decisions—when the next wave arrives.

From Outcomes to Process

On 4 November 2022, at 10:47 a.m. in Singapore, a thirty-year-old engineer named Daniel closed his laptop and stared into nothing. The value of his portfolio had collapsed by more than 80 per cent in a week. He had tracked every uptick during the boom; he now refreshed his screen compulsively, hoping recovery would appear by force of will. Yet his behaviour could not influence the chart. He was living inside a contradiction: the more attention he paid, the less control he had. A market he could not govern had been allowed to govern him.

That same week, a quieter story passed unnoticed. In Helsinki, a developer marked his Friday routine: a ten-minute review of his research log, a brief check against predefined triggers, and a note on whether his thesis still held. His capital was down too. But his stress was not. Because his system had already decided which variables mattered and which did not, the panic could not dictate his week. The difference between Daniel and the developer was not intelligence or timing. It was focus. One was captive to outcomes. The other was anchored in process. One was *watching*. The other was *working*.

Markets create a powerful illusion: that outcomes are the product of attention. Look longer, predict better, and profit follows. Yet the relationship is often inverse. Behavioural finance researchers such as Terrance Odean and Brad Barber (2000) have shown that frequent monitoring and trading correlate with lower performance. The reason is simple: excessive outcome focus induces action without thesis, distraction without insight. When every price move feels like a verdict on competence, the investor stops learning and starts reacting. A five-word sentence captures the trap: **Screens don't teach you anything.**

To shift from outcomes to process, we must show what control truly means. Control is not predicting direction. Control is defining method. The Harvard psychologist Ellen Langer named this move *active control*: placing agency where effort changes trajectory. In markets, this manifests as rules that decide what information enters the mind and how it is turned into decisions. A process is not a guarantee. It is a boundary. It protects attention from the noise that would consume it.

History offers compelling demonstrations. In 1974, amid a brutal downturn, the investment firm Wellington Management in Boston rebuilt its entire research workflow. Rather than chase prices, it instituted structured review cycles—meeting every two weeks to assess theses against clear criteria. Performance stabilised, even as markets remained hostile. System first, outcome later. Decades later, the Bridgewater team in Westport adopted a related principle in 1985: document every assumption, test every rule, refine or discard based on evidence. The visible behaviour: writing, not watching. The implication: confidence grounded in knowledge, not luck.

Crypto, by contrast, remains addicted to immediacy. Notifications replace notes. Volatility feels like progress. The investor whose identity depends on price becomes fragile to price. This ecosystem amplifies emotional feedback loops: social feeds turn guesses into gospel within minutes. Copycat trades swarm into positions without understanding the mechanism that supports them. When the mechanism buckles, regret arrives with its usual companion—silence. There is no record of why a choice seemed rational at the time. Without record, learning dies.

A weekly review rescues intelligence from hindsight. It is simple, structured, and brutally honest. It asks three questions: What did I believe? What happened? What will I adjust? Daniel's counterpart in Helsinki wasn't calm because he was a stoic genius. He was calm because the week's work was defined and finite. Process assigns winners and losers by iteration, not by fortune. Each adjustment is visible. Progress becomes measured in clarity rather than coins.

A critic might object: process cannot eliminate uncertainty. Correct. Process cannot prevent loss. It can prevent **repeat loss**. The counterexample strengthens the argument. In July 2021, several funds holding GBTC—Grayscale's Bitcoin trust—trusted a price discrepancy would close quickly. It did not. Firms with documented risk frameworks reduced exposure methodically. Others froze, hoping. Those who had a process navigated pressure. Those who did not endured chaos. The limitation of process is that it cannot erase consequences. The power of process is that it converts consequences into change.

The motif here is attention. What we measure dictates what we become. If the only metric that matters is net worth, net worth will govern our self-worth. A weekly review shifts attention to decisions, to reasoning, to evidence. The locus of achievement shifts from "What did the market give me?" to "What did I build?" The deepest implication: stress becomes diagnostic rather than existential. It tells you where a rule is missing or misaligned. It does not tell you that you are broken.

Some habits sound trivial until they are tested. Writing one's thesis in a paragraph before entering a position. Conducting a post-mortem within 48 hours of a thesis break. Limiting screen checks to pre-set windows. These rituals are not about restraint for its own sake. They are about constructing a life the market cannot hijack. The mark of a mature participant is not who predicted the rally. It is who can still think when the rally ends.

The weekly review provides a rhythm of control. But its real value is cumulative. After six months, patterns emerge: which sources mislead, which states of mind distort, which signals matter. Decisions stop being improvisations and become research-backed commitments. You start to see your own fingerprints on outcomes—whether good or bad. A record of thinking becomes a record of growth.

There is a quiet question that returns throughout this chapter: *What are you optimising for?* If the answer is a number, the market will shape you. If the answer is a system, you will shape the market's role in your life. The choice is not abstract. It is visible in where you place your attention tomorrow morning. A screen or a notebook.

Anxiety or improvement. A reactive story or a deliberate one.

The next cycle will arrive. It always does. The real question is whether your method will be ready before the headlines declare the return of euphoria. So as you close this section and look outward again, ask yourself the forward test: Which process—small, repeatable, tracked—will you commit to by next Friday?

Community and Calm

On 16 March 2008, as the collapse of Bear Stearns became public in New York, a small gathering of analysts met in an unremarkable conference room on Park Avenue. Phones buzzed. Screens glowed red. Yet the most striking feature of the room was its tone. No shouting. No doom-laden predictions. Just a deliberate exchange of questions: *What failed? Why now? What can be learned?* The meeting lasted fifty minutes. Not one trade was executed in that time. But every participant left with a clearer head. Within a week, several wrote that those fifty minutes were the most valuable of the entire crisis. The power was not in information. It was in the room.

Contrast this with a digital chatroom I observed in November 2021, during the meme-coin frenzy. A single rumour—fabricated, as it turned out—spread through the group in seconds. Members copied each other's fear, then each other's enthusiasm, then each other's confusion. No one paused to ask who first posted the claim or what evidence supported it. Within an hour, most had taken positions they could not justify. Within a day, several had lost savings they could not replace. The difference between the Park Avenue analysts and this chatroom was not access. Both had imperfect information. The difference was composure. Calm is not the absence of noise. Calm is the presence of discernment.

The motif that threads through this subchapter is simple: *the room shapes the mind.* Good rooms slow down thinking just enough to let reasoning appear. Bad rooms accelerate emotion until thinking disappears. The behaviour is visible. In better rooms, participants ask clarifying questions, challenge premises, and cite sources. In poorer ones, people rush to agreement, recycling language they barely understand. A community is not a collection of people. It is a collection of habits.

To see why community quality matters, consider the work of psychologist Solomon Asch, whose landmark 1951 experiments in New York showed how easily individuals conform to group errors even when the truth is visually obvious. One of the most cited observations is that the presence of a single dissenting voice slashed conformity rates by 80 per cent. A solitary question—"Are we sure?"—reshaped the entire group dynamic. The implication is sobering: if a room punishes scrutiny, accuracy collapses. If it rewards curiosity, clarity improves.

Crypto markets have recreated Asch's pressures but at digital velocity. Airdrop speculation groups in 2020–2023 became mini echo chambers: identical predictions, identical language, identical fears. The behaviour gave away the underlying psychology. People checked their feeds every few minutes. They followed strangers' lists without understanding the criteria. Their attention narrowed until only one thing mattered: *missing out*. FOMO is not born from ignorance. It is born from insecure rooms.

Yet the counter-example enriches the point. Some online communities cultivate discipline rather than frenzy. The research-focused forums that studied the Merge in 2022—Ethereum's transition from proof-of-work to proof-of-stake—demonstrated this. In Berlin, London, Lagos and Singapore, developers and analysts held weekly calls where claims required code references, and disagreements were resolved through testnets rather than rhetoric. These rooms kept pace with markets yet refused to adopt the market's tempo. They stayed slow enough to think.

To build an environment that improves judgement, we must name its components. First: epistemic hygiene. This is visible in behaviours such as citing transaction data, linking to audited contracts, or sharing meeting notes rather than opinions. Second: emotional temperature. Good rooms modulate intensity. Participants speak in measured tones. They admit uncertainty. They ask for clarification instead of approval. Third: incentives. Communities with skin in shared learning, not shared speculation, produce far better forecasts. When success is judged by the quality of arguments rather than the speed of trades, people act differently. They measure twice. They compare sources.

A sceptic might argue that communities inevitably drift into mimicry because people prefer belonging to accuracy. There is truth here. Social pressure can corrode discernment. But well-constructed rooms delay that erosion. They create friction against impulsive behaviour. They encourage challenge without hostility. They support silence when silence is wiser than commentary. The limitation is that no room is perfect. The reconciliation is that perfection is not required. What matters is whether the environment consistently nudges you toward reflection rather than reaction.

Calm is not a personality trait. It is a practice enabled by context. When people around you model slow breathing, deliberate speech, and evidence-based analysis, your cognitive tempo drops. The metric is simple: how often do you check for updates? In a poor room, dozens of times an hour. In a good one, perhaps a handful. That difference changes everything. When attention is reclaimed, fear loses its grip. Anxiety becomes a cue, not a command.

Historical precedent reinforces the point. During the 1997 Asian financial crisis, the Monetary Authority of Singapore convened cross-disciplinary working groups to analyse currency pressures. These meetings were deliberately small and conspicuously sober. Participants were required to articulate reasoning before offering conclusions. This structure reduced panic-driven decisions and helped coordinate a measured response. The lesson transfers seamlessly to crypto: governance processes matter because people matter, and people think better when surrounded by standards.

The quiet question to ask when joining any community is: *What behaviour does this room reward?* If the room rewards predictions, speed and bravado, it will shape you accordingly. If it rewards modesty, method and reference to verifiable data, it will refine your mind rather than rattle it. The quality of your environment determines the quality of your attention. The quality of your attention determines the quality of your decisions.

What, then, does it mean to curate who you learn from? It means selecting voices not for their confidence but for their clarity. It means observing how people respond to stress: do they accelerate rumour, or do they slow down inquiry? It means noticing whether they admit error or defend it. These signals, tiny but telling, reveal whether a person is cultivating understanding or chasing identity. The stronger the identity attachment, the weaker the analysis.

Rooms shape narratives. Narratives shape behaviour. Behaviour shapes outcomes. The chain is inescapable. If you want to change the final link, change the first. Place yourself among people who think in systems, not stories; in questions, not slogans; in evidence, not excitement. Better rooms beat better tips because tips expire. Rooms endure.

A future cycle will test this again. New assets will surge. New rumours will spread. New communities will appear, promising insight and belonging. The tension you must carry forward is simple and sharp: will you choose rooms that strengthen your judgement, or rooms that soothe your fears?

Long-Term Curiosity

On 31 October 2008, when Satoshi Nakamoto released the Bitcoin white paper to a small cryptography mailing list, barely a dozen people responded. The document was nine pages. The world was in the middle of a financial crisis. The message arrived from an unknown author, at an unknown location, with no credentials beyond clarity. Yet within hours, a few readers began parsing the code snippets, questioning the incentive design, and testing the assumptions. They were not chasing a price. There was no price. They were chasing an idea. Those early responses, still archived, show a kind of patient curiosity that looked out of place amidst collapsing banks and political noise. But it is precisely that kind of curiosity—slow, thorough, structural—that outlasts every hype cycle.

Compare this with a Telegram group I observed in February 2021. A new token had launched on a major exchange. Within minutes, hundreds of messages appeared: screenshots, emoji, breathless claims. Almost no one asked for the contract address. Almost no one inspected the GitHub repository. Nobody checked whether the liquidity was locked or whether the team had disclosed their governance keys. The room was ablaze with confidence and devoid of investigation. Within four days, the project vanished. The difference between the readers of 2008 and the speculators of 2021 is not intelligence. It is discipline. Curiosity that endures is curiosity that slows down.

Long-term curiosity is best understood as a craft, not a mood. It requires behaviours that can be seen and measured: reading source code rather than summaries; comparing two protocol versions rather than repeating a slogan; studying the incentives of validators rather than retweeting a chart. These actions reveal a commitment to understanding the machinery of systems rather than the drama of prices. They also reveal a willingness to return to first principles when noise overwhelms signal. The quiet motif running through this subchapter is a simple question: *What is actually happening under the hood?*

To see how enduring curiosity works in practice, consider the case of the 2016 Ethereum hard fork, triggered by the DAO collapse. In Berlin and Toronto, developers and researchers convened to audit the vulnerability. They read the recursive call exploit line by line. They reconstructed the attack path. They debated the implications for immutability and governance. Crucially, they distinguished their emotional reaction from their analytical one. The process became a model for how to investigate failure without surrendering to panic. Curiosity was the stabiliser: it kept attention on technical facts rather than tribal rhetoric.

A contrasting example helps sharpen the lesson. During the 2017 ICO surge, many projects published glossy white papers with no working code. Investors, intoxicated by rising prices, treated prose as proof. They repeated each other's talking points. They treated buzzwords as engineering. Only later, once public scrutiny increased, did it become clear that many teams lacked even basic repository structure. The limitation is obvious: in environments dominated by promotion rather than production, curiosity becomes inconvenient. It slows people down. But that friction is exactly what protects judgement. The reconciliation is that curiosity may not prevent mistakes, but it reduces the frequency and magnitude of avoidable ones.

To cultivate research disciplines that survive hype cycles, we must name their forms. One is primary-source bias: the habit of starting with the raw material. Code, block explorers, audited reports, version histories. When someone claims a protocol is "decentralised", curiosity asks: *How many validators? Where? With what client diversity?* Metrics replace metaphors. Assertions become questions. A second form is comparative reading. Instead of absorbing a single project's claims, a curious reader compares it to predecessors. How does this AMM differ from Uniswap v2? How does this oracle design differ from Chainlink's architecture in 2020? Curiosity is not vague enthusiasm. It is specific investigation.

Yet a sceptic might object that not everyone can read code, nor should they need to. That critique contains truth. Technical literacy has a gradient, and expertise takes time. But curiosity is not synonymous with expertise. It is a posture: a refusal to outsource thinking. A person may not write Solidity, but they can inspect a contract's verified status, check commit frequency, or examine whether the top contributors are individuals or bots. They can observe whether a repository contains testing frameworks or merely marketing files. These small behaviours, easily performed, signal a commitment to reality over rhetoric.

Long-term curiosity also thrives on slowness. In January 2022, when rumours spread about vulnerabilities in cross-chain bridges, thoughtful analysts in Singapore and Zurich paused before commenting. They examined the block explorers. They looked at sequence numbers. They checked whether the paused contracts had been upgraded recently. The behaviour is instructive: they waited for evidence. Waiting is a skill. It requires resisting the social pressure to speak merely because others are speaking. The metric is simple: do you read before you react? Those who wait tend to outlast those who rush.

Curiosity's most reliable ally is repetition. Weekly reviews, understated but powerful, create muscle memory. They shift focus from price charts to process charts. They prompt questions such as: *What did I learn this week? What assumptions changed? What claims deserve further scrutiny?* These reviews turn scattered attention into structured inquiry. They build archives of understanding that compound quietly over months and years. They also expose blind spots. When a topic appears repeatedly yet remains unclear, curiosity signals that deeper study is required.

A historical parallel clarifies the stakes. During the early days of the internet, from 1993 to 1999, technologists like Tim Berners-Lee and Vinton Cerf emphasised protocol literacy over market speculation. They encouraged engineers and curious amateurs to read RFCs, inspect packet flows, and test interoperability. Prices fluctuated wildly, but the underlying research culture remained steady. That culture outlived the dot-com crash. The communities that treated the web as an engineering challenge, not a speculative theatre, became the foundation of modern infrastructure. The same pattern appears in crypto: projects grounded in sustained inquiry tend to survive, while those rooted in hype tend to fade.

Still, long-term curiosity faces a persistent threat: attention hijacking. Social platforms reward speed, outrage and novelty. They punish nuance. They amplify certainty even when certainty is unwarranted. The limitation is that curiosity cannot flourish when attention is always fragmented. But a disciplined reader can reclaim attention. One technique is silent inspection: reading a contract, a commit log, or a research paper without commentary or chatroom influence. Silence restores signal.

When curiosity matures, it produces a distinctive orientation. The curious person measures what they can see, names what they cannot, and withholds judgement when evidence is insufficient. They compare claims across cycles. They commit to understanding how systems function rather than how crowds feel. Over time, this orientation produces intellectual resilience. Hype cycles rise and fall, but discipline persists.

The quiet motif returns: *What is actually happening under the hood?* The future will offer new narratives, new instruments, new temptations. Some will glitter. Some will threaten. The unresolved tension you must carry forward is whether your curiosity will be episodic or enduring. Will you choose the discipline that outlasts the cycle, or the excitement that evaporates with it?

An Operating Manual for the Next Cycle

When Coinbase froze withdrawals for several minutes on 27 October 2021, during a period of surging retail activity in San Francisco and London, the reaction was instantaneous. Social feeds filled with rumours of insolvency. Screenshots circulated faster than facts. Within an hour, trading volume across major exchanges had swung by billions of dollars. The halt was brief, the explanation mundane—system congestion—but the behavioural shock was lasting. People realised how thin their preparation had been. They had plans for profit, but none for pause. They had studied market narratives, but not their own response rhythms. It was a small disruption that exposed a large gap: enthusiasm often exceeds readiness.

Contrast that scene with a quieter one, recorded in March 2020, in a basement office in Copenhagen. A small team at a crypto research firm ran timed drills as markets convulsed at historic speed. They simulated exchange downtime, oracle delays, and accidental position exposure. They used spreadsheets and whiteboards, not dashboards. They rehearsed calm. When liquidity dried up across several venues and price dislocations widened, the team did not react faster than others—they reacted cleaner. They had pre-set triggers for when to stand back, when to exit, and when to simply observe. Their advantage was not superior information. It was a mindset built through rehearsal.

These two moments reveal the same pattern: the next cycle does not reward the loud; it rewards the prepared. Yet preparation is often misunderstood. Many imagine it as a set of predictions, forecasts, and grand narratives. But the kind of preparation that survives repeated cycles is quieter. It deals in routines, not revelations. It commits to scenario thinking rather than certainty. It treats each cycle as a laboratory for refining systems, not a referendum on personal genius. The motif that will guide this subchapter is a simple test: *What do you want to have already decided before the next wave hits?*

Preparation begins with clarity of constraints. During the 2022 stablecoin crisis centred on TerraUSD in Singapore and New York, the projects that adapted swiftly were not the ones with the most elaborate models but the ones with pre-defined thresholds for scrutiny. They had already listed which metrics warranted further investigation: redemption queues, collateral composition, time-weighted deviations from the peg. These metrics provided structure when emotions surged. The visible behaviour is unmistakable: when uncertainty rises, disciplined actors look inward to their frameworks before looking outward for opinions. They measure. They compare. They commit to a process rather than a personality.

A parallel example comes from traditional finance. In October 2008, when several British banks faced liquidity stress, the Bank of England published conditional guidelines for capital support. The guidelines did not predict contagion; they delineated the steps institutions needed to demonstrate before assistance. The structure itself was stabilising. It turned panic into procedure. The implication transfers elegantly to volatile digital markets: structure acts as ballast. Where noise increases, scaffolding becomes signal.

Yet any operating manual faces a limitation: excessively rigid plans break. The 2021 gas-fee spikes during periods of NFT mania across Paris, Seoul, and Los Angeles exposed this. Users who relied on fixed expectations for transaction timing, rather than ranges, faced unexpected liquidation risks. Some attempted to adapt mid-flight—raising gas bids, switching networks, moving collateral—but the speed of improvisation could not overcome their lack of margin. The reconciliation lies in designing manuals that flex without folding. You decide principles, not presets. You choose boundaries, not scripts.

Preparation also requires that you name the behaviours that matter. When sentiment overheats, participation should slow. When liquidity fragments, execution should shrink. When information feels overwhelming, intake should tighten. The manual you build is not a list of trades; it is a choreography of posture. This choreography becomes visible in practice. Consider a group of researchers in Tokyo who, during the post-merge months of Ethereum in late 2022, ran a weekly review ritual. They asked the same questions every week: *What confused us? What did we assume? What did we verify?* Over time, the ritual sharpened their insight and narrowed their blind spots. Their performance improved not because the market rewarded them, but because their process corrected them.

Participation in a cycle is not neutral. It shapes your psychology as much as your portfolio. This is why the most enduring manuals incorporate deliberate pauses. In May 2021, during a rapid drawdown across major tokens, a fund in Zurich enforced a 24-hour reflection window before any major allocation change. The team had pre-committed to this rule in calmer months. It slowed decision-making precisely when speed felt seductive. Critics argued that hesitation risked missing opportunities. But when post-event analyses were published in December 2021, the fund's discipline showed its worth: most large moves made in the first hour of panic were reversals driven by stress, not insight. The implication is not moralistic. It is mechanical. Humans under strain confuse urgency with importance. A robust manual distinguishes them.

Still, the counter-example is worth addressing. There are circumstances—such as cascading liquidations or systemic oracle delays—where urgent action is necessary. For instance, during the 2020 Black Thursday Ethereum crash, liquidation auctions failed to clear, and rapid response was essential to prevent permanent loss. In such environments, a forced pause would be harmful. The reconciliation is subtle. Pauses must be contextual, not absolute. They require criteria. The manual must encode when to stop and when to accelerate. Routines are guardrails, not handcuffs.

A distinguishing feature of effective operating manuals is that they blend behavioural foresight with technical literacy. Before the 2023 emergence of modular blockchain designs gained traction, several Berlin-based teams had already drafted if-then statements regarding data availability risks. They tested hypothetical timelines: *If the DA layer stalls, then how many blocks until settlement risk becomes unacceptable?* Their preparation did not predict which chain would stumble. It simply defined how they would observe, interpret, and decide. The visibility of their method mattered more than the correctness of their forecast.

The manual for any next cycle must also attend to the rhythms of attention. Markets will accelerate. Narratives will proliferate. Feeds will demand reaction. A manual that ignores attention patterns is incomplete. One group of researchers in Boston experimented with a simple metric in mid-2021: the "interrupt count". They tallied how often they switched tabs, chats, or dashboards during high-volatility days. Their finding was unglamorous but illuminating: as interrupt count rose, reasoning clarity fell. They added a rule: no commentary while measuring. It sounds trivial, but it transformed their focus. Good manuals domesticate distraction.

Cycles also bring fatigue. During long consolidations, motivation wanes. Curiosity dips. Information loses flavour. Manuals compensate by embedding renewal. One example comes from a London engineering team who introduced quarterly "reset weeks" in 2022. They paused execution, re-read core protocol papers, updated threat models, and archived obsolete assumptions. Renewal became routine. This was not nostalgia; it was maintenance of clarity. The visible metric was the number of assumptions retired each quarter.

A manual that survives multiple cycles must engage with uncertainty without pretending to eliminate it. In late 2020, several DeFi protocols began publishing incident post-mortems. These documents, whether from Yearn or Harvest, shared a common structure: a clear timeline, identified faults, and proposed changes. The practice did not immunise them from future events, but it institutionalised learning. It also modelled intellectual honesty. An operating manual for the next cycle should echo this discipline: record decisions, record reasoning, and revisit both when conditions change.

The quiet motif returns: *What do you want to have already decided?* The next cycle will tempt you with novelty, velocity, and spectacle. But your manual will not care. It will ask: *What is your threshold? What is your check? What is your pause? What is your signal to step back?* The unresolved tension you must carry forward is whether you will design such a manual before the market demands it. The test is simple but uncomfortable: will you wait for chaos to clarify your priorities, or will you clarify them now, while clarity is still possible?

About the Author

Tarek Omraneh writes about technology, markets, and the messy human behaviours that connect them. After years spent documenting product launches, security incidents, and community governance debates, he became convinced that cycles teach more than slogans do. His work blends practical observation with a historian's eye for repeated patterns, drawing on case studies from payments, exchanges, and open-source projects. Raised around multilingual dinner-table arguments about trade and trust, he brings a cultural curiosity to financial manias and the stories we tell about them. His aim is not to sell certainty, but to help readers build habits that survive noise, whether prices rise or fall.

www.ingramcontent.com/pod-product-compliance
Lightning Source LLC
Chambersburg PA
CBHW031335230926
51848CB00002B/245
* 9 7 8 9 3 7 4 5 9 2 9 3 9 *